Wind Chamber Music

For Two to Sixteen Winds

An Annotated Guide

Barbera Secrist-Schmedes

The Scarecrow Press, Inc.
Lanham, Maryland • Toronto • Oxford
2002

SCARECROW PRESS, INC.

Published in the United States of America
by Scarecrow Press, Inc.
A wholly owned subsidiary of
The Rowman & Littlefield Publishing Group, Inc.
4501 Forbes Boulevard, Suite 200, Lanham, Maryland 20706
www.scarecrowpress.com

PO Box 317
Oxford
OX2 9RU, UK

British Library Cataloguing in Publication Information Available

Library of Congress Cataloging-in-Publication Data Available

ISBN 0-8108-4246-7 (cloth : alk. paper)

To my son, Eron, who brings great joy to my life.

To my friend and colleague Julie Spencer,
who has been a loving supporter and collaborator
in my chamber music adventure.

CONTENTS

PREFACE

This bibliography of chamber music for two to sixteen winds serves as a companion book to my first wind chamber music bibliography which covers wind quintets and winds with piano. It has been compiled from a variety of sources: music publishers and dealers, internet research, catalogues, reference books, composers and musicians. For the most part, I have included only those works that are currently in print, with the exception of a few works that I have personal knowledge of and felt their quality warranted inclusion. In those cases I have indicated a source for the music.

Works with the following instruments are included in this book: flute, oboe, clarinet, bassoon and French horn. Works using only instruments from the same sub group (i.e., all double reeds or all clarinets) are not included since there are other sources that already provide that information and their inclusion would have made this book too large. The instrumentation is listed in standard orchestral instrumentation format. For example: 1111/1 would indicate one player each on flute, oboe, clarinet, bassoon and French horn in that order. 0202/1 would indicated no flute, two oboes, no clarinets, two bassoons and one French horn.

I have arranged the composition on three lines. The first line relates to the composer: name, nationality and birth date. The second line concerns the composition: name, arranger (if any) and date written (if known) or copyright date. The third line details performance and publisher information: publisher, performance length (if known), instrumentation and difficulty level (if known).

When using the copyright date instead of the actual date the work was written, I have used a lower case "c" prior to the date. I have used a commonly accepted grading system of numbers one to five with one being the easiest and five being the most difficult works. In a few instances where I found a work listed without publisher information I have listed a music distributor instead. There are a number of works listed solely by the last name of the composer because that was all the

vii

information provided by publisher or distributor catalogs. After substantial effort to find the missing information, I decided nevertheless to include those works in an effort to create as comprehensive a resource guide as possible.

The descriptive information about the music or the composer's general style given with many of the entries was derived from record jackets, composer biographies, reference books, fellow musicians, the internet and my own experiences with the music.

Works listed under the "Miscellaneous" heading in each section include music whose composer is unknown (such as many of the traditional Christmas carols or folk songs) or a set of music by multiple composers

At some point I hope that both volumes of this bibliography will become available on the internet so that the information can be more easily accessed and continually updated.

If there are inadvertent omissions or errors, I welcome feedback from readers and subsequent editions can be revised. Send email to: bschmedes@earthlink.net

ACKNOWLEDGMENTS

Special thanks once again to my mother, Katherine Secrist, for her diligent proofreading and warm encouragement of my musical career. I also want to thank Florida State University and Kennesaw State University for the use of their library facilities and services.

TWO WINDS

Addison, John English/American 1920-1998
Five Dialogues; c1992; ESM; 8 mins; 1010; C/D
Addison was a composer of great skill and versatility whose music covered a wide spectrum of genres including ballet, film, TV, chamber music and solo literature. He won an Oscar for the musical score to the movie *Tom Jones*.

Alexander, Josef American 1907-1989
A Brace of Duets; GMP; 0011
A graduate of the New England Conservatory in piano, Alexander studied composition with Piston, Boulanger and Copland.

Alldahl, Per Gunnar Swedish 1943-
Rorverk 80; 1980-81; SMI; 12.5 mins; 0011
Bass clarinet is required.

Allen, Harold English 1917-1983
Duo; 1969; ESM; 11 mins; 0110

Althouse
Hymns of Prayer; SHA; 1010/1; B

Ames, William T. American 1901-
Pieces; ACA; 0110

Two Sketches; ACA; 1001

Amos, Keith English 20th C.
Raquettes; ESM; 1010; D

Anderson
Echoes; 1987; BBM; 0101; E

Andraud, Albert J.
Twelve Duets; c1935; SMC; 0110

Andriessen, Jurriaan Dutch 1925-
Aulos; c1959; DNA, PRC; 5 mins; 1100; C
Andriessen's music shows sound professional skill in a style that draws on diverse techniques without being bound to any specific system. Jurriaan is the brother of Louis Andriessen and son of Hendrik.

Arma, Paul   Hungarian/French   1905-1987
Three Transparencies; 1961; LEM; 11 mins; 1010
Born in Hungary, Arma also lived in the United States and France,
where he became interested in the folklore of these countries, concentrating particularly on American Negro spirituals and French songs.
Arma, a student of Bartok, wrote numerous orchestral, solo, chamber,
and vocal pieces. Arma's real name was Weisshaus, but he worked
under the pseudonym of Paul Arma after 1930. Oboe may be used in
place of flute.

Arrieu, Claude   French   1903-1990
Trois Duos Faciles; c1954; PRC, BIL; 3 mins; 1001; B/C
Arrieu studied at the Paris Conservatoire with Caussade, Long, Roger-
Ducasse and Dukas, taking a Premier Prix for composition in 1932.
Her subsequent career was in teaching and various kinds of work for
French radio, which she joined in 1946.

Asia, Daniel   American   1953-
Five Images; PRC; 1001
Asia has received numerous grants and fellowships including Meet the
Composer/Reader's Digest Commission, Fulbright Arts Award, Gug-
genheim Fellowship, National Endowment for the Arts Composer's
Grant and M.B. Rockefeller Grant. "An intense rhythmic construction
is the paramount characteristic of this inventive duet."—*The Instru-
mentalist*

Bach, Jan Morris   American   1937-
Four Two-Bit Contraptions; GLM; 1000/1; D/E
Bach holds degrees from the University of Illinois and is currently a
Distinguished Research Professor at Northern Illinois University. He
won first prize in the New York City Opera Competition. This difficult
work is a delight to both performers and audiences.

Bach, Johann Sebastian   German   1685-1750
Cantabile; Coolidge; KED; 1001; B/C
The most famous of the Bach family, Johann wrote primarily sacred
music and works for keyboard. He also was a master organist and instructor.

Concerto #3 in D Minor, BWV 1043; Langenus; CFI; 10 mins; 1010;
C/D
Originally for two violins and piano, this arrangement may be played
either with or without piano accompaniment.

Five More Two-Part Inventions; Conley; KED; 1010; D

Five Two-Part Inventions; Conley; KED; 1010; D
This set includes Inventions #1, 4, 8, 10, and 14.

Two Part Inventions, #12 and #13; Conley; KED; 0011

Two Part Inventions, #3 and #14; Conley; KED; 0011

Bach, Wilhelm Friedemann   German   1710-1784
Duo Sonata, F Major; Maganini; ESM; 1010; B/C
W.F. Bach, a son of Johann Sebastian, was a composer of superior talent. This work is a good example of two-part canonical writing with technical perfection and real emotional depth. It may be played on two like instruments or flute and oboe.

Baines, Francis   English   1917-
Comic Variations; ESM; 0011; C/D
Baines is one of England's leading double-bass players. He studied at the Royal College of Music in London where he later became a professor.

Baksa, Robert Frank   American   1938-
Three Trifles for Clarinet and Bassoon; PRC; 0011
A graduate of the University of Arizona with a degree in composition, Baksa has written over 400 works and is best known for his chamber music choral pieces. A student of Foss, Baksa began composing at the age of thirteen.

Balbastre, Claude   French   1727-1799
Noel, With Four Variations; Smim; ESM; 1001; C
Balbastre studied with Rameau and wrote music for piano, voice and organ. There is an alternate clarinet part for the bassoon.

Ball
Homage to Haydn: Sonatina in C; NOV; 1100; C
There are alternate oboe and clarinet parts to replace the flute and oboe parts respectively.

Homage to Mozart: Sonatina in C; NOV; 1100; C
There are alternate oboe and clarinet parts to replace the flute and oboe parts respectively.

Homage to Rossini: Sonatina in F; NOV; 1100; C
There are alternate oboe and clarinet parts to replace the flute and oboe parts respectively.

Homage to Schubert: Sonatina in D; NOV; 1100; C
There are alternate oboe and clarinet parts to replace the flute and oboe parts respectively.

Three Miniatures; NOV; 1100; C
There are alternate oboe and clarinet parts to replace the flute and oboe parts respectively.

Barrell, Christopher
Suite for Tom, Dick and Harriet; PIP; 1100; B
There are alternate versions (flute, clarinet, oboe) for both parts.

Bauer, Marion   American   1897-1955
Duo, Op. 25; 1932; PTE; 7 mins; 0110; D
Bauer studied with Boulanger, Ertel and Rothwell. Her music was basically impressionistic, showing clarity of texture and a strong sense of form. This work is in four movements titled *Prelude, Improvisation, Pastoral, Dance.*

Improvisation and Pastoral, Op. 22; c1997; EDV; 3 mins; 0110; C

Bavicchi, John Alexander   American   1922-
Six Duets for Flute and Clarinet, Op. 27; c1962; OUP; 11 mins; 1010
Bavicchi studied at the New England Conservatory with McKinley and Cooke and later at Harvard with Piston. His music is Neo-Baroque while using Classical forms.

Bayford, Frank   English   1941-
Scherzo, Op. 41; ESM; 0011; D/E
Bayford, a composer, music critic and concert promoter, wrote music for chorus, ensembles and orchestra.

Becker, John   American   1886-1961
Soundpiece, No. 6; 1942; PTE; 6 mins; 1010; C/D
Becker, together with Ives, Ruggles, Cowell and Riegger, belongs to the group called the "American Five" of avant-garde music. His music, bold and ultra modern, includes works for orchestra, ballet, chorus and chamber music.

Beekum, J.
Due Duetti; ESM; 1010; B/C
Oboe may replace flute.

Duets for Treble and Bass; ESM; 1001; B
There are alternate oboe or clarinet parts in place of the flute.

Easy Duets; ESM; 0110; B

Beethoven, Ludwig van   German   1770-1827
Allegro and Minuet; ESM; 1100; C
Beethoven's early achievements show him to be extending the Viennese Classical tradition. Later he began to compose in an increasingly unique musical style, and at the end of his life he wrote his most sublime and profound works.

Three Duos, WoO 27; Wildgans/Kirkbride; SCI, IMC; 5 mins each; 0011; C

Benjamin
Four By Two; SMC; 0011

Bennett, Robert Russell   American   1894-1981
Suite for Flute and Clarinet; WBP; 1010
After studies with Boulanger in Paris, Bennett worked as an orchestrator on Broadway, writing more than 300 musicals in 40 years.

Bentzon, Niels Viggo   Danish   1919-
Duettino, Op. 343; SCI; 4 mins; 1100
Bentzon studied at the Copenhagen Conservatory and began teaching there in 1949. His development, which shows the influence of Nielsen and Hindemith, includes works for orchestra, piano and chamber ensembles. His later works use many avant garde procedures. This work requires alto flute and English horn.

Berger, Arthur   American   1912-
Duo; 1952; PTE; 9 mins; 0110; D/E
Berger studied with Piston and Milhaud. Heavily influenced by Stravinsky, Berger's music is usually categorized as Stravinskian Neo-Classical. There is also a version for clarinet and piano transcribed by the composer.

Berkeley, Michael   English   1948-
American Suite; OUP; 1001
Michael is the son of Lennox Berkeley.

Besozzi, Alessandro   Italian   1702-1793
Divertimento in E Minor; MED; 0101
Son of Cristoforo Besozzi, Alessandro is best known as an oboist and teacher. Besozzi performed at the Ducal Chapel in Parma from 1728 to 1731 and toured with his brother, bassoonist Girolamo Besozzi. This work is written in the late Baroque style of the northern Italian school.

Sonata in F; MED; 0101; D

Besozzi, Carlo   Italian   1738-1791
Sonata in C; NPR, ESM; 0101; D
Carlo, a virtuoso oboist, was the son of Antonio Besozzi. He wrote in
a style similar to Haydn. This work is in standard sonata form.

Beyer, Johanna   German/American   1888-1944
Suite for Oboe and Bassoon; 1939; AMC; 0101
Beyer studied with Rudhyar, Crawford, Seeger and Cowell. Her style is
dissonant counterpoint.

Suite for Oboe and Clarinet; 1939; AMC; 0110

Binkerd, Gordon   American   1916-
Duo; c1970; BHI; 7 mins; 1100; D/E
Binkerd studied with Bernard Rogers, Piston, Kubik and Russell Dan-
burg. His music is usually written in a Neo-Classical idiom. This
moderately easy work dedicated to Charles Delaney and Baline Edlefsen
is in three multimeter movements.

Bischof, Rainer   Austrian   1947-
Duo, Op. 3; c1971; DBM; 7 mins; 1010; E
Bischof studied composition at the Vienna Academy of Music and privately with Apostel. His music follows the tenets of the Second
Viennese School. This twelve-tone work in three movements is based
on the following sequence: E, D, A-flat, C, B, F, A, D-sharp, B-flat, F-
sharp, G, C-sharp.

Blank, Allan   American   1925-
Bicinium II; AMC; 0011
Blank attended Juilliard then performed on violin with the Pittsburgh
Symphony before resigning to devote his time to composition. He has
published more than 60 works and received numerous grants and
awards. This work uses clarinet in A.

Four Bagatelles; SEE; 0110; D/E

Games in Space; 1987; RIC; 7 mins; 1010; D
This work was commissioned by the Virginia Music Teachers
Association and is dedicated to its first performers, David Niethamer
and Patricia Werrell, members of the Roxbury Chamber Players.
Using many twentieth-century musical devices, this work is divided
into five sections titled *Introduction, Divisions, Interlude, Passing the
Impulse* and *Coda*.

Boccherini, Luigi   Italian   1743-1805
Sonata; Sciannameo; SPR; 0011
Boccherini's style was very similar to Haydn's, and almost all his works are for instrumental chamber ensembles.

Borris, Siegfried   German
               1908-1987
Duo for Flute and Oboe, Op. 116 #1; 1964; BAR; 1100
Borris studied with Hindemith at the Berlin Hochschule für Musik. His musical style features lively dance-like rhythms with functional tonality.

Bosmans, Arthur   1908-
Tropicana 1; c1980; MOS; 6 mins; 1001; E
This is a very difficult, multimeter work in two movements: *Improviso and Chorinho.*

Boucard
Suite Champetre Leloir; PRC, BIL, ESM; 1000/1; D

Bozza, Eugene   French   1905-1991
Contrastes 1; c1977; LDA; 12 mins; 1001; D/E
Bozza studied with Busser, Rabaud, Capet and Nadaud at the Paris Conservatory where he won the Premiers Prix for the violin (1924), conducting (1930) and composition (1934), and also the Prix de Rome in 1934. Though his larger works have been successfully performed in France, his international reputation rests on his large output of chamber music for winds. His works display at a consistently high level the characteristic qualities found in mid-20th century French chamber music: elegant structure, melodic fluency and an awareness of the capabilities of the instruments for which he writes. This is a moderately difficult work in eight movements.

Contrastes II; c1977; LDA; 11 mins; 0101; D/E
The first movement is difficult, but the remaining two movements should not present too many problems.

Contrastes III; c1977; LDA; 14 mins; 0011; D/E

Sonatine; 1938; LDA; 1001; D/E

Trois Mouvements; c1974; LDA; 15 mins; 1010; D/E

Pieces; LDA, PRC; 1100; C
The oboe part could be played on flute.

Braun, Carl Anton Philipp   German   1788-1835
Six Duets; Dishinger; MED; flexible
Braun, an oboist and composer, was a member of the well known
Braun family of musicians. Though primarily known as a virtuoso,   he
also composed light pieces for a variety of combinations. Various
instrumentation may be used with flute, oboe, clarinet and bassoon.

Brockman, Jane   American   1949-
Shadows; c1985; ARP; 6 mins; 1010

Brod, Henri   French   1799-1839
First Sonate; c1976; BIL; 0101; D

Brosh, Thomas Denton   1946-
Dialogue for Treble Clef Instruments; SHA; 1100
Any treble clef instruments could be used.

Brown, A.
What Claude Did Next (Debussy); ESM; 0101; C
English horn required.

Brown, Newell Kay   American   1932-
Four Pieces; c1967; PRC; 5.5 mins; 1010; D
Brown writes in a natural, seemingly effortless style that transfers well
to other media, and he has penned many chamber works.

Burkhard, Willy   Swiss   1900-1955
Serenade, Op. 92 in B-Flat Major; 1953; BAR; 12 mins; 1010; D
During his early years Burkhard evolved a contrapuntal, imitative style
similar to Hindemith and Bartok. His harmony is based on church
modes and chromaticism, and there is a strong relationship between
harmony and melody. The movements in this five movement work are
titled *Dialog, Cavatine, Elegie, Perpetuum Motion* and *Marsch.*

Cage, John   American   1912-
Duet for Oboe and Horn; c1961; HNP, PTE; 0100/1
Cage studied composition with Weiss, Cowell, Schoenberg and Varese. He initiated the use of "prepared piano," which places an object
on a piano string to alter the tone color. He has written music for
piano, orchestra and chamber ensembles.

Call, Leonard   Austrian   1767-1815
Drei Duos, Op. 12; c1987; ESM; 1001; C
There is an optional oboe part to replace the flute.

Cambini, Giuseppe Marie   Italian   1746-1825
Six Sonatas, Vol. 1 and 2; ESM; 1001; C
Cambini was one of several composers who contributed greatly to the development of the string quartet. His works are charming and facile though somewhat limited in imagination. Cambini's many compositions also include symphonies, instrumental solos and other ensembles including the first three woodwind quintets every written, antedating Anton Reicha's quintets by more than ten years.

Campbell, Thomas
Ragged Diversion, No. 2; KED; 0011; D/E

Carastathis, Aris   Canadian   20th C.
Crosswind; 1994; CPI; 6 mins; 0011
Carastathis is on the faculty at Lakehead University in Ontario. In 1995 he was admitted as an Associate Composer of the Canadian Music Centre. A composer of more than fifty works, he has received numerous commissions and his works have been performed throughout the world. Counterpoint and rhythmic contrast define *Crosswind*. Primarily in a three part form, the piece makes extensive use of imitation. Pronounced rhythms and dance-like movement are complemented by lyrical passages. Both instruments read from a score.

Carroll, James   1950-
Five Little Canons; MMM; 1001; D/E

Cartan, Jean   French   1906-1932
Sonatine; 1930; LDA; 6 mins; 1010
Cartan studied with Rousseau and Dukas. Written in three movements (*Pastorale, Berceuse, Rondeau*), this witty work received a lot of enthusiasm at its premiere at the 1931 ISCM Festival in Oxford.

Carter, Elliott   American   1908-
Esprit Rude/Esprit Doux, #1; 1985; BHI; 4 mins; 1010; D/E
Carter's reputation is derived mainly from a few large-scale works. He studied with Piston, Hill and Boulanger. Carter has been the recipient of the highest honors that a composer may receive and has honorary degrees from many universities. His best music has an energy of invention that is unmatched in contemporary compositions.

Chagrin, Francis   English   1905-1972
Six Duets; NOV; 1100

Childs, Barney American 1926-
Duo; AMC; 1001
A student of Ratner, Chavez, Copland and Carter, Child's music incorporates improvisation and more traditional multi-section pieces. He has written music for orchestra, band, chamber music and chorus.

Horn and Oboe Music; AMC; 0100/1

Cirri, Giovanni Battista Italian 1724-1808
Divertimento in C Major; MED; 0101
Cirri served as a chamber musician to the Duke of Gloucester in England then returned to his native land sometime before his death. His works include string quartets, trio sonatas and duets for celli. This three movement work is part of a collection of music for small combinations of instruments. The style of the work indicates a possible keyboard source though there is no mention of such an adaptation on the title page.

Clarke, Henry American 1907-
A Game That Two Can Play; 1966;WIM; 1010; C
Clarke graduated from Harvard and studied with Boulanger in Paris. He uses many twentieth-century musical devices in his works. This is a single movement, moderately easy work, appropriate for students.

Cortes, Ramiro American 1933-1984
Duo; 1966; EVI, PRC; 1100; D
Cortes studied with Henry Cowell, Halsey Stevens and Ingolf Dahl. Until the late 1960s his music was serially organized. Thereafter it became more freely structured while remaining fully chromatic. This work requires English horn and alto flute.

Couperin, François French 1668-1733
Couperin Suite; Maganini; ESM; 1100; B/C
Couperin is considered one of the greatest French composers of his time with music for voice, chamber ensemble and harpsichord.

Cowles
Two-Getherness; FML; 1010; C

Cranmer, Philip 20th C.
Variations on a French Tune; NOV; 1010

Crosse, Gordon   English   1937-
Three Inventions, Op. 3; 1965; OUP; 5 mins; 1010; D/E
Crosse studied at Oxford and Egon Wellesz. His music reflects his
interest in both early music and modern techniques.

Curtis, Mike   20th C.
Duo Suite on Mexican Themes; ESM, MSS; 1010; C

Eight More Original Jazz Duos; MSS; 0101 or 0011

Eight More Original Jazz Standards; MSS; 0101

Cytron, Warren A.   1944-
Dances for Two Trebles; c1983; MMM; 6 mins; 1100; D/E
This work features two movements titled *Symetradanc* and *Tronner*.

Mixed Duos; MMM; 0101

Danfelt, Douglas
Divertimento for Flute and Clarinet; SHA; 1010; B/C

de Groot
Serenade; 1949; ESM; 0101; D

De Smet
28 Duos; FML; 1010; B/C

Deak, Csaba   Hungarian/Swiss   1932-
Duo-Svit; 1960; NMS; 1010
Deak studied clarinet and composition in Budapest and Sweden where
he was a student of Hilding Rosenberg. His music uses dodecaphonic
techniques.

Demersseman, Jules   French   1833-1866
William Tell-Duo Brilliant, Op. 37; PRC; 14 mins; 1100
Demersseman trained at the Paris Conservatory under the famous
Tulou.

Devienne, François   French   1759-1803
Six Duos, Op. 21; Mullers; 1788-1803; ESM; 0011; C/D
Devienne's compositions did much to raise the musical level of works
for wind instruments in late 18th-century France. He wrote concertos,
sinfonie concertantes, opera and chamber music. His music usually is
comprised of a single melodic line with accompaniment. The melodies
are elegant and graceful, and usually have sections intended to display
the performer's technique. A well-known flutist and bassoonist, he was

a prolific composer and showed a real interest in chamber music for wind instruments.

Six Duos, Op. 74, Vol. 1 and 2; MED, ESM; 1010; C/D

Symphonie Concertante #2; 1788-1803; EUL; 0011; C/D

Dijk, Jan Van   Dutch   1918-
Duo; DNA; 0011
Dijk studied composition with Pijper in Rotterdam and later taught at the Brabant Conservatory in Tilburg and the Royal Conservatory in Hague. He wrote hundreds of works for orchestra, piano and chamber ensembles.

Dobrzynski, Ignacy Feliks   Polish   1807-1867
Duet from Konrad Wallenrod; Kurkiewicz/Leloir; PWM; 0010/1
Dobrzynski was a prominent person in Warsaw musical life as pianist, composer, critic and teacher. He wrote a limited amount of music for orchestra, opera, chamber ensemble and piano.

Dominutti, Franco   20th C.
Petite Suite; c1983; LDA; 5 mins; 0101; C
This work features six movements titled *Prelude, Gavotte, Menuet, Sicilienne, Gigue* and *Conge (Postlude)*.

Donahue, Robert Lawrence   American   1931-
Five Canonic Duets; PRC; 1010; C
Donahue studied at the University of Wisconsin, University of Illinois and Cornell University. He is on the faculty of Spelman College.

Donatelli, Vincent   American   20th C.
Duet No. 1 for Flute and Clarinet; WIM; 2 mins; 1010; C/D
The flute part in this single movement work could be performed on oboe.

Duet No. 1 for Oboe and Clarinet; c1965; WIM; 3 mins; 0110; D

Duet No. 2 for Oboe and Clarinet; c1965; WIM; 3 mins; 0110; D
This two-movement work is a chromatic finger twister for both players.

Donatoni, Franco   Italian   1927-
Luci II; BHI; 10 mins; 0001/1
Donatoni studied with Ettore Desderi at the Milan Conservatory. His music has embraced serialism, electronic music and, later, an eccentric experimentalism.

Doppelbauer, Josef Friedrich   1918-1989
Duo Sonata; 1979; DBM; 12 mins; 0011; D

Dorff, Daniel   American   1956-
Andante con Variazioni; 1975; PRC; 5 mins; 1010
Dorff studied with Rochberg, Brumb, Husa and Wernicki at the University of Pennsylvania and Cornell University. He is the award-winning composer in residence for the Haddonfield, N.J., Symphony.

Dances and Canons; 1975; PRC; 7 mins; 1010; C
This work has nine movements titled *Waltz, Canon, Ballad, Canon, Invention, Dance, Nocturne, Canon* and *Dance*.

Douglas, Paul Marshall   Canadian   20th C.
Jamet De Saen-Troyes; 1989; NPR; 2 mins; 0101; D

Dubois, Pierre Max   French   1930-
Petite Suite; LDA; 1001; D/E
Dubois studied at the Paris Conservatoire and won the Prix de Rome in 1955. His main musical influences have been Milhaud, Françaix and Prokofiev, and he has written music for orchestra, dance and chamber ensembles.

Durieux, Frédéric   French   1959-
Alliances; DUR; 1010

Duvernoy, Victor Alphonse   French   1842-1907
Sonata #2; KAL, ESM; 0001/1; D/E

Eben, Petr   Czech   1929-
Duettini; GMP; 1100
Eben studied at the Academy of Music Arts in Prague and has written a large quantity of music for orchestra, organ, chorus and chamber ensembles.

Eklund, Hans   Swedish   1927-
Smaprat; 1965; GMF; 7 mins; 1010
Eklund, a student of Larssen and Pepping, wrote music that shows the influence of Hindemith as well as Baroque and Classical procedures. He wrote music for opera, orchestra and chamber music.

Elliot, Willard   American   1926-
Five Canonic Duets; BMP; 0101
Elliott, a renowned bassoonist, studied at North Texas State University and the Eastman School.

The Penguins; ESM; 0101; B

Erixon, Per Anders   Swedish   1930-
Divertimento, Op. 11; 1964; SMI; 9 mins; 0100/1

Duo, Op. 9; SMI; 5.5 mins; 0110
This work requires English horn.

Lento Och Allegro, Op. 3; 1964; SMI; 10 mins; 0011
This work requires clarinet in A.

Etler, Alvin D.   American   1913-1973
Duo; c1964; NVM; 0110
Etler studied with Hindemith while teaching woodwinds and conducting the band at Yale. He used serialism, but usually with a tonal center, and jazz is sometimes evident in his music. He wrote music for
orches-tra, chamber ensembles and chorus.

Eyser, Eberhard   Polish/Swedish   1932-
The Missing Link: Duo; 1993; ECB; 10 mins; 0110
Eyser studied at the Music Academy in Hanover and later became a
violist with the Royal Opera House Orchestra in Stockholm. English
horn and bass clarinet are required.

Favre, Georges   French   1905-1993
Pnyx; LDA; 1000/1
Favre writes in a very tuneful and rhythmically varied style.

Feld, Jindrich   Czech   1925-
Duo; LDA; 1001; E
Feld studied at the Academy of Music in Prague and later taught at the
Prague Conservatory. His early works are Neo-Classical while later mu-
sic uses serialism and aleatory. He wrote music for opera, orchestra and
chamber music.

Fenner, Burt L.   1929-
Suite; SEE; 1001

Fernandez, Oscar Lorenzo   Brazilian   1897-1948
Tres Invencoes Seresteiras; PIC; 0011
In his music, Fernandez adopted a strongly national style, derived from
Brazilian folksongs, but without actual quotation.

Ferrara, Anthony   20th C.
Divertimento #1; c1991; ALE; 1001; C
A unique new work linking traditional Mozartean style with contemporary techniques, this very playable work is an excellent addition to the repertoire. There is an optional oboe part to replace flute.

Ferstl
18 Duets; ESM; 1010; B/C

Fétis, François-Joseph   Belgian   1784-1871
Five Sonatinas; ESM; 0001/1; C/D

Fiala, Joseph   Czech   1748-1816
Duo Concertante #1 in F Major and #2 in C Major; c1979; NPR, ESM; 1001; C
Fiala was a friend of Mozart and an oboist in orchestras in Munich, Salzburg and Vienna. He composed a number of string quartets, symphonies and concertos, as well as numerous wind serenades which Mozart described in glowing terms. The flute part could be played on oboe.

Fischer
Bicinien; EAM; flexible instrumentation
Any two melody instruments may be used in this arrangement.

Fischer, Johann Christian   German   1733-1800
Duet in G Major; 1780-90; UNE; 8 mins; 0101; C/D
Fischer was one of the most popular oboists of his time, and his oboe concertos were famous, inspiring many composers, including Mozart, to make arrangements of his music. The oboe part could be played on flute.

Françaix, Jean   French   1912-
Sept Impromptus; 1977; EAM; 17 mins; 1001; D/E
A brilliant piano virtuoso, Francaix's music shows an innate gift for invention and an ability to express the freshness and wonder of childhood. "The *Impromptus* are witty, whimsical pieces of immense difficulty, and they are written with the possibilities of both instruments firmly in mind. Clever arpeggiation gives the semblance of chords; there is much use of elaborate dialogue between players. This work is a valuable addition to the repertoire."—*Seattle Times*

Frank, Andrew   American   1946-
Pastorale Duo; 1982; MOB; 3.5 mins; 1100; D

Freund, Donald Wayne   1947-
Pas de Deux; SEE; 0011

Fuchs, Georg-Friedrich   French   1752-1821
Three Duos; 1799; ESM; 1010; C/D
Fuchs, a clarinetist, studied with Haydn and Christian Cannabich. His compositions include pieces for military band, fanfares, a few orchestral works and numerous chamber music works, most of them involving clarinet.

Furrer-Munch, Franz   Swiss   1924-
Dialog; BHI; 8 mins; 0110

Gabaye, Pierre   French   1930-
Sonatine; c1692; LDA; 1001; D
This work is a light work appropriate for children's demonstrations or as a filler for a concert.

Gallay, Jacques François   French   1795-1864
Three Sonatas; PRC, BIL; 0001/1; C/D

Gallon, Noel   French   1891-1966
Sonata; LDA; 1001; E
Gallon studied at the Paris Conservatory and won the Prix de Rome in 1910. He was a renowned teacher and is best known as a composer for his dramatic and orchestral works. His compositions are noted for their elegance and clarity with a subtle impressionistic quality.

Garnier, Francois Joseph   French   1755-1825
Three Duos, Op. 4; Voxman; c1983; NPR, KZE, ESM; 0101; D
The first and third duos are in the key of F Major and the second duo is in C Major.

Gearhart, Livingston   20th C.
Duet Sessions; c1964; SHA; 1100

Gebauer, François Rene   French   1773-1845
Six Duos Concertante, Books 1 and 2; Allard; PRC; 0011; C/D
Gebauer, son of a German military bandsman, studied bassoon at the Paris Conservatory where he later served as professor of bassoon from 1796 to 1802 and later from 1826 on. Between 1802 and 1826 Gebauer played bassoon at the Grande Opera in Pairs. In his numerous compositions he concentrated especially on woodwind instruments.

Three Duos, Op. 17; BIL, ESM; 1001; D

Geminiani, Francesco   Italian   1687-1762
Sonata in E minor; BAR; 7 mins; 1001
Geminiani was a student of Corelli and was one of the greatest violin virtuosos of his time. He was a highly original composer and a teacher whose influence reached beyond his students through his treatises. This composition is written in standard, four-movement Baroque style. The flute part could be played on oboe.

Gerber, Steven R.   American   1948-
Prelude and Fugue; 1999; ACA; 7 mins; 0101

Ghent, Emmanuel   Canadian/American   1925-
Two Duos; 1962; OUP; 1010; D
Although influenced by Shapey and Varese, Ghent concentrates on the harmonic and melodic exploration of fixed interval groups. The flute part could be played on oboe.

Ginastera, Alberto   Argentine   1916-1983
Duo for Flute and Oboe; 1945; PRC; 1100; D
Ginastera graduated from the Williams Conservatory with a gold medal in composition and later graduated from the National Conservatory with highest honors in composition. This duet uses a quartal-chromatic, compellingly rhythmic idiom.

Glaser, Werner Wolf   Swedish   1910-
Duo; 1984; SMI; 6 mins; 1010
Glaser studied composition with Jarnach and Hindemith, and later became a choral conductor. His compositions for opera, orchestra and chamber groups are in a Neo-Classical style.

Liten Duett; 1967; SMI; 2 mins; 0110

Goepfert, Karl Andreas   English   1768-1818
Duo Concertante, Op. 19 #1; ESM; 0011; C/D

Goodman, Joseph Magnus   American   1918-
Jadis, In the Days of Yore; GMP; 8 mins; 1001
Born in New York City, Goodman has for many years been on the faculty of Queens College of the CUNY. He was also head of the Composition Department of the School of Sacred Music of Union Theological Seminary from 1958 to 1973. His teachers include Paul Hindemith, Walter Piston and Gian Francesco Malipiero.

Goossens, Sir Eugene   English   1893-1962
The Old Music Box; Schmidt; c1996; WIM; 1 min; flexible instrumentation; B/C
Goossens studied with Stanford at the Royal College of Music in London. He is perhaps best known as a conductor. His eclectic musical style includes works for opera, orchestra and chorus. Various instrumentations are possible using flute, clarinet, oboe and bassoon.

Gordon, Christopher   English   1949-
Sonatina; NPR; 1010; D
The flute part could be played on oboe.

Vienna 1791; ESM; 1010; D

Gould, Morton   American   1913-1996
Benny's Gig, Eight Duos; 1962-79; SCI; 16 mins; 0011
Gould integrated jazz, blues, gospel, country/western and folk elements into his compositions. Actually written for double bass instead of bassoon, this version works well. The final movement of the work was written as a birthday present for Benny Goodman's 70th birthday, while the first movement was a celebration of Goodman's 1962 Russian tour.

Duo; 1972; SCI; 10 mins; 1010; B
Written as a wedding present for friends, the six movements are titled *Unison, Song, March, Waltz, Hora* and *Lullaby*.

Gounod, Charles   French   1818-1893
March of a Marionette; Griffiths; ESM; 0011; B/C
Gounod, a leading figure in the revival of chamber music in France during the 1870s, wrote this piece specifically for the famous flute virtuoso, Paul Taffanel. It has been compared with the divertissements of Mozart and the septet and octet of the youthful Beethoven. Certainly the freshness and clarity of both melody and part-writing were inspired by those works.

Grabner, Hermann   Austrian   1886-1969
Kleine Serenade, Op. 47; KIS; 1001
Grabner studied music with Reger and Hans Sitt at the Leipzig Conservatory, later serving on the faculties of Strasbourg Conservatory, Mannheim Conservatory, Leipzig Conservatory, Hochschule für Musik in Berlin and the Berlin Conservatory.

Grahn, Ulf   Swedish   1942-
Chanson; 1969; SMI; 3 mins; 1010
Ulf studied composition with Gunnar Johanson and Hans Eklund at the Royal College of Music in Stockholm, later moving to America where he founded the Contemporary Music Forum which presents modern music by American and European composers. His music incorporates contemporary techniques that are accessible to most audiences.

Dialog; 1969; SMI; 7 mins; 1010

Grandert, Johnny   Swedish   1939-
Prego II; 1978; SMI; 8 mins; 0011
Grandert studied with Lidholm at the Royal College of Music in Stockholm. His music often uses startling contemporary effects and titles that are meant to intrigue audiences.

Gray
Relativity; ESM; 1010; E

Grimm, Carl Hugo   American   1890-1978
Alla Sarabanda; SMC; 0011; C/D
Grimm taught composition at the Cincinnati Conservatory from 1907 to 1931 and wrote music for orchestra, chamber ensembles, organ and voice.

Guerra, O. D'Estrade
Sonatine Pastorale; JMC; 0110

Haager, Max   1905-
Spielmusik; MFS; flexible instrumentation; A/B
This work may be performed on any two instruments in the same range.

Haan, Stefan de   1921-
Divertimento; PTE; 0011

Haieff, Alexei   Russian/American   1914-
Three Bagatelles; 1939; BBL; 6.5 mins; 0101; B/C
Haieff studied at the Juilliard School with Jacobi and Goldmark. His music is Neo-Classical, with some Stravinsky influence apparent. While there are some possible endurance challenges, this three-movement, multimeter work (originally written for piano) is otherwise not difficult.

Hall, Richard   English   1903-1982
Two Diversions; c1960; BHI; 1001; C/D
This modernistic work is fun to play and good for developing sight
reading skills for college and advanced high school students.

Hamel, Peter Michael   German   1947-
Tagtraum; 1979; BAR; 7 mins; 1010

Handel, George Frideric   German/English   1685-1759
Nine Duets from Concerti Grossi, Op. 6; Dishinger; MED; 1010
Handel's music featured grand design, lush harmonies and a certain
eloquence. He wrote works for opera, oratorios, chamber ensembles and
orchestra.

Harris, Robert A.   African American   1938-
Two by Two Duets for Flute and Clarinet; FMI, SCI; 1010; B
Harris received degrees from Wayne State University, the Eastman
School and Michigan State University. His teachers included Bernard
Rogers and H. Owen Reed.

Hart, Weldon   American   1911-1957
Interlude; 1945; SPR; 2 mins; 1001; C
Hart studied with Howard Hanson and Bernard Rogers at the Eastman
School. Written for Murray Panitz and Loren Glickman, this is a mod-
erately easy work in one movement.

Hartman, Christian   German   1750-1804
Nine Duets; Dishinger; MED; 1100; B/C

Hartzell, Eugene American   1932-
Workpoints #1; DBM; 9 mins; 1001; E
Hartzell studied at Kent State University and Yale University. He uses
the twelve-tone method.

Workpoints #2; 1977; DBM; 0110; E

Workpoints #3; 1978; DBM; 1000/1; E

Workpoints #4; 1978; DBM; 8 mins; 1100; E

Workpoints #5; c1982; DBM; 7.5 mins; 0010/1

Workpoints #6; 1979; DBM; 8 mins; 0101; E
This is a single-movement, multi-section work of considerable difficulty.

Workpoints #7; c1983; DBM; 0001/1

Workpoints #8; c1984; DBM; 7.5 mins; 0011

Workpoints #9; 1982; DBM; 7 mins; 0100/1; E

Workpoints #10; 1983; DBM; 9 mins; 1010; E

Harvey, Paul   1918-
All At Sea; c1965; BHI; 3 mins; 0110; C/D
This two-movement work (*Hornpipe, Shanty*) is interesting, light en-
tertainment.

Ten for Two, Vol. 1 and 2; FML; 1010; B/C

The Summer Belles; WBP; 1010; C

Hasquenoph, Pierre   French   1922-1982
Sonata Espressa; EME; 1001

Hauta-Aho, Teppo   Finnish   1941-
Duettino; FMC; 4 mins; flexible instrumentation
The treble part could be played on flute, oboe or clarinet; bassoon is
required.

Hayden, Paul
Hambridge Quavers; PRC; 0101; E

Haydn, Joseph   Austrian   1732-1809
Three Sonatas; Maganini; ESM; 1010
Haydn is considered the creator of the Classical form of the symphony
and string quartet. He played an historic role in the evolution of
harmony by adopting four-part writing as the compositional foundation.
A prolific composer, Haydn wrote music for orchestra, chamber ensembles, concertos, dramatic works, masses and oratories.

Witches' Canon; Skolnik; ESM; 1010; B/C

Hedwall, Lennart   Swedish   1932-
Duos; 1952/55; SMI; 0011
Hedwall studied composition with Back and Blomdahl.

Five Epigrams; 1959; HAN; 6 mins; 1010; C/D
These five short movements are *Lento, Allegro, Andantino, Allegro
vivace* and *Lento.*

Liten Duo; 1975; SMI; 1 min; 1001
Alternate oboe or clarinet part may replace flute.

Sonatina; 1964/75; HBM; 6 mins; 1100; B

Variations and Fugue; 1975; NMS; 7 mins; 1100; C

Heinichen, Johann David   German   1683-1729
Sonata in C Minor; c1985; ESM; 4 mins; 0101; C/D
Written in standard Baroque form, this work includes three movements
titled *Vivace, Largo* and *Presto.*

Hekster, Walter   Dutch   1937-
Setting #9; 1988; DNA; 8 mins; 0011
After graduation from the Amsterdam Conservatory, Hekster was a
clarinetist with the Connecticut Symphony Orchestra and later taught
clarinet and composition at Brandon University (Canada), Utrecht
Conservatory and Arnhem Conservatory. This work requires doubling
on English horn and bass clarinet.

Hermanson, Christer   Swedish   1943 -
Applikatur; 1976/93; SMI; 1001

Heussenstamm, George   American   1926-
Ambages; SEE; 1010
Heussenstamm was a recipient of a 1976 National Endowment for the
Arts grant and is on the faculty of California State College at
Dominguez Hills.

Hoffding, Niels Finn   Danish   1899-
Dialogues, Op. 10; 1927; CHE, HAN; 8.5 mins; 0110; C/D
Hoffding initially drew his inspiration from Nielsen's modernism as
well as Stravinsky, Bartók and Hindemith. He is perhaps best known
for his choral arrangements and songs.

Hoffmeister, Franz Anton   Austrian   1754-1812
Drei Duos for Flute and Oboe, Op. 38; HOF; 1100; C/D
Hoffmeister, a well-known music publisher in his time, was also a prolific composer. He wrote music for orchestra, concertos, stage and
chamber ensembles.

Hofmann, Leopold   Austrian   1738-1793
Divertimento in C Major; Biba; EUL; 1001
Hofmann composed a large number of vocal works, symphonies and
chamber music.

Holcombe, Bill   American   20th C.
Intermediate Jazz Etudes; MPI; 1010; D

Hook, James   English   1746-1827
Hornpipe; Emerson; c1995; ESM; 1001; B/C
A child prodigy, Hook played harpsichord at the age of four, performed concertos when he was six and composed a ballad opera at eight. He later served as organist at Vauxhall for more than fifty years. This work, good for encores, is fun to play and not very difficult. Clarinet may replace the flute.

Hovhaness, Alan   American   1911-
Prelude and Fugue, Op. 13; c1967; PTE; 0101
Although most of Hovhaness's music is instrumental, almost every work is religious in nature. His melodies are clear and modal, harmonies are consonant but progress chromatically rather than tonally, and he uses counterpoint from a variety of periods.

Sonata for Oboe and Bassoon; PIC; 0101

Suite, Op. 21; c1968; PTE; 0101
English horn is required.

Suite, Op. 23; c1968; PTE; 0101

Hughes, Kent   20th C.
Second Chance; WIM; 1100; D

Hunt, G.
Duo in F Major; DCM, ESM; 0101; C/D

Hyams, Alan
Prelude, Blues and Fugue; c1973; SMC; 6 mins; 1010; C/D
There is another version of this work for clarinet and bassoon.

Ibert, Jacques   French   1890-1962
Trois Pieces; LDA; 1100
Ibert studied at the Paris Conservatory with Paul Vidal for composition, and won several prizes there in 1914. He won the Prix de Rome in 1919, after serving in WWI. He made important contributions in all musical genres except oratorio. He used Classical forms as a foundation, but made them flexible, always with a strong sense of balance and restraint. Flute may replace oboe.

Inwood, Mary B.   American   20th C.
Seven Bagatelles for Wind Trio; 1981; SEE; 1010/1
Inwood studied at Queens College, New York University and City University of New York.

Suite for Clarinet and Bassoon; 1985; SEE; 0011

Jacob, Gordon   English   1895-1984
Three Inventions; c1951; ESM; 1100; C/D
Jacob studied with Stanford and Howells at the Royal Academy of Music and Dulwich College and later joined the faculty of the RAM. His works are deeply rooted in tradition and display fine craftsmanship.

Three Little Pieces; c1968; MRI; 3 mins; 0101; C
Dedicated to Evelyn Rothwell and Archie Camden, this is a delightful concert piece suitable for professionals and students.

Jalkanen, Pekka Finnish   20th C.
Asca; 1983; FMC; 11.5 mins; 0101

Jansson, Johannes   Swedish   1950-
Duo; 1991; SMI; 12 mins; 1001

Johnsen, Hallvard Olav   Norwegian   1916-
Suite, Op. 41; 1964; HAN; 1000/1; D/E
Johnsen studied composition with Brustad at the Oslo Conservatory and later with Karl Andersen and Holmboe.

Johnson, Hunter   American   1906-
Serenade for Flute and Clarinet; NVM; 1010
Johnson studied at the University of North Carolina and Eastman. His compositions show the influence of jazz and include music for orchestra, concertos, piano and chamber ensembles.

Johnson, Robert Sherlaw   English   1932-
The Monuments of the Emperor of China; 1991; OUP; 4 mins; 1010

Jolivet, André   French   1905-1974
Sonatine; 1961; BHI; 8 mins; 1010; D/E
Jolivet wrote a great quantity of music for stage, orchestra, voice, chamber ensembles and solo instruments. He greatly admired Debussy and Stravinsky and this influence is apparent in his music.

Sonatine; 1963; BHI; 0101; D/E

Jones, David Evan   20th C.
Later That Same Evening #1 and #2; 1987; NHP; 1010; E

Joplin, Scott   African American   1868-1917
Easy Winners, a Ragtime Two Step; Kauffman; ALE; 1001; B
Named the "King of Ragtime", Joplin was largely self-taught though he briefly attended the Smith College for Negroes in 1895 to gain tech-

nical skills in composition. A traditional favorite Joplin two-step, this arrangement is perfect for social events and encores.

Kaplan, Lloyd   American   20th C.
Two Part Invention; PMP; 0011
Kaplan was primarily known as a jazz musician.

Karkoff, Maurice   Swedish   1927-
Cinque Caratteri, Op. 138; 1978; SMI; 9 mins; 1010
Karkoff's teachers included Blomdahl, Larsson, Koch, Holmboe, Jolivet and Vogel. His music reflects his interest in many cultures.

Duo, Op. 3; 1951; SMI; 6 mins; 0011

Kay, Ulysses   African American   1917-
Suite for Flute and Oboe; 1964; MCA; 5 1/2 mins; 1100; C/D
Kay studied with Hindemith and Luening. He is regarded as one of the important American composers of his generation and the leading black composer of his time. His works include music for orchestra, chorus, band and opera. His career has included many awards such as the Prix de Rome, Fulbright and Guggenheim.

Keal, Minna   English   1909-1999
Duettino, Op. 6; 1996; ESM; 1010; E

Kelterborn, Rudolf   Swiss   1931-
Incontri Brevi; 1967; BAR; 9 mins; 1010; E
Kelterborn's early works are firmly based in the Neo-Baroque tradition. Later works incorporate unusual techniques of the 1950s and 1960s.

Kennis, Willem Gommaire   Netherlands   1717-1789
Divertimento in E Major; Thomas; MED; 3.5 mins; 0101
Kennis, his first name is sometimes spelled Guillaume, was a violin virtuoso and composer. This work may have been adapted from another medium since the bassoon (cello) part is more accompanimental in character and may perhaps be a figured bass in the original version. The style of the work indicates an origin more late Baroque than Rococo or Classical though Kennis lived into the third quarter of the century.

Kenny, Terry   20th C.
Street Wise; PRC; 1010; C

Keuler, Jeno   20th C.
Piccola Partita; 1936; MBP; 3 mins; 0011; C/D

Kibbe, Michael   American   1945-
Three Canons; SEE; 1010
Kibbe studied at San Diego State University, New Mexico State University and California State University at Northridge. He has written music for orchestra, band, chamber ensemble, choral and solo pieces.

Kiel, Friedrich   German   1821-1885
Five Duos; Sikorski; 1850; SCI; 0011
Kiel is known for the masterly command of counterpoint in his choral works. These five duets, transcribed from the *Fifteen Canons for Piano, Op. 1,* offer some of the few Romantic period pieces available for this combination of instruments.

Knussen, Oliver   Scottish   1953-
Elegiac Arabesques, Op. 26; 1991; FMI, ESM; 4 mins; 0110
Knussen studied with Schuller and wrote music for opera, orchestra and chamber ensembles. English horn is required.

Koch, Erland V.   Swedish   1910-
Dialogue; 1975/79; DNP; 4 mins; 1010

Kocsar, Miklos   Hungarian   1933-
Ungaresca; BVP; 1010
Kocsar studied with Farkas at the Budapest Academy.

Koechlin, Charles   French   1867-1950
Confidences d'un Joueur, Op. 14 #2, 8, 9, 10, 12 and 18; PRC; 0001//1
A student of Faure, Koechlin is considered a revolutionary Classicist and has gained a place for himself alongside the greatest innovators of his time by his harmonious synthesis of numerous musical trends. He was a member of "Les Nouveaux Jeunes" along with Roussel, Milhaud and others. Among his hundreds of works are pieces for stage, orchestra, chorus, cinema, chamber and solos.

Sonatine Modale, Op. 155; 1935-6; PRC; 6 mins; 1010; C

Koivula, Kari   Finnish   20th C.
Reeds; 1985; FMC; 0110
Bass clarinet is required.

Komorous, Rudolf   Czech/Canadian   1931-
Duettino; 1954; ESM; 3.15 mins; 0011; C/D
Komorous attended the Prague Conservatory and Academy of Music where he studied bassoon with Pivonka and composition with Borkovec. His music incorporates a wide variety of twentieth-century compositional techniques.

Konig, Herbert
Duo for Flute and Clarinet; TBM; 1010; C

Krenek, Ernest   Austrian/American   1900-1991
Sonatina, Op. 92 #2b; 1942; BAR; 7 mins; 1010; D
Krenek grew up in Vienna and his development as a composer went through a number of stylistic periods: Post-Romanticism, experimentation, Neo-Classicism and atonality combined with elements of jazz.

Kubik, Gail   American   1914-1984
Five Birthday Pieces; 1974; KAL, EAM; 1010
Kubik studied composition with Rogers and Royce at the Eastman School. While basically tonal, his music uses modern techniques. This work is originally for two recorders.

Kummer, Kaspar   German   1795-1870
Deux Duos Concertantes, Op. 46; PRC; 5 mins each; 1010; C/D
Kummer is best known as a flutist and composer of music for flute.

Kunert, Kurt   1911-
Sonate in G Major, Op. 15; c1944; HOF, BBL; 15 mins; 0011; C

Sonate, Op. 20; HOF; 0011; C

Kupferman, Meyer   American   1926-
Available Forms; GMP; 0011
Kupferman studied at Queens College of the City University of New York and later taught at Sarah Lawrence College. He received awards from Guggenheim and the American Academy and Institute of Arts and Letters. His works make use of Neo-Classicism, serialism, jazz and electronics.

Dovely Duo; 1998; SSP; 1010

Duo Divertimento; GMP; 0011

Four Charades; GMP; 1010

Four Constellations; GMP; 1010

Kurz, Walter
Suite of Variations; DBM; 0011

Lacome, Paul Jean Jacques   French   1838-1920
Passepied: Duo; DUR; 1001
Lacome is best known for his operettas though he also wrote orchestral suites, chamber music, piano pieces and songs. There is an alternate oboe part in place of the flute.

Leech, Alan   American   1944-
Ranch-On Danzon; 1986; ALE; 2 mins; 1001; B/C
Leech has been on the music faculty at Montana State University since 1972. This work, originally written for performance by jazz quartet in 1981 and transcribed for flute and bassoon by the composer in 1986, has a somewhat South American rhythm with an ostinato background and floating melody. Unique and lots of fun to play, this is a great addition to a recital.

Lees, Benjamin   American   1924-
Three Duos; 1973; BHI; 1010
Lees studied at the University of Southern California with Halsey Stevens, Ernst Kanitz and Ingolf Dahl. His music is basically traditional in approach and his artistic creed is to be original but comprehensible.

Leichtling, Alan   1947-
Nachtmusik; SEE; 0011
This work requires bass clarinet in place of B-flat clarinet.

Lemeland, Aubert   French   1932-
Suite Dialogue, Op. 65; c1977; PRC; 10.5 mins; 0110
Lemeland's works comprise more than a hundred pieces of chamber, instrumental and orchestral music. This single-movement, multimeter work presents some endurance problems but otherwise should not be difficult.

Levy, Frank Ezra   French/American   1930-
Duo; SEE; 0011
Levy, son of Ernst Levy, holds degrees from the Juilliard School and Uni-versity of Chicago. He was a cello student of Rose and Starker.

Lewin, Gordon   English   20th C.
Caribbean Sketches; BHI; 1010; D

Nostalagie d'Espana; BHI; 1010; D

Three Latin American Impressions; BHI; 4 mins; 1010; C
Written in three movements *(La Chica, El Burro Pequeno, Bailecito Mexicano)*, this is fairly easy other than some occasional rhythmical challenges.

Lindgren, Par   Swedish   1952-
Ioga: Inventions; 1993; SMI; 1001

Linn, Robert   American   1925-
Five Pieces; 1950; SHA; 1010; C/D
Linn studied composition with Milhaud, Halsey Stevens and Roger Sessions.

Loeillet, Jean-Baptiste   Flemish   1680-1730
Sonata, Op. 5 #1 - #3; 1717; 10 mins each; 1001
Loeillet recognized the flute as the instrument of the moment and wrote this set of flute/bassoon duets due to this increased demand for flute music. The flute part may be played on oboe.

Lowry, Robert   American   1826-1899
Farce and Fantasy; SMC; 3 mins; 1010; D
Best known for writing hymn music, he was also a Baptist preacher.

Lunde, Jr., Ivar   Norwegian/American 1944-
A L'Ecole At School, Op. 11; c1978; SHA; 0110; C/D
Lunde, an oboist, has served on the faculties of the University of Maryland and University of Wisconsin. Laid out as six hours of classes at school, this work includes movements titled *Song Lesson, Mathematics Lesson, History Lesson, Gymnastics Lesson, English Lesson* and *French Lesson*.

Lutek, Peter A.   1962-
Duo; MMM; 0101; E

Lyons, Graham
Short Sonata; ESM; 0011; D/E

Maasz, Gerhard   German   1906-1984
Duo in G; MOS; 7 mins; 1100; B/C
This five-movement work should present no significant technical difficulties.

Five Inventionen; MOS; 7 mins; 1010

Maganini, Quinto   American   1897-1974
Canonico Espressivo; ESM; flexible instrumentation; C
A composer, conductor and flutist, Maganini studied with Boulanger and performed with the New York Symphony Orchestra. He wrote an opera and many orchestral and chamber music works.

Petite Suite Classique; ESM; 3 mins; 1010; C
This work could also be performed with flute duet, flute and oboe or oboe and clarinet.

Makovecky
Duo Concertante #1; ESM; 0010/1; D

Mangs, Runar   Swedish   1928-
Six Bagatelles; SMI; 1010

Margola, Franco   Italian   1908-1992
Partita for Flute and Oboe; 1965; EDC; 1100
After studies at the Parma Conservatory and the Accademia di Santa Cecilia, he taught at conservatories in Cagliari, Bologna, Milan, Rome and Parma. He wrote music for opera, orchestra and chamber groups.

Massias, Gerard   1933-
Dialogues; BIL; 1100; E

McBride, Robert   American   1911-
Hot Shot Divertimento; ACA; 0110
A prolific composer of more than 1,000 works in various genres, McBride frequently used American or Mexican themes with a jazz influence. A student of Luening, he was awarded a Guggenheim Fellowship in 1937 and the Pulitzer Prize in 1942.

McGuire, Edward   Scottish   1948-
Four Two-Part Inventions; SMP; 1010
McGuire studied at the Royal Academy of Music and the State Academy of Music in Stockholm.

McLeod, John   Scottish   1934-
Sonatina for Flute and Oboe; SMP; 10 mins; 1100
McLeod studied with Berkeley at the Royal Academy of Music and is currently a Visiting Professor at the Royal Academy of Music. He won the Guinness Prize for British composers in 1979.

Mellnas, Arne   Swedish   1933-
Vaxlingar; 1961; SMI; 9 mins; 1010
Mellnas studied with Larsson, Blomdahl and Wallner at the Stockholm Musikhogskolan. Privately he worked with Deutsch, Ligeti and Koenig. He is considered one of Sweden's most innovative avant-garde composers. This work requires piccolo and bass clarinet.

Michalsky, Donal Ray   American   1928-1975
Sonatina for Flute and Clarinet; KAL; 1010
Michalsky studied with Dahl and Halsey Stevens at the University of Southern California and did post-graduate work in Germany with Wolfgang Fortner on a Fulbright grant. His music is characterized by lyric lines, effective use of counterpoint and generally conservative harmonies and phrasing. His forms paraphrase traditional styles.

Mignone, Francisco   Brazilian   1897-
Invention; 1961; EDV; 2 mins; 0011; C/D

Migot, Georges   French   1891-1976
Suite in Three Movements; BAR; 1010
Migot was an accomplished composer, poet and visual artist. His music uses diatonic melodies but avoids any suggestion of definite tonality. The flowing quality of Migot's music is in the tradition of Debussy and Couperin.

Miller
Just Desserts; SMC; 1001

Miscellaneous
Baroque and Classical Duets; Elkan; EVI; 1001; C
There is an optional oboe part to replace flute.

Christmas Companion; Hobbs; ESM; 1010; B

Christmas for Two, #1-#3; Conley; c1996; KED; 1010; B
This collection of traditional carols would be good for light holiday concert programs, church services and caroling excursions. Arrangements also available in a variety of other instrumentation.

Christmas Jazz; Cathrine; ESM; Flexible instrumentation; B/C
Any combination of flute, oboe and clarinet may be used for these arrangements.

Duos Concertants #1-#3 Series; Andraud; SMC; 1010; C
There are three sets of books with music by Bach, Handel, Mozart and others.

Duo Ho Ho!; Isaacson; ALE; 1100; C
This collection of twelve familiar Christmas carols is suitable for any two treble instruments.

Eight Duos of Chanukah; Isaacson; ALE; 1100; C
Any two treble instruments may be used on this set of Chanukah songs including *Sevinon, Mi Y'mallel, Chanukah, I Have a Little Dreidle, Oh Chanukah Oh Chanukah, Light the Legend, Ner Li* and *Ma Oz Tsur.*

From A to Z; Arbatsky; MMM; 1010; C
Arbatsky studied with Grabner at the Conservator of Leipzig. He wrote works for orchestra, chorus and chamber ensembles. Oboe may replace flute. This is a collections of original and unoriginal arrangements of music by Tschaikovsky, Rheinberger, Purcell, Paganini, Mendelssohn, Liszt, Haydn, Couperin and Bach.

Get Reel: Jigs, Reels and Strathspeys; McConnell; ESM; 1010

Holidays for Two; Conley; KED; 1010; B/C

Jiggery Folkery; McConnell; PRC; 1010

Kol Nidre; Kaplan; ALE; 1001; B/C
This traditional Jewish song, used in High Holiday Services, is a beautifully arranged plaintive and touching melody.

Londonderry Air: British Folksongs; Kenny; ESM; 1010; B/C

Nine Christmas Songs; Ferstl; HOF; 1010; B/C

Seventeen Short Duets; Frank and Forbes; OUP; 1010; C

Seventy-Eight Duets, Vol. 2; Voxman; Rubank; 1010
This set include music by Mozart, Bach, Chedeville and more.

Take Your Partner for Christmas; Cramer; CRA; 1010; B

Three Duos; OUP; 1010; D/E
This collection includes duets by Rutter, Kelly and Dodgson.

Tunes for Two; Tambling; ESM; Flexible instrumentation; A/B
Various combinations of flute, oboe, clarinet and bassoon could be used.

Twelve Duets; SMC; 1001
Oboe may be used to replace flute on these duets by Mozart, Handel and Bach.

Woodwind Duets II; Weston; FML; 1010; B/C

Monaco, Richard   American   1930-1987
Five Short Pieces; SHA; 5.5 mins; 1010; C/D
Monaco received the BA, MA and DMA degrees in composition from
Cornell University. He studied with Hunter Johnson, Robert Palmer
and Roberto Gerhard. He was the recipient of the ASCAP composition
award for three consecutive years.

Morawetz, Oskar   Czech/Canadian   1917-
Four Duets; OUP; 14 mins; 1001; D
This work was commissioned by members of the New York Philhar-
monic through the Ontario Arts Council.

Morigi, Angelo   Italian   1725-1801
Duetto in B-Flat Major; Voxman; NPR; 0101; C/D
Morigi had an excellent reputation as a teacher of composition with
many works for violin solo, trio sonatas and a number of concerti.

Morthenson, Jan W.   Swedish   1940-
Intimi; 1978; EDR; 0011
Tape is required.

Moszumanska-Nazar, Krystyna   Polish   1924-
Five Duets; 1959; PWM, PRC; 1010
Moszumanska-Nazar studied composition with Wiechowics at the State
College of Music in Krakow. Her music uses harmonic dissonance with
formal Classical structure.

Mozart, Wolfgang A.   Austrian   1756-1791
Four Short Pieces for Two Diverse Instruments; TIE; flexible instrumentation
Mozart was a musical genius whose works in virtually every genre are
unmatched in lyrical beauty and rhythmic variety.

Seven Menuets, K.65A; Dishinger; MED; 1100; C

Sonata in B-Flat Major, K. 292; Emerson; ESM; 0011; C/D
This work was originally for bassoon and cello.

Sonatina in C Major; NOV; 1100

Twelve Duets, K.487; Ball; 1785; NPR; 20 mins; 1100
These duets were originally written for two basset horns. Oboe and
clarinet could replace the flute and oboe respectively.

Muczynski, Robert   American   1929-
Duos; SCI; 1010
Muczynski studied with Alexander Tcherepnin at DePaul University.
He has won fourteen ASCAP awards and two Ford Foundation grants.

Muczynski received both Bachelor and Masters degrees from De Paul University in piano and composition.

Muir
Six Duets; ESM; 0110; B

Mullins, H.
Duets; CFI; 1010

Murto, Matti Jrjo Juhani   Finnish   1947-
Duo; 1972; FMC; 0110
Murto studied at the Sibelius Academy and the University of Helsinki. He wrote music for orchestra and chamber ensembles.

Musgrave, Thea   Scottish/American   1928-
Impromptu #1; 1967; CHE, SCI; 4 mins; 1100; D/E
Musgrave studied with Boulanger and Copland. Her numerous awards include the Koussevitzky and a Guggenheim fellowship. The composer described her writing style as "dramatic-abstract: that is dramatic in the sense of presentation, but at the same time abstract because there is no programmatic content." Musgrave describes this piece as follows: "It is a short work and, as its title implies, lighthearted. The music grows out of a very short idea heard at the outset. Each time this motive returns there is a different continuation. The final coda, marked as fast as possible, brings the work to a virtuosic close."

Naumann, Siegfried   Swedish   1919-
Duet in B-Flat; c1954; SIK; 0101; C
Naumann studied with Pizzetti, Malipiero and Orff. His music uses serialism and aleatory techniques.

Duo; 1948; SMI; 13 mins; 0011

Nelhybel, Vaclav   Czech/American   1919-
Four Duets for Woodwinds; GMP; flexible instrumentation
Nelhybel, best known for his symphonic band music, used harmonic dissonance with tonal centers.

Nemiroff, Isaac   American   1912-1977
Duo; MMM; 0110; C/D
Nemiroff studied at Cincinnati Conservatory and with Stefan Wolpe at the New York College of Music. Bass clarinet is required.

Nixon, Roger   American   1921-
Four Duos; 1966; PRC; 6 mins; 1010; C
Nixon studied with Bliss, Bloch, Sessions and Schoenberg, later joining the faculty of San Francisco State University. A prolific composer, he writes in a consistent contemporary idiom with a distinctly American flair. His numerous awards and grants include the NEA and ASCAP. The flute part could be played on oboe.

Two Duos; c1981; GLM; 2.5 mins; 1010; C/D
Piccolo and E-flat clarinet are required.

Noble
Chit Chat; ESM; 1010; C

Norre, Dorcas   1911-1985
Pastorale; SMI; 1100
Could be performed on any two treble instruments.

Nuorvala, Juhani   Finnish   20th C.
Five Pieces; 1994; FMC; 1010

Olsen, Sparre   Norwegian   1903-1984
Aubade, Op. 57#3; HAN; 1000/1; C
Olsen studied music with Percy Grainger and Fartein Valen. He represents the continuation of the Grieg tradition and Norwegian nationalism. He is particularly known for his vocal works.

Nocturne, Op. 57#2; HAN; 1000/1; D

Otten, Ludwig   Netherlands   1924-
Duo; DNA; 4 mins; 1001

Paciorkiewicz, Tadeusz   Polish   1916-
Twenty Two Preludes; PWM; 1001; C/D
Paciorkiewicz studied with Sikorski and later taught in various music schools including the Warsaw State College of Music.

Parry-Jones, Gwyn   Welsh/English   1891-1963
Welsh Rarebit; ESM; C
Jones studied at the Royal College of Music and is best known as a singer.

Pearson, William Dean   1905-
Three Pastorale Fugues; c1965; BHI; 1100

Phillips, Gordon   1908-
Suite in B-Flat Major; c1949; EAM; 6 mins; 0110; C/D
This work has four movements titled *March, Pastoral, Lydian Hymn*
and *Menuetto.*

Pillin, Boris   American   1940-
Sonata for Clarinet and Bassoon; 1922; WIM; 0011
Pillin received degrees from the University of California in Los Angeles
and University of Southern California and is perhaps best known for his
book about Schoenberg's music. He has written music for orchestra,
piano, and chamber ensembles. Regarding his music, Mr. Pillin states:
"I feel that my music is imbued with an urban quality, reflecting the
complexity and multi-faceted moods of the big city, often in a jazz-like
manner."

Pirani, Osvaldo
Momento Dinamico; ESM; 0011; D

Pisk, Paul Amadeus   Austrian/American   1893-1990
Duo, Op. 106; 1966; AMC; 0011
Pisk describes his style as "linear, not atonal but free in tonal centers
and using the traditional structures and motivic development." He co-
wrote a book on musical style and history.

Plumby, Donald   1919-
Picture of a Hunt; CPP; 1001; C/D
There is an alternate oboe part in place of flute and an arrangement for
four clarinets.

Poulenc, Frances   French   1899-1963
Sonata; 1922/rev.1945; CHE, SCI; 8 mins; 0011; D/E
Influenced by Ravel's Neo-Classicism, Poulenc wrote music for voice,
piano, organ and sacred works. His style is deceptively simple with
tonal melodies laced with quickly passing dissonance. This difficult,
three-movement work has a wandering quality reminiscent of Debussy.

Poulteau, Pierre   French
Sonatine, LDA, 12 mins, 0011, D
This four-movement, moderately difficult work should not present
problems for the ensemble aside from the final movement which is in
5/8 meter. Cello could be used in place of bassoon.

Pregnitz, Hans   German   1913-
Duettini; ESM; 1010; D/E

Presser, William Henry   American   1916-
Five Duets for Flute and Clarinet; 1987; PRC; 6.5 mins; 1010; C
Presser studied with Bernard Rogers, Burrill Phillips, Roy Harris and
Gardner Read at the Eastman School. He has won numerous awards
and grants and has served on the faculties of Florida State University,
West Texas State College and the University of Southern Mississippi.
Al-though he didn't start composing until age 25, Presser has written
well over 200 works, of which over 120 have been published.

Five Duets for Oboe and Bassoon; 1966; PRC; 7.5 mins; 0101; C/D

Primosch, James   American   1956-
Exchanges for Flute and Clarinet; 1981; PRC; 8 mins; 1010; D
Primosch is a student of Crumb, Wernick and Davidovsky while
studying at the University of Pennsylvania and Columbia University.
Among the many awards he has received are the Guggenheim Fellowship, a grant from the NEA and two prizes from the American Academy
and Institute of Arts and Letters.

Prinz
Dialog; ESM; 1001; D/E

Puccini, Giacomo   Italian   1858-1924
La Boheme for Two; Simpson; 1896-1904; INT; 0101; C
Flute or clarinet may be substituted for oboe.

Madam Butterfly for Two; Simpson; 1896-1904; INT; 0101; C
Flute or clarinet may be substituted for oboe.

Rae, James   English   20th C.
Easy Jazzy Duets; UNE; 1010; B
Rae wrote *Modern Studies in Rhythm and Interpretation for Solo Sax*.

Jazzy Duets; UNE; 1010; B/C
This is part of a series of pieces that gives young players experience
with the syncopated patterns of jazz, rock and pop music. This book
provides valuable duet experience in the jazz idiom. Both parts are of
equal importance and difficulty but written in "comfortable" keys.

Raihala, Osmo Tapio   Finnish   20th C.
Kaleidoscope; 1989; FMC; 12 mins; 1010

Ransom, Don   American   20th C.
Pavanne; WIM; 1010; C/D

Prelude and Samba; c1978; TGM; 2.5 mins; 1010; C/D

Raphling, Samuel   American   1910-1988
Sonatina; ESM; 6 mins; 1010; C
Raphling has composed numerous works for opera, orchestra, concertos, piano and chamber ensembles.

Variations; 1955; ESM; 1010; C/D
Originally composed for two flutes, this transcription by the composer is a single-movement, multimeter work.

Regt, Hendrik de   Dutch   1950-
Musica, Op. 31; DNA; 12 mins; 0110

Pastorale, Op. 43; 1974-75; DNA; 9 mins; 1100
After studies with Otto Ketting in The Hague, Regt wrote music primarily for chamber groups.

Reiche
Miniaturen; ESM; 0011; E

Reizenstein, Franz   German/English   1911-1968
Duo; 1965; ESM ; 0110; C/D
Reizenstein's output of Neo-Romantic music for wind instruments was large. His clarity of style, melodic invention and underlying wit, together with a natural understanding of the instruments, produced a number of works that have become part of the standard repertoire.

Reynolds, John
Airs and Dances; ESM; 1010; C/D

Richardson, Alan   Scottish   1904-1978
Three Inventions; ESM; 1100; D

Ridderstrom, Bo   Swedish   1937-
Duo; 1981; SMI; 6 mins; 1010

Ridout, Alan   English   1934-1996
Dandelion Days; PRC, ESM; 1010; C

Rieti, Vittorio   Italian/American   1898-1994
Recital for Young Chamber Players: Canon; GMP; 1010
Rieti studied with Frugatta and Respighi. His music is generally Neo-Classical in style and demonstrates an elegant charm and technical mastery.

Rieunier, François   French
Antienne; LDA; 1010

Rivier, Jean   French   1896-1987
Duo; 1968; BIL; 1010; E
Rivier won the premier prix in counterpoint and fugue in 1926 at the Paris Conservatory. He wrote in an Impressionistic style. Using robust counterpoint and vigorous rhythms and concentrating on the development of a small number of thematic ideas, Rivier's music shows the influence of Roussel.

Rochberg, George   American   1918-
Duo for Oboe and Bassoon; 1946/1979; PRC; 15 mins; 0101; C
Rochberg studied with Szell, Mannes and Menotti. He taught at the Curtis Institute and the University of Pennsylvania and has written music for theatre, orchestra, chamber ensemble, chorus and piano. He is author of the book *The Hexachord and Its Relation to the Twelve-Tone Row*. The 1979 revised version is dedicated to Sol Schoenbach.

Roy, Klaus   Austrian/American   1924-
Duo, Op. 2; 1947; PRC; 7 mins; 1010
Roy studied at Boston University and Harvard. He is best known as a writer and teacher. His works include music for chamber opera, orchestra and chamber ensembles. Using clarinet in A, this work includes three movements titled *Sonatina, Canon* and *Fughetta*.

Russell, Robert
Duo; GMP; 1010

Rutland
Forty Duets; ESM; 0011; B

Rutter, John   English   1945-
Three American Miniatures; c1981; OUP; 1010; D
The three movements are titled *Fanfare and Proclamation, Blues* and *Rag*.

Sagvik, Stellan   1952-
Antigonia, Op. 79; 1978; SMI; 10 mins; 1010
Requires E-flat clarinet and alto flute.

Samter, Alice   German   1908-
Mobile; Furore; 0101

Sangiorgi, Alfredo   20th C.
Sonatina; 1950; FLC; 9 mins; 1010; D/E

Scarlatti, Domenico   Italian   1685-1757
Neopolitan Suite; Skolnik; ESM; 8 mins; 1010; C
A prolific composer, Scarlatti composed over 500 works for solo keyboard. This arrangement of the suite could also be performed by two clarinets.

Schmidt, William   American   1926-
Duo with Credenzas; WIM; 8 mins; 0110; D
Schmidt, best known as a saxophonist and music publisher, writes in a compositional style influenced by Halsey Stevens and Ingolf Dahl.

Schonberg, Stig Gustav   Swedish   1933-
Dialoger, Op. 18; 1960; HAN; 10 mins; 1010
Schonberg studied with Larsson, Blomdahl and Erland von Koch. He wrote music for organ, orchestra and chamber groups.

Duo, Op. 16; 1959; SMI; 0011

Schubert, Franz   Austrian   1797-1828
Sonatina in D Minor; NOV; 1100
Schubert produced great masterpieces in virtually every field of composition. His music is rich in melody and expressive harmony.

Schudel, Thomas   1937-
Intermezzo; ALE; 1010; A/B
This work is a brief conversation between the flute and clarinet with a simple melodic flow.

Schwadron, Abraham A.   1925-
Duo for Flute and Oboe; PMP; 1100

Duo for Oboe and Clarinet; c1966; PMP; 0110

Schwartz, Elliot Schelling   American   1936-
Ninas; CFI; 1100
Schwartz studied with Luening and Douglas Moore at Columbia University, and later with Paul Creston at Teachers College in Columbia. Piccolo, alto flute and tape required.

Schwartz, George W.   20th C.
Three Duets; c1980; SMC; 8 mins; 0011
This work may also be performed with bass clarinet instead of bassoon.

Schwarz, Ira Paul   American   1922-
Bachatti in a Baroque Style; AMC; 1010
Schwarz is emeritus professor of music and theatre and composer-in-residence at State University of New York College of Brockport. He studied with Boulanger, Phillip Bezanson, Thaddeus Jones and Richard Herwig.

Chopinesquea a la Chopin; AMC; 1010

Dialogue, An Aleatoric Happening; AMC; 1010

High on a Claude; a la Debussy; AMC; 1010

Klozartina in a Classical Style; AMC; 1010

Lyric Piece on a Twelve-Tone Row; AMC; 1010

Variations on a Folk Tune in a 20th Century Modal Style; AMC; 1010

Schweizer, Klaus   1939-
Klappentext; 1976; BAR; 1100
Piccolo and English horn are required.

Seeger, Peter
Zehn Duos; MFS; flexible instrumentation; C

Segger
Three Duets; ESM; 0101; D

Sehlbach, Oswald Erich   1898-
Duo for Flute and Oboe, Op. 53 #2; MOS; 1100

Serebrier, Jose   Uruguayan/American   1938-
Manitowabing; PIC; 4 mins; 1100; C
Serebrier studied with Giannini and Copland. "Manitou" is an Indian word for "place of the Great Spirit." The composer states that he "has attempted to reflect this spiritual element in the music, as well as the more playful side of my stay" at a resort on the banks of the Manitou-Wabing River.

Sermila, Jarmo   Finnish   1939-
Danza 4B; 1993; FMC; 8.5 mins; 0110
Sermila studied with Tauno Marttinen, Joonas Kokkonen and Frantisek Kovaricek. He organized a group of Finnish composers of electronic music, and his music shows a very experimental style, particularly in the instrumentation.

Siennicki
Four Pieces; ESM; 1000/1; D

Silverman, Faye Ellen   American   1947-
Conversations; SEE; 1010
This work requires alto flute.

Simons, Netty   American   1923-
Design Group II; MNM; 1001

Smith, Leland C.   American   1925-
Two Duets; AMC, SAP; 0011
Smith studied with Milhaud, Messiaen and Sessions, and has taught at
the University of California (Berkeley), Mills College, the University of
Chicago and Stanford. He writes in a modern and eclectic composi-
tional style.

Smith, Stuart   American   1948-
Faces; 1979; Smith Publications; 0110; D/E
Smith studied percussion and composition at Hartt College of Music
and the University of Illinois.

Smith, William Overton   American   1926-
Five Pieces; MJQ; 10 mins; 1010
Also known as a jazz clarinetist, Smith studied at the Juilliard School,
Mills College and the University of California at Berkeley. His teachers
included Milhaud and Sessions. He received the American Prix de
Rome in 1957 and a Guggenheim grant in 1960. His music uses a
variety of contemporary techniques within an organized structure.

Jazz Set; MJQ; 10 mins; 1010

Straws; MJQ; 10 mins; 1001

Sommerfeldt, Oistein   Norwegian   1919-
Three Dialogues; HAN; 0011; D
A student of Boulanger, Sommerfeldt also worked as a music critic in
Oslo. He wrote music for orchestra and chamber ensembles.

Sonstevold, Knut   Swedish   1945-
Perfugio; 1977; SMI; 0011
Bass clarinet and tape are required.

Stearns, Peter Pindar   American   1931-
Nocturne; AMC; 1010

Three Short Studies; AMC; 0110

Stevens, Halsey   American   1908-1989
Five Duos; 1966; PIC; 6 mins; 1010; C/D
Stevens studied with Berwald and Bloch and later taught at the
University of Southern California in Los Angeles. A prolific composer,
Stevens has written for a wide variety of choral and instrumental
combinations. His music features brilliant, vigorous rhythms and clear
tonal centers.

Invention; EDH; 2 mins; 0011; C/D
This piece is a transcription from *Seventeen Piano Pieces #12*.

Six Canons for Two Equal Instruments; ACA; 1100

Stewart, Don   American   1935-
Concert Duet; TRI; 1010
Stewart, a member of the Boehm Quintette, studied with Harris, Hei-
den and Schuller. This work requires bass clarinet.

Stich, Jan Vaclav   Czech   1746-1803
Sonata for Horn and Bassoon; EKW; 0001/1
Mozart and Beethoven wrote music specifically for Stich, a famous
horn player. He wrote a great quantity of chamber music with horn and
a horn method book.

Stucky, Steven   American   1949-
Movements III; 1976; SHA; 18 mins; 1010
Stucky studied with Husa, Burrill Phillips and Robert Palmer. He has
won numerous awards and has written music for orchestra and chamber
ensembles. *Movements* is an interlocking series of free and strict pieces:
*Fantasy, Fugue, Cadenza, Invention, Cadenza, Passacaglia, Perpe-
tuum Mobile*. Even the strict movements, however, are only distantly
related to their eighteenth-century namesakes. Closest to traditional pattern perhaps is the *Fugue*, the only movement to be notated strictly and
metrically.

Suter, Robert   Swiss   1919-
Duetti; c1970; PTE; 1100
Suter, a pupil of Geiser, taught at the Berne Conservatory and the Basle
Academy. His music shows a highly controlled contrapuntal style
influenced by Bartók. Many of his works are cantatas and chamber
pieces.

Swack, Irwin   American   20th C.
Four Burlesques; 1979; SHA; 5 mins; 1010; D
Swack's music shows the influence of popular culture expressed through the idioms of jazz, dance and folk music. He attended the Cleveland Institute, Juilliard School, Northwestern University and Columbia University.

Sydeman, William J.   American   1928-
Music for Oboe and Clarinet; c1965; PIC; 8 mins; 0110; D
Sydeman studied with Felix Salzer and Sessions and he later joined the faculty of Mannes College in New York. His compositions, which show the influence of Mahler and Berg, are atonal, linear, motivic and use complicated rhythms.

Szalowski, Antoni   French   1907-1973
Duo; CHE; 1010
Szalowski studied with Sikorski at the Warsaw Conservatory and with Boulanger in Paris. He wrote in an elegant Neo-Classical style, mostly orchestral and chamber pieces.

Tausch, Franz J.   German   1762-1817
Three Duos, Op. 21; Voxman; 1812; MRI; 0011; C/D
Tausch was a violinist and clarinetist in the Mannheim Court Orchestra at the early age of eighteen years. He later entered the Royal Prussian service and founded a conservatory for wind instruments in 1805. Among Tausch's compositions are concertos for clarinet and orchestra and a variety of chamber works.

Tepper, S.D.
Suite for Clarinet and Bassoon; MCA; 0011

Thorne, Nicholas   1953-
Three Folk Song Settings; 1984; SCI; 9 mins; 0110

Tivenius, Olle   Swedish   1956-
Luscinia Suecica Svensson; SMI; 2.5 mins; 1010
Piccolo and E flat clarinet are required.

Tulou, Jean-Louis   French   1786-1865
Six Duet Etudes; ESM; 1100; C/D

Turk, Daniel   German   1756-1813
Cuckoo; Dishinger; STU; 0110; A/B
Turk studied harmony and counterpoint with Homilius and later
worked as a cantor, organist, teacher and composer.

Tustin, Whitney   1907-
Thirty Duets, Books I and II; PIC; 1100
These duets could be played by any two like treble instruments.

Tuthill, Burnet   American   1888-1982
Duo, Op. 18 #2; 1940; SPR; 2 mins; 0011; B/C
Tuthill, son of William Burnet Tuthill who was the achitect of Carne-
gie Hall, composed numerous works in various genres.

Sonatine in Canon, Op.7; 1933; PRC; 3 mins; 1010 or 1100
This two-movement work presents no problems and would be good for
training student groups in playing mixed duple/triple meter and canon
form.

Ulrich, J.
Five Duets for Winds; HAN; flexible instrumentation

Van Appledorn, Mary Jeanne   American   1927-
Reeds Afire; 1994; SMC; 0011
Van Appledorn has degrees from the Eastman School of Music and is
horn professor at Texas Tech University. She has received com-
missions from the New York City Ballet and the International Trumpet
Guild.

Van Hulse, Camil   1897-
Duet Sonata; SHA; 1010; D

Van Slyck, Nicholas   American   1922-1983
Pairs; 1978; SMC; 11 mins; 1010; C/D
Van Slyck had a national reputation as an educator and administrator
and as a composer was popular among music educators. He received
both bachelor and master degrees at Harvard. His music shows the
influence of Bartók, Bach, Piston and Prokofiev. This work is written
in five movements titled *Duettino Concertante, Siamese, Two-Step,
Two Party Line* and *Double Time*.

Van Vactor, David   American   1906-1994
Canons on Various Intervals, #1; c1976; RML; 2 mins; 1100
Van Vacter, a graduate of Northwestern University, studied also with
Franz Schmidt and Paul Dukas and later played flute with the Chicago
Symphony, conducted the Knoxville (TN) Symphony and taught at the

University of Tennessee. His inventive music is tonal and rhythmically energetic.

Villa-Lobos, Heitor   Brazilian   1887-1959
Bachianas Brasileras #6; 1938; SCI; 8 mins; 1001; D/E
Villa-Lobos, one of the most original composers of the twentieth century, had a remarkable ability to recreate native melodies and rhythms in large instrumental and choral forms. This work was originally written for orchestra and piano. Part of a series of nine Bachianas composed between 1930 to 1945, this is the only one of the series that can be considered true chamber music. There are some particularly challenging rhythms that may create problems for the ensemble.

Choros No. 2; 1924; EAM, PRC; 2.5 mins; 1010; E
This modest, but charming duet, composed during the first year of Villa Lobos' stay in Paris (1923-30), is thought to express his nostalgia for Brazil. The first half of the work is a poignant flute soliloquy set to a fitful, tentative clarinet accompaniment. The second half is a country dance, characterized by a delightful ostinato figure for the clarinet which provides a solid underpinning to the free, soaring song of the flute.

Duo; 1957; PRC; 13 mins; 0101; D/E

The Jet Whistle; PIC; 1001; E
Written originally for flute and cello, bassoon may easily replace cello and this becomes a welcome addition to the flute/bassoon repertoire.

Vogel, Roger   American   1947-
*Suite in G Major;*1976; PRC; 10.5 mins; 0101
Vogel received BM, MA and PhD degrees in composition from Ohio State University where he studied with Norman Phelps, Marshall Barnes and Jay Huff. This piece was dedicated to John Corina and James Burton, members of the University of Georgia faculty.

Vredenburg, Max   Dutch   1904-1976
Variaties, "Daer Was Een Snnewit Vogheltje"; DNA; 4 mins; Flexible instrumentation
Vredenburg studied with Paul Dukas in Paris, later returning to the Netherlands where he established the National Youth Orchestra.

Wain, George
Duets for Flute and Clarinet; KMC; 1010; B

Walker, Richard   American   1912-
Three Miniatures; KED; 5 mins; 1010; A/B

Walter, Johann   German   1496-1570
Canons in the Church Modes; KAL; 1100
Walter was one of the earliest composers of the Lutheran church. This
piece could also be played by any two like instruments.

Wanek, Friedrich K.   1929-
Three Burlesque Pieces; EAM; 6 mins; 1001; D/E

Waters, Charles   English   1895-
Classic Dances; PTE; flexible instrumentation; B/C
This work may be performed by any two equal pitch instruments.

Watson
Duo Gems; ESM; 0110; C

Weaver, Thomas   American   1939-
Seven Dialogues; c1964; SHA; 8 mins; 1010; D
Weaver studied at the Juilliard School and with Nadia Boulanger. He
has served on the faculties of Furman University and the University of
Georgia. This work is a conversation between the flute and clarinet employing dissonant techniques of twentieth-century composition. It is
similar to the twelve-tone style evolved by Schoenberg, but without
strict adherence to the serial or twelve-tone systems.

Weber, Alain   French   1930-
Sonatine; c1955; LDA; 8 mins; 1001; D
Weber was a student of Aubin and Messiaen at the Paris Conservatory
and won the Prix de Rome in 1952. This three-movement, multimeter
work is written in early twentieth century French style.

Weegenhuise, Johan   Netherlands   1910-
Pezzi 3; DNA; 8 mins; 1010

Wehner
Twenty Modern Duets; SMC; flexible instrumentation

Weinzweig, John   Canadian   1913-
Intermissions; c1964; PIC; 1100
Weinzweig studied with Leo Smith and Bernard Rogers, later teaching
at the University of Toronto and founding the Canadian League of
Composers.

Weiss, Adolph   American   1891-1971
Fantasia; c1997; EDV; 2 mins; 0011; B
Weiss studied with Schoenberg in Berlin and was one of the first to introduce twelve-tone techniques in the USA, composing mostly chamber, orchestral and piano music.

Welander, Svea   Swedish   1898-1985
Divertimento; 1963-64; SMI; 1100
Could also be played by any two like instruments.

Liten Fuga Och Dialog Over B-A-C-H; 1970; SMI; 0011

Sonatine; 1966; SMI; 0011

Welcher, Dan   American   1948-
Mill Song: Four Metamorphoses after Schubert; 1987; PRC; 0101; C
Welcher, a bassoonist and graduate of the Eastman School and the Manhattan School, has written numerous compositions in almost every imaginable genre including opera, concerto, symphony, vocal, piano and chamber music. He has served on the faculties of the University of Louisville and Aspen Music Festival, and now teaches at the University of Texas/Austin. A former composer in residence with the Honolulu Symphony, Welcher has been commissioned by the Dallas Symphony and Boston Pops.

Reversible Jackets in Conjugal Counterpoint; 1987; PRC; 6 mins; 1010; C

Welin, Karl-Erik   Swedish   1934-1992
Sermo Modulatus; 1960; SMI; 6 mins; 1010
Welin studied with Gunnar Bucht and Lidholm, later joining the experimental group "Fylkingen" in Stockholm. His music incorporates extreme avant-garde techniques.

White, David   American   1944-
Suite; 1968; SMC; 8 mins; 0110; C/D
White studied with Horvit, Bonelli and Kurtz. His varied output consists of vocal music and works for chamber and large ensembles.

Wigglesworth, Frank   American   1918-1996
Duo; 1961; PRC; 4 mins; 0110
Wigglesworth studied with Luening and Cowell. His music is basically contrapuntal with clear lines and structure. This single-movement work is dedicated to Robert Bloom and Walter Trampler.

Wilder, Alec   American   1907-1980
Twelve Duets; c1974; MAR; 0001/1; C
Wilder, a remarkably gifted composer, studied with Inch and Royce at
Eastman School of Music. He writes both serious and popular music,
all in a melodious, pleasant style. These are a collection of twelve short
single movement pieces.

Wildgans, Friedrich   Austrian   1913-1965
Three Inventions; 1935; ESM; 0010/1
Wildgans wrote in all musical genres, in an ultramodern style includ-
ing twelve-tone technique.

Williams, Adrian   Welsh   1956-
Three Miniatures; 1971; PRC; 3 mins; 1100; C
Williams, winner of the 1978 Menuhin prize for composition, studied
with Bernard Stevens, Alan Ridout, John Lill and John Russell at the
Royal College of Music. His works include a variety of genres and
styles. Written at the age of fourteen, this work won first prize at the
Watford Music Festival. A second flute may replace oboe part.

Wilson, Jeffrey
Three Duets; PRC; 1010; B/C
There is an optional oboe part to replace flute.

Wilson, Richard   American   1941-
Dithyramb; 1982; SMC, PIC; 4 mins; 0110
Wilson studied at Harvard, Rutgers and the American Academy in
Rome. A dithyramb is a song in honor of the god of fertility, wine and
drama—Dionysus. It dates back at least to the seventh century BC.
From the fifth century BC, it was commonly accompanied by the most
important of ancient Greek instruments, the aulos. The composer
describes the piece as ceremonial, lyrical and only mildly "dionysian"
at one point: a passage near the end in which the instruments alternate,
in rapid succession, a grace-note figure. The work was given its premiere in Carnegie Recital Hall in 1983 by Margaret Helfer, oboe, and
Meyer Kupferman, clarinet.

Wolpe, Stefan   German/American   1902-1972
Suite in Hexachord; 1936; MMM; 13 mins; 0110; D
German-born Wolpe settled in America in 1938 where he devoted
himself to teaching and composing, producing works in virtually every
medium. Two copies of the score are needed for performance.

Woodbury, A.
Three Brief Pieces; SMC; 0011
Bass clarinet may substitute for bassoon.

Wright, Maurice   American   1949-
Duo; 1974; MOB; 6 mins; 1010; C/D

Wurzburger, Walter   20th C.
Fanfare-Toccata; c1984; ESM; 0110; D/E
There is an optional flute part to replace oboe.

Wyttenbach, Jurg   Swiss   1935-
Serenade; 1959/rev.1979; EAM; 10 mins; 1010; D
Wyttenbach's early works show the influence of Bartok and Stravinsky
while later works use serialism and variation form. This work is writ-
ten in four movements: *Little March in Broken Steps; Duettino in
Unequal Voice; Waltz in Added Values and Trio in False Unisons;
Chasse in Slow Motion and Accelerated.*

Zettervist, Hans V.A.
Canon Per Motu Contrario; SMI; 0011

Zonn, Paul   American   1938-
Dance Set; ACA; 0011

THREE WINDS

Alain, Jehan   French   1911-1940
Invention a Trois Voix; 1937; LDA; 3 mins; 1110; C/D
Alain studied at the Paris Conservatory and won the Premiers Prix for
harmony and fugue in 1934 and again in 1939 for organ. He studied
with Dukas and Roger-Ducasse. Although killed at the age of 29 in
WW II, he produced a number of charming chamber works and songs
including this one for wind trio.

Albéniz, Isaac   Spanish   1860-1909
Tango from *Espana*; 1890; INT; 1011; D
Albeniz studied with Reinecke, Dukas and d'Indy. Virtually all of his
music written for piano is inspired by Spanish folklore. He is credited
with establishing the modern school of Spanish piano literature which
is derived from original rhythms and melodic patterns, rather than
imitating the Spanish music by French and Russian composers. This
is the *Tango* movement from the *Espana, Op. 165* solo piano
collection, here arranged for woodwind trio. Oboe may replace flute.

Allen
Diversions, Op. 20 Books 1-4; ESM; 0111; C

Allgen, Claude Loyala Swedish   1920-1990
Maria Semper Virgo; SMI; 0102

Trio; 1987; SMI; 1101

Amos, Keith   English   20th C.
A Croquet Party; ESM; 1110; C/D

Trifolium; ESM; 1110; C

Andriessen, Jurriaan Dutch   1925-
Trio #4; 1957; DNA, PRC; 11.5 mins; 1101; C
Andriessen's music shows sound professional skill in a style that
draws on diverse techniques without being bound to any specific system. Jurriaan is the brother of Louis Andriessen and son of Hendrik.

Andriessen, Louis   Dutch   1939-
Aanloop en Sprongen; 1961; DNA; 4 mins; 1110
Andriessen studied with Berio. This single-movement, multimeter work offers only moderate challenges for the ensemble.

Anonymous
Grant Us Peace; Schaeffer; KAL; flexible

Antoni, Thomas
Three Encores; SCI; 1110

Two Easy Fanfares; SCI; 1110

Two More Easy Fanfares; c1976; SCI; 1110

Apostel, Hans Erich   Austrian   1901-1972
Five Bagatelles, Op. 20; c1953; KAL; 1011
Apostel studied with Schoenberg and Berg. His early works were written in a dissonant, expressionistic style with later works using a twelve-tone system. Good for training in rhythmic and ensemble skills, all players in this trio use a score.

Archer, Violet   Canadian   1913-2000
Divertimento #1; 1949; DNP; 9.5 mins; 0111; B/C
Archer's teachers include Bartok and Hindemith. She was chosen Composer of the Year in 1984 by the Canadian Music Council and has written over 200 works.

Arma, Paul   Hungarian   1905-1987
Trois Mouvements; 1949; PRC; 10 mins; 0111; D/E
Born in Hungary, Arma also lived in the United States and France, where he became interested in the folklore of these countries, concentrating particularly on American Negro spirituals and French songs. Arma, a student of Bartók, wrote orchestral, solo, chamber and vocal music. Arma's real name was Weisshaus, but he worked under the pseudonym of Paul Arma after 1930. Bartók's influence is apparent in this work. Syncopated rhythmic figures and irregular accents are used, especially in the third movement. There are solo passages for all three instruments and the thematic material explores the instruments' most extreme registers.

Arnold, Malcolm   English   1921-
Divertimento, Op. 37; 1952; CFI, NOV; 8 mins; 1110; D
Arnold's music is basically diatonic and the main attraction lies in catchy tunes, interesting orchestration and the pleasure that the music

gives to the performers. This trio is a merry bit of pops concert virtuosity.

Arrieu, Claude   French   1903-1990
Suite en Trio; 1936; BIL; 9 mins; 0111; D
Arrieu studied at the Paris Conservatoire with Caussade, Long, Roger-Ducasse and Dukas, taking a Premier Prix for composition in 1932. Her subsequent career was in teaching and work of various kinds for French radio, which she joined in 1946. This work is stylistically conservative, highly spirited and very light in character. Optimistic in nature, this difficult work is written in the keys of C and G major.

Auber, Chantal   1931-
Contraste; DUR, PRC; 0111

Auric, Georges   French   1899-1983
Trio; 1935; EOL; 12 mins; 0111; D
Auric studied at the Montpellier and Paris Conservatories. He was a student of Caussade and d'Indy. He was a member of the famous "Les Six," a group of six renowned French composers. He wrote music for ballet, film, piano, orchestra, vocal and chamber ensembles. This work has a light, witty character, lively tempi and rhythms, attractive melodies and an overall brilliant style. Clarinet in A is required.

Averitt, William   American   1948-
Trio; 1970; DNP; 1011; D/E
Averitt studied at Murray State and Florida State Universities and since 1973 has been on the faculty at the Shenandoah Conservatory of Music.

Avison
Sonata a Trois; Lancelot; BIL; 0021

Baaren, Kees Van   Dutch   1906-1970
Trio; 1936; DNA; 9 mins; 1011; D/E
A student of Pilper, Van Baaren fulfilled an important link in passing on the techniques of Arnold Schonberg. The *Trio* is an angular, exciting and colorful work.

Bach, Erik   Danish   1946-
Departure; 1978; MRI; 18 mins; 1011

Theme and Three Variations; 1985; MRI; 8 mins; 1101

Bach, Johann Sebastian   German   1685-1750
Adagio; CON; 1101

The most famous member of the Bach family, Johann wrote primarily sacred music and works for keyboard. He also was a master organist and instructor.

Allegretto; CON; 1011

Allegro; CON; 1101

Canonic Fugue from Musical Offering; Glasel; c1962; BHI; 0111; C
This traditional melody with a counter-melody and harmony, arranged for woodwind trio, is suitable for contests or light programs. There is an alternate clarinet part for the oboe.

Fifteen Three Part Inventions; Cochran; CFI; flexible instrumentation; C/D
There are versions with varying combinations of flute, oboe, clarinet, bass clarinet and bassoon.

Four Fugues; Winkler; DBM; 0111; C

Fuga Canonica; Schwadron; WIM; 0021; D
Bassoon part could be played on bass clarinet.

Fuga #8, Art of the Fugue; Schmidt; WIM; 0011/1; C/D

Fuga #13, Art of the Fugue; Schmidt; WIM; 1011; C

Fugue in C Minor; Benyas; INT; 1011
Oboe may replace flute.

Goldberg Variations, Five Canons; PTE; 0111
This arrangement contains variations 3, 9, 15, 18 and 21.

Inventions #1-4, 8, 9, 11; Johnson; PTE; 1011; C/D
Oboe may substitute for flute.

Jesu, Joy of Man's Desiring; Weller, Holcombe; ALE, ESM; flexible instrumentation; C
This arrangement may be played on any two treble instruments and one bass instrument.

Little Bach Suite I; Morsch; KAL; flexible instrumentation
There are alternate parts that could be played on any three instruments.

Little Bach Suite II; Morsch; KAL; 1101
There are alternate parts that could be played on any three instruments.

Now Awake, We Hear a Voice Cry; Conley; KED; 1011; B/C

Polonaise; Williams; SMC; 1011; B/C
Oboe may replace flute.

Prelude and Fugue; Oubradous; c1938; EOL; 0111

Sheep May Safely Graze; Weller; 1713; ALE; 1101; B

Siciliano from Flute Sonata #2 in E-Flat Major; PRC; 1011; C

Sonate En Trio; Poulteau; LDA; 0111
There are lternate parts for flute, violin and cello.

Three Fugues; Dundas-Grant; ESM; flexible instrumentation; C/D
Parts for flute, oboe, English horn and clarinet are available for the two upper voices, and the bass part may be played on cello, bass clarinet or bassoon.

Three Part Inventions; Manoukian; ESM; flexible instrumentation; C/D
Parts for flute, oboe, saxophone and clarinet are available for the top voice; clarinet or English horn for the second voice; bass clarinet and bassoon parts for the low voice.

Three Trios; Dundas-Grant; ESM; flexible instrumentation; C/D
Parts for flute, oboe and clarinet are available for the top voice. Clarinet and bassoon are required for the two remaining parts.

Two Bach Fughettas; Sharpe; ESM; 0021; C

Two Gavottes; Andraud; SMC; 1110; C

Wachetauf; Schmidt; WIM; 0011/1; C

Bach, Wilhelm Friedemann   German   1710-1784
Siciliano; Dorff; PRC; 1011; C/D
W.F. Bach was a son of Johann Sebastian and a composer of superior talent.

Baden, Conrad   Norwegian   1908-1989
Trio; c1965; PTE; 7 mins; 1110; C/D
Baden studied with Honegger and Rivier. His early music was influenced by sixteenth-century polyphony and his later works showed a grow-ing interest in twelve-tone techniques. This moderately difficult work is in three movements.

Badings, Henk   Dutch   1907-1987
Trio; 1948; DNA; 16 mins; 0111; D
Badings embraced the German musical idiom, using colorful harmonies, strong tonality and simple rhythmic formulas. This difficult work is written in four movements: *Allegro, Scherzo, Theme and Variations, Rondo.* It is primarily homophonic and all the fast movements are light in character and highly rhythmical.

Baeyens, August   Belgian   1895-1966
Concertino; 1951; CFI; 13 mins; 0111; D

Baeyens combines tonality, polytonality and atonality along with equally diverse melodic writing. The independent nature of the individual parts makes ensemble precision a challenge, and the last movement requires a high level of technical skill from all three players.

Bailey, Marshall   American   20th C.
Two Structures; AMC; 0201
This work requires English horn.

Baines, Francis   English   1917-1999
Divertimento; ESM; 1011; C/D
Baines is one of England's leading double-bass players. He studied at the Royal Conservatory of Music in London where he later became a professor.

Baksa, Robert Frank   American   1938-
Running Tune, Lullaby and March; c1967; SHA; 6 mins; 1110; B/C
A graduate of the University of Arizona with a degree in composition, Baksa has written over 400 works and is best known for his chamber music choral pieces. A student of Foss, Baksa began composing at the age of thirteen. *Running Tune, Lullaby and March* is a transcription of some of those early efforts.

Trio #1 in E-Flat Major; 1973/77; PRC; 12 mins; 1011; C/D
This work was originally written for trumpet, horn and tuba.

Trio in G Major, Op. 37; PRC; 12 mins; 1011; C/D
This highly sophisticated contrapuntal piece has been described by New York critic Peter Davis as an "innocent charmer."

Barboteu
Burlesque; ESM; 1101

Barraud, Henry   French   1900-1997
Trio; c1938; EOL; 9.5 mins; 0111; C/D
Barraud studied composition with Auric at the Paris Conservatory. The emphasis of this work is on the cantabile melodic writing shared by all three instruments. Rhythmic interest is maintained by use of a wide variety of rhythmic figures. Clarinet in A is required.

Barta, Jiri   Czech   1935-
Trio; 1989; CMI; 13 mins; 0111
Barta studied piano at the Bruno Conservatory and composition at the Janacek Academy. Now on staff at the Bruno Conservatory, Barta has re-ceived awards from the Czech Composers and Performing Artists and the Czech Music Fund.

Bartók, Béla   Hungarian   1881-1945
Bartok Suite; Schmidt; WIM; 0011/1; C/D
Bartók, a student of Koessler, began collecting folk songs in 1906 from Hungary, Romania, Slovak, Bulgaria and Croatia. He used these in much of his music in either substance or spirit.

Dance of the Slovaks; Dishinger; STU; 1101; A/B

Bartos, Frantisek   Czech   1905-1973
Trio; c1964; BHI; 0111
Bartos studied with Jirak and Kricka at the Prague Conservatory. He wrote works for stage, chamber ensembles and orchestra.

Bauernfeind, Hans   German   1908-
Gay Play; DBM; 1011
Bauernfiend's style is conservative, rhythmically uncomplicated and melodious.

Heitere Musik; 1955; DBM; 13 mins; 0111; C/D
The first and last movements are written in a standard three-part format with the principal theme stated at the beginning of each movement. Though technically not very difficult, there could be endurance challenges for all players.

Baumann, Herbert   German   1931-
Divertimento; c1961; SIK; 9 mins; 0111; D
This melodious, four-movement work combines lively rhythms and formal clarity. A spirited folk melody is featured in two movements with an ostinato style and theme with variations found in other movements.

Baur, Jurg   German   1918-
Kontrapunkte on a Theme by Bach; c1978; BKH; 1101
Baur studied with Jarnach in Cologne and taught at the Dusseldorf Conservatory and in Cologne. His music, while conservative, shows the influence of the younger composers in the 1950s. English horn is required in this work.

Beck, Jochen   1941-
Trio; c1971; MOS; 1011

Beclard d'Harcourt, Marguerite French   1884-1964
Rhapsodie Peruvienne; LDA; 0111

Beekum
Instrumental Trios; ESM; 1110; B/C

Miniature Trios; ESM; 1011; A/B

Trios; ESM; 1101; A/B

Beethoven, Ludwig van   German   1770-1827
Scherzo, Op. 9; Grant; 0111
Beethoven's early achievements show him to be extending the Viennese Classical tradition. Later he began to compose in an increasingly unique musical style, and at the end of his life he wrote his most sublime and profound works.

Six Minuets; ESM; 2001; C

Minuet in G Major; Tustin; CPP; 1110; B/C

Ode to Joy; Halferty; 1824; KED; 1110; B/C

Prelude and Fugue; Merriman; SMC; 0021; C

Rondo from Sonatina in F Major; Morris; c1974; 1110

Trio, Op. 87; Langenus; 1795; MRI, BIL, IMC; flexible instrumentation; C/D
This work was originally for two oboes and English horn. Several versions of this work are now available for three treble instruments.

Variations on "La ci darem la mano"; 1795; MRI; 1011; C/D
This work is a theme and variations format from the *Don Giovanni* aria of the same title. Oboe may be used in place of flute.

Bennett, Richard Rodney   English   1936-
Trio; 1965; UNE; 11 mins; 1110
Bennett, considered one of the most brilliant and versatile of English composers, attended the Royal Academy of Music in London where he studied with Berkeley and Ferguson. Written in six movements, this difficult multimeter work is played without pause between movements.

Bentzon, Jorgen   Danish   1897-1951
Racconto No. 3, Op. 31; 1937; SKI, SCI; 3 mins; 0111; C/D
Bentzon, cousin of Niels Viggo Bentzon, studied with Carl Nielsen and then briefly at the Leipzig Conservatory. He wrote music that ranged from witty, sometimes ironic entertainment to works of highly crafted polyphony. This single-movement work shows the influence of Nielsen. The harmonies are somewhat dissonant, although always tonal, and emphasis is placed on the lyric quality of the instruments. This work requires clarinet in A.

Sonatina, Op. 7; 1924; HAN, SCI, CHE; 1011; D

Berger, Jean   German   1909-
Divertimento for Three Treble Instruments; BBL; 8 mins; flexible instrumentation; D/E
This work may be performed by various combinations of the following treble instruments: flute, oboe, clarinet, violin.

Berkeley, Lennox   English   1903-1989
Piece; 1930; CHE; 1011
Lennox studied with Boulanger and was influenced by Ravel and Stravinsky.

Berlinski, Herman   German/American 1910-
Three and Four Part Canons and Rounds; c1988; MER; 2100
Berlinski was an instructor at Hebrew Union College, then later became organist and music director at Washington Hebrew Congregation, D.C. Any three like instruments could be used.

Berthelemy
Rondo Pour Rire; ESM; 0021; C/D

Bertouille, Gerard   Belgian   1898-1981
Prelude and Fugue; 1957; EAM; 3.5 mins; 0111; C/D
This two-movement work is atonal and contrapuntal. Though technically challenging, it is still within the capabilities of advanced high school students. Clarinet in A required.

Besozzi, Carlo   Italian   1738-1791
Trio Sonata, Op. 7 #6; c1976; MMM; 0201; B/C
Carlo, a virtuoso oboist, was the son of Antonio Besozzi. He wrote in a style similar to Haydn. This work is in standard sonata form.

Beurle, Jurgen   German   1943-
Six Easy Pieces; c1968; BAR; 2100
Beurle studied philosophy and music in Stuttgart, Tubingen and Utrecht. His musical design is considered constructionist.

Bialosky, Marshall   American   1923-
Suite; WIM; 5 mins; 1110; B/C
Bialosky studied with Lionel Nowak, Ernst Bacon, Robert Delaney and Luigi Dallapiccola. This easy work in three movements *(March, Aria, Fughetta)* is appropriate for student ensembles.

Variations on an Elizabethan Lute Theme; SEE; 1101

Biersack, Anton   1907-
Divertimento; EAM; 1011

Bizet, Georges   French   1838-1875
Three Pieces; SMC; 1101; C
Primarily known for his French operas, but Bizet also composed music
for piano and orchestra. Clarinet may be used in place of oboe, and horn
may substitute for bassoon.

Bjorkman, Rune   Swedish   1923-1976
Liten Musik; 1972; SMI; 3 mins; 1001/1

Soave i Viston; 1974; SMI; 1001/1

Trio; SMI; 1001/1

Bjorn
Alley Cat; Jarvis; KED; 1110; D

Blank, Allan   American   1925-
Three Related Pieces; 1962; AMC; 7 mins; 1011
Blank attended The Juilliard then performed on violin with the
Pittsburgh Symphony before resigning to devote his time to
composition. He has published more than 60 works and received
numerous grants and awards.

Blezard, William   1921-
A Pair of Pieces; ESM; 2010

Four Piece Suite; ESM; 1011
There are alternate parts for clarinet and horn to replace flute and bassoon.

Blomdahl, Karl-Birger   Swedish   1916-1968
Trio; 1938; SMI; 15 mins; 0111
Blomdahl studied composition with Rosenberg in Stockholm and later
taught at Stockholm's Royal College of Music. His early music shows
the influence of Neo-Classicism and Hindemith, while later music uses
twelve-tone and electronic techniques.

Blumenthal, Jakob   German   1829-1908
Trio; PTE; 1101
Blumenthal, known primarily as a pianist, composed many melodious
pieces in the salon style.

Blyton, Carey   English   1932-
A Little Trio, Op. 18B; 1954; ESM; 5 mins; 1011; D/E
Originally written for violin, cello and clarinet, this arrangement has
alternate parts for oboe and bass clarinet.

Boccherini, Luigi   Italian   1743-1805
Terzetto; Waln; c1951; KMC; 1110; B
Boccherini's style was very similar to Haydn's and almost all his works are for instrumental chamber ensembles. There is an optional clarinet part to replace oboe.

Boder, Gerd
Wind Trio, Op. 1; c1965; PRC; 12 mins; 0111; D/E
The most striking features of this work are its atonal idiom and varied rhythmic figures. While there is a clear twelve-tone influence, it does not appear to be serial. All movements are in a loose ternary form and multimeters are used in the first two movements. Rhythmic accuracy is difficult even for advanced groups.

Bodinus, Sebastian   Dutch   1700-1760
Trio in G Major; Delius; ESM; 1002; C

Bois, Rob du   Dutch   1934-
Trio; DNA; 7 mins; 1110
Bois's works are contrapuntal in texture using the classical Flemish tradition but with ultramodern techniques including serialism.

Bolz, Harriett   American   20th C.
Festive Fantasia; c1995; HPC; 4 mins; 0011/1

Bonneau, Paul   French   1918-
Three Noels Anciens; 1949; LDA; 2.5 mins; 0111; C
This single-movement work presents a clear, chordal setting of three familiar Christmas carols. English horn could be used instead of clarinet. The key signature of five sharps for clarinet in the final carol, and use of the low register for oboe, could present some challenges for young players. There is another version of this work for oboe, English horn and bassoon.

Booren, Jo van den   Dutch   1935-
Trio, Op. 2; DNA; 1101
Booren studied composition with Kees van Baaren and Klaus Huber. His music is considered sonorous structuralism.

Borris, Siegfried   German   1908-1987
Partita; MOS; 1020; C
Borris studied with Hindemith at the Berlin Hochschule fur Musik. His music uses lively dance-like rhythms with functional tonality.

Bourguignon, Francis de   Belgian   1890-1961
Suite, Op. 80; 1944; EAM; 14 mins; 0111; D
This work features a variety of melodic and rhythmic materials within
a primarily atonal style. Technical requirements are fairly challenging
and endurance could be a problem for all three players.

Boutry, Roger   French   1932-
Divertissement; c1956; LDA; 10.5 mins; 0111; D/E
Boutry studied at the Paris Conservatoire with Boulanger, Long and
Aubin. He won first prizes in piano, composition and conducting and
in 1954 won the Prix de Rome. His music is deeply influenced by
Debussy and Ravel, and is notable for its uncommonly expressive
melody. This work is highly chromatic; technical agility is required of
all players. Ensemble precision is challenging, and much of the
bassoon part is written in the tenor range.

Bove, J. Henry   1897-1963
Petite Trio; c1934; CFI; 2 mins; 1011; B
Dedicated to Lamar Stringfield, this easy work is good for training
young ensembles. It is conservative in every aspect and the three
instruments share the melodic material. Oboe may substitute for flute.

Boyce, William   English   1711-1779
Andante Dolce from *Symphony #1*; 1760; CON; 1011
Boyce's style has a fresh energy which is apparent in this work. He
uses middle movements that are quick, light and soft rather than slow.
In the nineteenth-century Boyce's reputation depended mainly on his
Cathedral Music, a three-volume collection of sacred music by English
masters of the sixteenth through eighteenth centuries. However, in the
early twentieth-century interest in his music was revived when a
number of Boyce's overtures were published by Constant Lambert.

Boyd, Anne Elizabeth   Australian   1946-
Synchromy #1; 1964; FMI; 0111
Boyd studied at the New South Wales Conservatorium, University of
Sydney and York University. Her compositional style is sparse and
disciplined, placing contemporary techniques at the service of a
personal and individual manner.

Bozza, Eugene   French   1905-1991
Fugue, Siciliano and Rigaudon; 1933; Tres/EPR; 7 mins; 0111; D/E
Bozza studied with Busser, Rabaud, Capet and Nadaud at the Paris
Conservatory where he won the Premiers Prix for the violin (1924),
conducting (1930) and composition (1934), and also the Prix de Rome
in 1934. Though his larger works have been successfully performed in

France, his international reputation rests on his large output of chamber music for winds. His works display at a consistently high level the characteristic qualities found in mid-twentieth century French chamber music: elegant structure, melodic fluency and an awareness of the capabilities of the instruments for which he writes. The titles of the movements suggest their character and rhythmic style. Except for occasional dissonance, this piece is written in a Baroque style.

Serenade En Trio; c1971; LDA; 14 mins; 1011; D/E
This challenging piece from one of the French school masters is well worth the effort. There are three movements titled *Entree, Fuguette* and *Gigue.*

Suite Breve En Trio, Op. 67; 1947; LDA; 10.5 mins; 0111; D
As with much of Bozza's writings, this work features rapid chromatic scales, modal harmonies, pentatonic scales, jazz rhythms and an over-all emphasis on brilliance. Demanding technique, complex rhythms, rapid articulation and complete control of the dynamic range are required by all players.

Braga, Luiz Otavio   20th C.
Micro Suite; 1988; BMP; 1011
There are three movements titled *Pequena polka, Valsa pequena* and *Pequena choro.*

Brahms, Johannes   German   1833-1897
Lilac Hillsides; Dansby; KED; 0120
One of the greatest masters of music, Brahms composed works for orchestra, voice, piano, chorus and chamber ensembles.

Brasher, John   20th C.
Diadelphos; c1973; WIM; 3.5 mins; 1011; D
This complex work appears to offer significant ensemble and individual rhythmic challenges.

Bravnicar, Matija   Yugoslavian   1897-1977
Trio Quasi Fantasia; 1930; GER; 8 mins; 1011
Bravnicar uses a Neo-Classical style with a strong influence of Slovenian folk music. He studied at the Ljubljana Conservatory and later taught at the Ljubljana Academy of Music.

Brettingham Smith, Jolyon   English   1949-
Wind in the Reeds, Op. 12; 1975; BBM; 0111; E
This is a difficult work with many twentieth-century devices. Bretingham studied with Isang Yun.

Brod, Henri   French   1799-1839
Fantasie sur le "Crociato"; RIC; 1101

Brons, Carel   Dutch   1931-1983
Serenata II; 1964; DNA; 4 mins; 0111; D
Brons studied theory with Johan Vetter and later worked for Radio
Holland. This single-movement, contrapuntal work uses pitch serial-
ism in many sections. The technical requirements are not excessive.

Brown, Charles F.   1898-
Trio; BIL; 0111

Browning, Zack   American   20th C.
Suite Time; 1988; BXP; 7 mins; 1011; C
Of the four movements (*Imaginary Time, Real Time, Easy Time* and
Hard Time), only the last should present any significant difficulties.

Bruns, Victor   1904-
Trio, Op. 49; BKH; 0111
This is a difficult, four-movement work.

Buchtel, Forrest L.   American   1899-1996
Wood Nymphs; c1965; KMC; 1110; B
Known as "Frosty" to his friends, Buchtell wrote more than 800 solos
and ensembles, 30 sets of band books, 30 overtures and 30 marches.

Buchwald, Roland   German   1940-
Trio; 1967-73; BBL; 5 mins; 1011
This is a multimeter, three-movement work with no significant ensem-
ble difficulties.

Buck, Ole   Danish   1945-
Sweet Summer Suite; ESM; flexible instrumentation; C
English horn or clarinet parts are available for the top voice; an alternate
bass clarinet part may replace bassoon.

Bull, Edvard Hagerup   Norwegian   1922-
Trois Bucoliques; 1953; PRC; 10 mins; 0111; D/E
Bull studied composition with Rivier, Messiaen and Milhaud. This
work has a light, cheerful and rhythmically spirited quality. It uses a
wide variety of rhythmic figures, and chromaticism is frequently used.
Extreme registers are used for both oboe and bassoon. Endurance for
the double reeds could be a significant factor in the middle movement.

Burghardt, Hans-Georg   1909-
Blaser-Trio, Op. 99; c1995; HOF; 0111; D

Butts, Carrol Maxton   American   1924-1980
Trio for Woodwinds; BEL; 1020; C

Cage, John   American   1912-
Trio for Flute, Clarinet, and Bassoon; c1961; HNP; 1011
Cage studied composition with Weiss, Cowell, Schoenberg and Varese. He initiated the use of "prepared piano" which places an object on
a piano string to alter the tone color. He has written music for piano,
orchestra and chamber ensembles.

Caldini, Fulvio
Guilame, Op. 10; ESM; 0111; C

Camara, Juan Antonio   Cuban   1917-
Suite; PIC; 1011

Cambini, Giuseppe   Italian   1746-1825
Trio, Op. 45 #1-6; 1785; MRI; 1101; B/C
Cambini was one of several composers who contributed greatly to the
development of the string quartet of which he wrote a large number. His
works are charming and facile though somewhat limited in imagination. Cambini wrote many symphonies, solos, string quartets and
other ensembles including the first three woodwind quintets, antedating
Anton Reicha's quintets by more than ten years.

Campione, Rob   English   20th C.
Sonata Notturna; ESM; 2001; C

Canteloube, Joseph   French   1879-1957
Rustiques; 1946; EOL; 15 mins; 0111; D/E
Canteloube studied with d'Indy at the Schola Cantorum and soon established himself as a composer of music descriptive of the landscape of
his native region. He used folksongs as the basis for much of his music.
This work is written in a Post-Romantic style characterized by rich
harmonies, varied tempi and use of modes. It is technically challenging
and presents some endurance problems for oboe which is featured
throughout the piece, but the beautiful lyrical lines make it work the
effort.

Carter, Elliott   American   1908-
Canon for Three: In Memoriam Igor Stravinsky; 1950; AMP; flexible
instrumentation

Carter's reputation is derived mainly from a few large-scale works. He studied with Piston, Hill and Boulanger. Carter has been the recipient of the highest honors that a composer can receive and has honorary degrees from many universities. His best music has an energy of invention that is unmatched in contemporary compositions. This work may be played by any three equal instrumental voices.

Carulli, Ferdinando   Italian   1770-1841
Trio, Op. 1 in C Major; c1974; EAM; 0021; B/C
Primarily known as a guitarist, Carulli published a famous guitar method and hundreds of guitar pieces.

Cazden, Norman   American   1914-1980
Trio #2, Op. 40; SPR; 1110; C
Cazden studied at the Musical Arts in New York and the Juilliard School, later studying with Piston and Copland at Harvard. He wrote contrapuntal, rhythmic music which often reflected his interest in folk music of the Catskills.

Chabrier, Emmanuel   French   1841-1894
Idylle; Schmidt; WIM; 1011; C/D
Trained first as a lawyer, Chabrier became a well-known composer and pianist. His music is written with a free treatment of dissonance, modality, bold harmonic contrasts, rhythmic energy and striking originality which inspired many subsequent French composers such as Ravel.

Chandler
Divertimento; ESM; 0111; C/D

Trio; 1967; ESM; 0110/1; C/D

Chaudoir, James   American   20th C.
Sept Vignettes; 1996; CPI; 9 mins; 0111
Chaudoir has composed a wide range of works for vocal and instrumental ensembles. A highly published and commissioned composer, his works have been performed in major cities throughout the world. This work is a suite of seven brief, but whimsically entertaining movements for reed trio. Filled with soft dissonances and periodic flirtations with tonal centers, unifying motifs can be heard throughout the movements.

Chedeville, Nicolas   French   1705-1782
Scherzo for Flute, Oboe and Clarinet; ESM; 1110

Cheetham, John   American   1939-
Four Miniatures; c1982; SHA; 6.5 mins; 1011; D
Cheetham, a native of Taos, NM, attended the University of New Mexico and the University of Washington. *Four Miniatures* was written for and premiered by the Mid-West Trio, a faculty group from the University of Missouri-Columbia.

Chemin-Petit, Hans   German   1902-1981
Trio in the Old Style; c1944; PTE; 20 mins; 0111; C/D
Written in Baroque style, this contrapuntal piece uses sequential melodies and cadential suspensions. Endurance could be a challenge for the double reed players, and ensemble precision may be difficult to achieve for younger groups.

Childs, Barney   American   1926-2000
Three Players I; AMC; 0011/1
A student of Ratner, Chavez, Copland and Carter, Child's music incorporates improvisation and more traditional multi-section pieces. He has written music for orchestra, band, chamber music and chorus.

Civil, Alan   English   1929-1989
Suite; PRC; 1110; D/E
A noted horn player, Civil was principal horn with various orchestras including the Royal Philharmonic, Philharmonia Orchestra and the BBC Symphony Orchestra.

Clementi, Aldo   Italian   1925-
Tre Piccoli Pezzi; 1955; EAM; 4 mins; 1110
Clementi studied composition with Sangiorgi and Petrassi at the Santa Cecilia Conservatory in Rome. His music incorporates many twentieth-century devices. This pointillistic work is performed from full scores.

Triplum; 1960; EAM; 4 mins; 1110

Constant, Marius   Romanian/French   1925-
Trio; c1949; CHE; 16 mins; 0111; D
Constant is perhaps best known for composing the signature theme of television's *Twilight Zone*. He studied at the Paris Conservatoire and won the Enesco Prize in 1944. This work features tonal, bitonal and atonal passages. It requires considerable technical agility from all players. Frequent low register writing for the oboe and high register for the bassoon offer challenges to the players.

Cooke, Arnold   English   1906-
Trio; ESM; 12 mins; 0111; D

Corelli, Arcangelo   Italian   1653-1713
Air and Dance; Maganini; ESM; 1110
Corelli's greatest achievement was the creation of the concerto grosso form. He was also known as a virtuoso violinist and is regarded as the founder of modern violin technique. Despite a small output of music, Corelli greatly influenced form, style and instrumental technique during his lifetime. While his music may seem rather predictable today, it was considered very original by his contemporaries.

Chamber Sonata, Op. 2 #1; Auslender; WIM; flexible instrumentation; C

Chamber Sonata, Op. 2 # 2; Schmidt; c1969; WIM; 0111 or 2001; C

Trio in D Minor; RIC; 1101 or 2001; C

Praeludium; Schaeffer; CPP, KAL; flexible instrumentation; B

Cormier
Sonatina #1 in C Major; ESM; 1101, 0201 or 2001; C

Cortes, Ramiro   American   1933-1984
Divertimento; 1953; PIC; 10 mins; 1011; C
Cortes studied with Henry Cowell, Halsey Stevens and Ingolf Dahl. Until the late 1960s his music was serially organized. Thereafter it became more freely structured while remaining fully chromatic. This moderately difficult work is in five movements titled *Allegro moderato, La Malaguena, Giocoso, La Petenera* and *Vivace.*

Cowell, John   1920-
Trio for Winds; 1960; COR; 6 mins; 0011/1; B
This is a three-movement, moderately easy work, written for an unusual instrumentation.

Coyner, Lou   American   1931-
Tertium Quid; c1981; AMC; 1020
Bass clarinet is required for this work.

Cruft, Adrian   English   1921-
Three Bagatelles, Op. 50; c1981; BHI; 8 mins; 1110; C
Cruft, a student of Jacob and Rubbra, wrote music for chorus, orchestra, band and sacred works.

Three Miniatures, Op. 70; c1976; 0111; D

Crusell, Bernhard Henrik   Finnish   1775-1838
Concert-Trio; 1814; HBM; 10 mins; 0011/1; D
Crusell studied clarinet with Tausch and Lefebvre, and composition
with Abbe Vogler, Berton and Gossec. This work is written in a single
movement, Classic period style.

Cuninghame
Serenade; ESM; 1110; C/D
Clarinet in A is required.

Curtis, Mike   20th C.
*Three Klezmer Trio*s; MSS; 0201
English horn is required.

Trio Suite on Mexican Themes; MSS; 0201
English horn is required.

Custer, Arthur   American   1923-
Terzetto for Flute, Oboe, Clarinet; SER; 1110; B
Custer studied with Boulanger and Hindemith. This easy work is ap-
propriate for student ensembles.

D'Hoir, Joseph   Belgian   1929-
Variations on A Child Is Born in Bethlehem; 1965; MAU; 6 mins;
0111; C/D
After a brief introduction by clarinet and bassoon, the oboe introduces
the main theme. Conventional variation technique is used. Good high
school players should be able to handle this piece.

D'Rivera, Paquito   Cuban   20th C.
Habanera; INT; 1011
This movement from the *Aires Tropicales* features challenging and unusual contrapuntal lines for all three instruments in a Latin style similar
to Ravel's *Habanera*. Oboe may replace flute.

Dandrieu, François   French   1682-1738
Les Tourbillons; Seay; SPR; 0111; B
Well-known as a harpsichord composer, Dandrieu also wrote trio sona-
tas, organ noels and airs.

Daniel-Lesur, Yves-Jean   French   1908-
Trio Suite; 1939; EOL; 13 mins; 0111; D/E
Daniel-Lesur studied at the Paris Conservatoire (1919-1929). In 1936
he was, along with Messiaen, Jolivet and Baudrier, a founder-member
of the group La Jeune France, dedicated to a "return to the human" and
opposed to the Neo-Classicism then prevalent in Paris. Daniel-Lesur's

music is unique among his more famous contemporaries, being more conventional in texture and rhythm and more directly diatonic. His music shows the influence of d'Indy, Dukas and Berlioz. This multimeter work is written in four movements: *Monodie et Beguine, Diaphonie, Berceuse* and *Scherzo*. Fast tempos and awkward technical passages make this an extremely difficult work.

Daniels, Mabel   American   1878-1971
Three Observations, Op. 41; 1943; CFI; 7.5 mins; 1011; D
Although never daring or very individualistic, Daniels was a competent composer who wrote well for both voices and orchestra. She was known principally for her choral works. Daniels studied with George Chadwick and Ludwig Thuille. The titles of the movements in this work suggest the character and the overall mood is light. It uses irregular scale patterns and complicated rhythms. Oboe may replace flute.

Danson, Alan   20th C.
Three Winds Go West; c1992; PRC; 5 mins; 0111; C/D
English horn required. The five movements are titled *A Roving, Blow the Man Down, Mermaid, Drunken Sailor* and *Bobby Shaftoe*.

Three Winds in a Boat; PRC; 0111; C/D
There is an optional English horn part.

Three Winds on the Rocks; c1992; PRC; 3 mins; 0111; C/D
English horn is required. The movements are titled *Drink to Me Only, 1 2 3 Drink Up, There's a Tavern in the Town* and *Show Me the Way to Go Home*.

Davidson, John H.   1930-
Row #1; PMP; 1020

de Bohun, Lyle   American   20th C.
The Americas Trio; ARP; 4.5 mins; 1011
Written in three movements, this work should not present any significant difficulties for student ensembles.

Deason, William David   1945-
Entropy; SEE; 1011

Debussy, Claude   French   1862-1918
Danse Negre Dite Danse de Gateau; Schmidt; WIM; 0011/1; C/D
Debussy studied with Chopin and later at the Paris Conservatory with Durand. He wrote music for opera, ballet, orchestra, piano and chamber ensembles. This work was originally part of a suite for solo piano.

Defossez, Rene   Belgian   1905-1988
Trio; 1946; 14 mins; 0111
Defossez studied at the Liège Conservatory and received the Belgian
Prix de Rome in 1935 for his opera *Le Vieux Soudard*. He wrote music
for opera and chamber ensembles.

Degen, Johannes   Swedish   1910-1989
Trialog, Op. 62; 1984; SMI; 4.5 mins; 0111

Delden, Lex van   Dutch   1919-1988
Sonata a Tre, Op. 59; 1957; DNA; 5 mins; 1101
Delden studied law then turned to music after WW II. Largely self-
taught, he has written oratorios, symphonies, and chamber music.
English horn is required.

Delmotte, Camille   Belgian   1914-
Trio; 1947; MAU; 6 mins; 0111; C/D
This work is written in an imitative, contrapuntal style. The varied
rhythms in the last movement would be a challenge to young players.
Alternate horn part to replace bassoon.

DeLorenzo, Leonardo   1875-1962
Trio Eccentrico, Op. 76; PTE; 7 mins; 1011; C/D

Delvaux, Albert   Belgian   1913-
Trio; 1948; EAM; 16 mins; 0111; C/D
Delvaux studied with Joseph Leroy at the Liège Conservatory. While
written in an atonal idiom, this work is nevertheless melodious with
lively rhythms and dissonance throughout.

Demachi, Giuseppe   Italian   1732-1791
Trio #1; Dishinger; MED; 1110; B/C
There is another version for oboe, clarinet and bassoon.

Denwood
Suite; ESM; 0111; C/D

Depelsenaire
Petite Concert; ESM; 0111; C/D

Dessau, Paul   German   1894-1979
Three Pieces; BKH; 0021; C
Dessau's early works show his interest in the twelve-tone method and
Jewish folk music, while his later music offers the opportunity for
political commentary. He wrote music for orchestra, chorus, chamber
music and piano.

Devienne, François   French   1759-1803
Sonatines, Vol. 1-4; ESM; 2001; C/D
Devienne's compositions did much to raise the musical level of works
for wind instruments in late eighteenth-century France. He wrote concertos, sinfonie concertantes, opera and chamber music. His music
usually is comprised of a single melodic line with accompaniment. The
melodies are elegant and graceful, and usually have sections intended to
display the performer's technique. A well-known flutist and bassoonist,
he was a prolific composer and showed a real interest in chamber music
for wind instruments.

Trio #2 in F Major; ESM; 0011/1; C

Trio #3 in D Minor; ESM; 0011/1; C

Trio in A Minor; ESM; 1011; C

Trio in C Major, Op. 61 #1; 1805; ESM; 0011/1 or 1011; C

Trio in D Major, Op. 19 #1; ESM; 2001; C

Trio in E-Flat Major, Op. 75 #3; ESM; 0021; C

Trio in F Major, Op. 75 #1; MRI; 0021; C

Trio in F Major,, Op. 61 #2; KZE; 0011/1 or 1011; C

Trios, Op. 27 #1-#6; Balassa; 1795; ESM; 0021; C

Trios, Op. 61 #1-#6; Balassa; 1795; MRI, EMB; 1011; C

Diemente, Edward Philip   1923-
Dimensions I; SEE; flexible instrumentation

Dobrowolski, Andrzej   Polish   1921-1990
Trio; 1956; PWM; 15 mins; 0111; B/C
Dobrowolski's early music is generally undemanding pieces based on
Polish folk dance themes. His later works have a more individual style
and show good craftsmanship and animated wit. *Trio*, a moderately
easy, multimeter work, is written in three movements.

Dodge, Charles   American   1942-
Solos and Combinations; 1964; 20 mins; 1110
Dodge, a student of Luening, Milhaud, Chou and Winham, has written
primarily computer music.

Dominutti, Franco   20th C.
Melos; c1992; LDA; 5 mins; 1011

Donatoni, Franco   Italian   1927-
Triplum; BHl; 5 mins; 1110
Donatoni studied with Ettore Desderi at the Milan Conservatory. His
music has embraced serialism, electronic music and, later, an eccentric
experimentalism.

Dondeyne, Desire   French   1921-
Suite d'Airs Populaires; c1962; EMT; 14.5 mins; 0111; D
This work features ten short movements based on popular French folk
songs. The melodies and harmonies are tonal and modal, while
rhythms are simple. There are some technical challenges in all parts
and intonation may be a challenge with many parts written in octaves
or unison.

Doppelbauer, Josef Friedrich   1918-1989
Trio #1; 1963; DBM; 8 mins; 1110; C/D
This challenging work offers much rhythmic variety and melodic inter-
est.

Trio for Two Clarinets and Bassoon; DBM; 0021

Trio in B Major; c1995; DBM; 15 mins; 1020; C/D

Dreyfus, George   German/Australian   1928-
Trio; 1956; AMP; 11 mins; 1011; C
Dreyfus's chamber music of the 1950s displays a gift for musical
parody and a preference for wind instruments.   After a period of
serialism, his musical style settled into a more profound lyrical
expression.

Dubois, Pierre Max   French   1930-1995
Trio D'Anches; 1958; LDA; 9 mins; 0111; D
Dubois studied at the Paris Conservatoire and won the Prix de Rome
in 1955. His music for orchestra, dance and chamber ensembles shows
the influence of Milhaud, Francaix and Prokofiev. He writes in a light,
humorous style, with chromatic scales, unusual harmonies and lively
rhythms.

Durey, Louis   French   1888-1979
Divertissement, Op. 107; 1966; PRC; 12 mins; 0111; C
Durey was greatly influenced by Debussy, Satie and Stravinsky, but his
music always has a somberness distinct from these composers. Written
in three movements, this work should present no ensemble problems.

Dusek, Frantisek Xaver   Bohemian   1731-1799
Six Parthias, Vols. 1 and 2; Komorous; 1763; SCI; 0201
Dusek, a popular keyboard player and teacher in Prague during his
lifetime, wrote instrumental music in the Galant style. He composed
more than forty symphonies, keyboard concertos, chamber music and
keyboard sonatas.

Duvernoy, Victor Alphonse   French   1842-1907
Three Trios; ESM; 0011/1; C/D

Ecklebe, Alexander   1904-
Wind Trio; 1975; GER; 15 mins; 0111; C/D

Edelson, Edward
Summer Winds; 2.5 mins; 1110; A/B

Eder, Helmut   German   1916-
Waechter Divertimento: Tower Music #18; PTE; 1011
A student of Johann N. David and Orff, Eder wrote music for opera,
ballet, orchestra, chamber ensembles and radio and television scores.

Eisenmann, Will   German   1906-
Divertimento; SIK; 0021

Eisma, Will   Dutch   1929-
Affairs III; 1965; DNA; 6 mins; 0111; D
Eisma studied with Stam and van Baaren at the Amsterdam Conservatory, then later with Petrassi in Rome. He has written music for
orchestra, chamber ensembles and tape. This avant garde work requires
considerable technical ability with a wide, flexible range.

Fleur Miroir; 1984; DNA; 0111

Reflections; 1989; DNA; 0111; C

Eler, André F.   French   1764-1821
Trio in F Major, Op. 9 # 1; Voxman; 1802-3; MRI; 1011; C/D
Eler can be noted as one who prepared the way for Romanticism in
France. Schooled in German Classicism, Eler's music demonstrates a
solid technique with pure harmonies, Classical melodies and strong

counterpoint. He wrote a large quantity of interesting chamber music, at a time when the genre was largely ignored in France. In the original version, this work used clarinet in C, but it is transposed here for B-flat clarinet.

Elkus, Jonathan   American   1931-
Five Sketches; 1954; MMB; 0021
The five movements are titled *Intrada, Alla Polacca, Notturna, Burlesca* and *Recitative-Capriccio.*

Elliott, Willard   American   1926-
Two Creole Songs; c1968; SMC; 3 mins; 0111
Elliott, a renowned bassoonist, studied at North Texas State University and Eastman School. This work features two movements titled *Mon L'aime Toi, Chere* and *O! Caitanne.*

Emmert, Adam Joseph   German   1765-1812
Trio; PRC; 0001/2

Erdmann, Dietrich   German   1917-
Blasertrio; 1944 REM; 1011
Erdmann studied with Hindemith and Paul Hoffer. Committed to the cause of contemporary music, he has written solo concerto, orchestral music, chamber music and vocal music.

Miniatures; 1972; 11 mins; 0111
This work in seven movements includes an oboe solo in the second and clarinet solo in sixth.

Erod, Ivan   Hungarian   1936-
Blasertrio, Op. 4; c1988; DBM; 1110

Escher, Rudolf   Dutch   1912-1980
Trio D'Anches, Op. 4; 1942; DNA; 14 mins; 0111; E
Escher studied with Pijper at the Rotterdam Conservatory. His music uses a broadened tonality in that the chromaticism is always tied to a tonal center. While one of the most interesting works for wind trio, this piece is also one of the most difficult. The harmony is chromatic and dissonant.

Etler, Alvin   American   1913-1973
Suite for Flute, Oboe and Clarinet; 1960; AMP; 1110; D
Etler studied with Hindemith while teaching woodwinds and conducting the band at Yale. He used serialism, but usually with a tonal center, and jazz is sometimes evident in his music. He wrote

music for orchestra, chamber ensembles and chorus. The *Suite* is a colorful and effectively written work.

Ewers, Jurgen   German   1937-
Trio, Op. 2; 1961; Krenn; 9.5 mins; 0111; D
The opening movement is multimeter, the middle movement is contrapuntal and the lively final movement is harmonically tonal. Endurance may be a factor for all players and a wide range is required of the double reed players.

Eyser, Eberhard   Polish/Swedish   1932-
Terzetto Polychrome; 1995; SMI; 11 mins; 1011
Eyser studied at the Music Academy in Hanover and later became a violist with the Royal Opera House Orchestra in Stockholm. flexible instrumentation for this work; alternates include saxophones or strings.

Faillenot, Maurice
Suite Breve; c1990; PRC; 3 mins; 0111; C

Falik, Yuri   Russian   1936-
English Divertimento; 1978; BHI; 1011; D
Known as both a cellist and composer, Falik's music shows a somewhat Romantic style with dissonance and angular rhythms.

Farkas, Ferenc   Hungarian   1905-2000
Mascarade; 1983; EMB; 7 mins; 0111; D
Farkas studied with Leo Weiner and Albert Siklos at the Academy of Music in Budapest and later with Respighi in Rome. He has served on the faculties of several schools including the State Conservatory at Szekesfehervar and the Academy of Music. Although there may be some endurance challenges for the players, this is an entertaining work with five movements titled *Il Capitano, Pantalone, Columbina, Povero Pulcinella* and *Arlecchino*.

Fasch, Johan Friedrich   German   1688-1758
Sonata in D Minor; SIK; 0201
Though none of his music was published during his lifetime, Fasch's early works show the influence of Telemann. He is best known today for his overtures, symphonies, concertos and chamber music, and musical scholars view him as an important link between the Baroque and Classical styles.

Sonata in F Major; Wojciechowski; c1956; SIK; 0201; D

Favre, Georges   French   1905-1993
Gouaches Suite; c1957; DUR; 9 mins; 0111; C/D
Favre writes in a very tuneful and rhythmically varied style. This work features four movements titled *Pastorale, Intermede, Grave* and *Danse*. All three parts are technically demanding, and ensemble precision is complicated by multimeters and challenging rhythmic patterns.

Felderhof, Jan   Dutch   1907-
Rondo; 1960; DNA; 5.5 mins; 0111; D
This single-movement work is harmonically chromatic and uses diverse rhythmic and melodic styles. The technical requirements are not extreme, but the tempo changes could present some ensemble difficulties.

Theme and Variations; 1943; DNA; 6 mins; 0111; D
This work features six short variations on a modal folk theme. All players are featured in various movements. There are technical demands on the oboe and clarinet players, and the bassoon part frequently goes into the extreme high register.

Feldman, Ludovic   Rumanian   1893-
Suite for Flute, Oboe and Clarinet; c1955; 1110
After a long career as a violinist, Feldman studied composition with Jihail Jora and wrote many works for orchestra and chamber groups. He wrote in a modern style within a Classical framework.

Fernandez, Oscar Lorenzo   Brazilian   1897-1948
Duas Invencoes Seresteiras; 1944; PIC; 7 mins; 1011
In his music, Fernandez adopted a strongly national style, derived from Brazilian folksongs, but without actual quotation. This work is challenging for its rhythmic ensemble in the second movement, and the remaining movements are pleasantly melodic with some chromatic dissonance.

Ferroud, Pierre Octave   French   1900-1936
Trio in E Major; 1933; DUR; 10 mins; 0111; D
Ferroud's music, greatly influenced by Bartók, shows a seriousness that was in contrast to the flippancy of much of the Neo-Classical style. While his music is sometimes cool and sarcastic, at other times he could be warmly lyrical and romantic. This work is highly chromatic, and multimeters are used throughout. Rhythmic precision and intonation could be challenging.

Filippi, Amedeo de   Italian/American   1900-
Corydon Suite for Flute, Clarinet, Bassoon; c1970; GMP, SER; 1011
De Filippi studied composition with Rubin Goldmark, and received a
four-year fellowship to the Juilliard School.

Flegier, Ange   French   1846-1927
Concert Suite; Voxman; Rubank; 13 mins; 0111; D/E
Flegier studied at the Marseilles and Paris conservatories. He wrote
music for opera, chorus, orchestra and voice. Aside from some fast
arpeggios and scales for the clarinet, this four-movement work should
present no ensemble problems. This work was originally written in B
minor, but later transposed by Voxman to C minor. This is one of the
earliest works written for the reed trio. It is written in a style similar to
the late nineteenth-century French overtures and features graceful melodies.

Trio in B-Flat Major; GAL; 0111

Flothuis, Marius   Dutch   1914-
Nocturne, Op. 11; 1941; DNA, CHE; 4 mins; 1110; D
Flothuis's music is usually lyrical and intimate, tonal and very contra-
puntal.

Focking
Uitnemend Kabinet, Het: Music for Three Instruments; ABM; flexible
instrumentation

Fontyn, Jacqueline   Belgian   1930-
Sept Petites Pieces; 1956; SCI; 8 mins; 0111; C/D
Fontyn (sometimes spelled Fontijn), awarded the Prix de Rome and
Prix oscar Espla, studied composition in Paris and Vienna. Her earlier
works are very traditional, but since 1959 she has written in a modern
idiom.

Foret, Felicien   French   1890-1978
Suite en Trio; c1953; BIL; 0111; C/D
This lyrical, rhythmically uncomplicated piece features frequent high
register passages for all players. The melody is shared by all three
players with the bassoon part particularly prominent.

Forsyth, Malcolm   Canadian   1936-
Melancholy Clown; KER; 5 mins; 1011; C/D
The composer writes: "Several images spring to mind as I listen to
these three little episodes of mine. One is of Petrushka, and indeed it
was after seeing Stravinsky's ballet for the first time that these were
written. Another is that of Picasso's clown, whose ludicrously jolly

make-up only half succeeds in masking a deeply tragic countenance, it is sometimes only such a picture that give any perspective to the charade of living. A third image is that of Marcel Marceau, the supreme mime artist, whose depth of humanity is unfathomable. I think my three pieces were inspired by something akin to that which moves him and they seem to invite choreographic treatment." This work has optional E-flat clarinet, bass clarinet, flute and bassoon parts.

Fortner, Wolfgang   German   1907-1987
Capricen; 1979; EAM; 10 mins; 1101; D/E
Fortner is important in West German music for his roles of both composer and teacher. His pupils have included many of the German composers who came to prominence after 1950, most notably Henze. Written in four movements, this difficult work utilizes multiphonics and frequent duple meter against triple meter passages.

Serenade; 1945; EAM; 10 mins; 1101; D
This six-movement work is perhaps more accessible to audiences than Fortner's *Capricen*.

Français, Jean   French   1912-1997
Divertissement; 1947; EAM; 10 mins; 0111; E
A brilliant piano virtuoso, Français's music shows an innate gift for invention and an ability to express the joy and wonder of childhood. Written in a charming and whimsical style, this difficult but graceful work makes virtuoso demands of all players.

Franck, Maurice
Deuxieme Trio d'Anches; c1960; ESM; 0111; D/E

Frangkiser, Carl   1894-
Inventriole; CPP; 0021

Frid, Geza   Hungarian   1904-
Dubbeltrio, Op. 73; 1967; DNA; 10 mins; 1101
A student of Bartók and Kodaly, Frid was a prolific composer with works for opera, orchestra, chorus, keyboard and chamber ensembles. This work requires piccolo, English horn and contrabassoon.

Fritter, Genevieve Davisson   American   1915-
Three Movements; c1989; ALE; 5 mins; 1101; C
The structure of *Three Movements* is based on contrapuntal treatment of the various themes and the motifs within them. There is a tonal center, but not necessarily a key. Occasionally there are short unison passages to tie the three parts together. It is concisely written and is more

consonant than dissonant. The rhythmic motifs are an important element.

Fritter, Jean
Eight Rondels; c1966; UNE; 1011; C

Fuchs, Georg-Fried   French   1752-1821
Trio; MRI; 0020/1; C/D
Fuchs, a clarinetist, studied with Haydn and Christian Cannabich. His compositions include pieces for military band, a few orchestral works and numerous chamber music works, most of them involving clarinet.

Trio, Op. 1 #1; ESM; 0111; C/D
The English horn part may be played on French horn.

Gagneux, Renaud   French   1947-
Trio d'Anches; DUR; 0111

Gallon, Noel   French   1891-1966
Suite en trio; 1933; SEL; 12 mins; 0111; C/D
Gallon studied at the Paris Conservatory and won the Prix de Rome in 1910. He was a renowned teacher and is best known as a composer for his dramatic and orchestral works. His compositions are noted for their elegance and clarity with a subtle impressionistic quality. Using a light character, this work uses a variety of harmonies and melodies based on both modes and major/minor scales. Technical agility and rapid articulation are required of all players.

Gannon, Lee   American   1960-
First Sonatine; 1983; AMC; 8 mins; 1110
Gannon studied flute and composition at the Eastman School where he studied with Adler, Baker, Morris and Schwantner.

Second Sonatine; 1985; AMC; 9 mins; 0111

Third Sonatine; 1986; AMC; 8 mins; 0011/1
This work was the winner of the 1988 Sigma Alpha Iota Composers Competition.

Gardner
A Suite of Sweets; ESM; 1011; B/C
The flute part could be played on oboe and bass clarinet may replace bassoon.

Gardonyi, Zoltan   Hungarian   1906-
Three Rondos; c1977; ZIM, PTE; 4.5 mins; 1101; C
Gardonyi studied with Kodaly and Hindemith and taught at the Academy of Music in Budapest.

Garscia, Janina   Polish   1920-
Theme with Variations, Op. 35; PWM, PRC; 1011

Gassmann, Florian Leopold   Czech   1729-1774
Trio in D Major; KZE; 0011/1
One of Vienna's most important eighteenth century musicians, Gassmann wrote music for opera, sacred choral works, secular cantatas, orchestra and chamber ensembles.

Gattermayer, Heinrich   1923-
Trio, Op. 62 #2; c1977; DBM; 9.5 mins; 0111; C/D

Gebauer, François Rene   French   1773-1845
Three Trios, #164A, B and C; c1977; EKW; 011/1; C
Gebauer, son of a German military bandsman, studied bassoon at the Paris Conservatory where he later served as professor of bassoon from 1796 to 1802 and later from 1826 on.   Between 1801 and 1826 Gebauer played bassoon at the Grande Opera in Paris. In his numerous compositions he concentrated especially on woodwind instruments.

Trio Concertante, Op. 32 #1 and#3; ESM; 1101; C/D
Clarinet may replace oboe.

Geraedts, Jaap   Dutch   1924-
Divertimento #1; 1943; DNA; 10 mins; 0111; D
This technically difficult, dissonant work is light in character and highly rhythmic.

Divertimento #2; 1946; DNA; 0111; C/D
Written in an unpretentious, dissonant style, this work matches the three instruments well.

Gerschefski, Edwin   American   1909-
America Variations, Op. 44 #4; ACA; 1011
Gerschefski studied at Yale and later with Schillinger in New York. His music includes works for orchestra, piano, chorus, chamber ensembles and incidental music and scores for films.

Gershwin, George   American   1898-1937
I Got Plenty of Nothing; Danson; 1935; ESM; 0111; C/D
Perhaps one of America's best known composers of music for stage,
Gershwin's musical style ranges from diatonic to chromatic with the
clear influence of jazz. This is an arrangement for trio of the well-known
song from the opera *Porgy and Bess*.

Jazzination: Gershwin for Three; Armitage; ESM; flexible instrumentation; C/D

Gethen, Felix
Scherzo; c1973; ESM; 0111

Gianella, Luigi   Italian   1778-1817
Nocturne in F Major, Op. 28 #2; Wienandt; SMC; 4 mins; 2001; C/D
This two-movement work is written in traditional Baroque style. The
second flute part could easily be performed on oboe.

Nocturne in G Major, Op. 28 #1; Wienandt; SMC; 4 mins; 2001;
C/D
In standard Baroque form, the second flute part could be performed on
oboe.

Nocturne in D Major; Wienandt; c1964; SMC; 2001
Written in three-movement sonata form, the second part could be
played on oboe.

Gibbons, Orlando   English   1583-1625
Fantasia; Clark; c1965; ESM; 1110; C

Gilson, Paul   Belgian   1865-1942
Trio; 1934; MMM; 0111
Gilson, a self-taught composer, won the Prix de Rome in 1889. He was
considered the most representative Belgian composer of his time. Although a Romantic in imagination, he was essentially a Classical composer using only traditional forms and harmonic language. His melodies rely heavily on folk music.

Giltay, Berend   Dutch   1910-1975
Trio Sonata; 1953; DNA; 13 mins; 0111; D/E
Written in a complex, chromatic style, this sonata uses short motives
which are then developed as the music unfolds. Ensemble precision is a
challenge due to multimeters and the independent character of the
various parts.

Gipps, Ruth   English   1921-1999
The Three Billy Goats Gruff; ESM; 0101/1
A pupil of Vaughan Williams, Gipps wrote concertos, chamber, choral
music and five symphonies.

Gluck, Christoph Willibald   German   1714-1787
Che faro senza Euridice from *Orfeo e Euridice*; Benyas; 1762; INT;
1011
Primarily self-taught, Gluck is best known for his stage works. This is
an elegant aria arrangement from Gluck's most famous opera. Oboe
may replace flute.

Dance of the Blessed Spirits; Stewart; TRI; 6 mins; 1011
This is an arrangement of music from *Orpheus and Euridice.*

Goeb, Roger   American   1914-1997
Suite; 1946; PIC; flexible instrumentation; C/D
Varying instrumentation of flute, oboe and clarinet may be used.

Golestan, Stan   Rumanian/French   1872-1956
Petite Suite Bucolique; c1953; DUR; 9 mins; 0111; D/E
Golestan's works use gypsy and other Rumanian folk ideas. He wrote
music for orchestra, piano and chamber ensembles. This three-movement work (*Humoresque, Lamento, Jeux*) is lyrical and chromatic. The
parts are equally technically demanding with the oboe and clarinet
sharing most of the melodic material.

Goodenough, Forret   American   1918-
Trio; AMC; 1101

Goodman, Joseph   American   1918-
Five Bagatelles for Flute, Clarinet, Bassoon; 1975; GMP, SER; 8
mins; 1011; C
Born in New York City, Goodman has for many years been on the
faculty of Queens College of the CUNY. He was also head of the Composition Department of the School of Sacred Music of Union Theological Seminary from 1958 to 1973. His teachers include Paul Him-
demith, Walter Piston, and Gian Francesco Malipiero. This multimeter
work is written in a straightforward manner and should present no
ensemble difficulties. Clarinet in A is required.

Gordon
Haydn at Eszterhaza; ESM; 1011; C

Gorner, Hans Georg   German   1908-1984
Trio for Winds, Op. 24; PRC; 1110; D
Clarinet in A is required.

Gould, Elizabeth   American   1904-
Disciplines for Woodwind Trio; c1964; EVI, PRC; 4.5 mins; 0111;
C/D
The composer states: "This composition consists of a melody limited
to the common range of the three instruments, followed by three
variations and a conclusion. All parts are constructed on a series of
seven scales or modes ranging in order from the darkest to the
brightest. At the same time other means such as rhythm and pitch are
used to increase the intensity of the music to a point just preceding the
conclusion. This was an attempt to make the music as meaningful and
interesting as possible while strictly observing a number of limita-
tions."

Graap, Lothar   Swedish   1933-
Divertimento; 1964; BBL; 8 mins; 1101; B/C

Grabner, Hermann   Austrian   1886-1969
Trio; 1951; KIS; 15 mins; 0111; D
Grabner studied music with Reger and Hans Sitt at the Leipzig Conservatory, later serving on the faculties of Strasbourg Conservatory, Mannheim Conservatory, Leipzig Conservatory, Hochschule für Musik in
Berlin and the Berlin Conservatory. This light, witty work is tonal and
rhythmically complex. The three parts are technically balanced, with
the oboe having frequent high register passages.

Grahn, Ulf   Swedish   1942-
Trio; 1967; SEE, EDN; 8 mins; 1110
Grahn studied composition with Gunnar Johanson and Hans Eklund at
the Royal College of Music in Stockholm, later moving to America
where he founded the Contemporary Music Forum which presents
modern music by American and European composers. His music
incorporates contemporary techniques that are accessible to most audiences.

Graun, Carl Heinrich   German   1704-1759
Trio #1 in D Major; c1959; MMM; 0101/1; C
Graun was one of the most important German composers of the pre-
Classical period. He was acquainted with J.S. Bach and gave violin
lessons to Bach's son, Wilhelm Friedemann. He worked at the court of
Frederic II of Prussia as concertmaster and later as Kapellmeister. This

version requires oboe d'amore but there is an alternate version with clarinet in A.

Trio #2 in E Minor; MMM; 0101/1; C
This version requires oboe d'amore but there are alternate versions with clarinet in A or oboe.

Griend, Koos van de   Dutch   1905-1950
Trio; 1929; DNA; 4.5 mins; 0111; D
This three-movement work features a non-tonal style with emphasis on texture and rhythm. The rapid tempo of the final movement makes it the most technically challenging.

Groot, Hugo de   Netherlands   1914-
Souvenir sud Americain; BVP; 0111; D

Grossi, Pietro   1917-
Composition #3; BRU; 0011/1

Haan, Stefan de   1921-
Divertimento on Folksongs; 1983; EAM; 4 mins; 0111; C
Haan has created three delightful arrangements of familiar folksongs from around the world including *Oh Enemy* (Flemish war song), *In The Wild Forest* (Swedish love song) and *Camptown Races* (American).

Sonatina I and II; ESM; 1011; B/C
Saxophone may be used in place of bassoon.

Three Easy Trios; ESM; 1011; B/C
Saxophone may be used in place of bassoon.

Trio; c1950; EAM; 6 mins; 1011; D/E

Halferty, Frank   20th C.
Demaray; KED; 1011; C
Bass clarinet may substitute for bassoon.

Fantasia on Lasst Uns Erfreuen; KED; 1110; C

Hall, Charles J.   American   1925-
Petite Suite; OPM; 7 mins; 1011
Hall studied with Charles Garland, Owen Reed and Paul Harder. This four-movement work uses twelve-tone technique.

Hallnas, Eyvind   Swedish   1937-
Serenata per Tre Musici; 1980; SMI; 5 mins; 1011

Trio; 1985; SMI; 1110
English horn and bass clarinet are required.

Handel, George   German/English   1685-1759
Andante-Larghetto from *Berenic;* Findlay; 1737; CFI; 1011; B
Handel's music featured grand design, lush harmonies and a certain eloquence. He wrote works for opera, oratorios, chamber ensembles and orchestra.

Bouree; Christiansen; KED; 1011; A/B

Chaconne in G Major: Theme and Variations; PMP; 0111

Five Trios; Voxman; SMC; 8 mins; 0111 or 0202; B/C
These are good training pieces for students.

Little Handel Suite; Morsch; UNE, KAL; 1101 or 1011

Minuet; Busto; CFI; 0111; C

Overture; EAM; 0020/1; C

Rigaudon, Bouree and March; MRI; 0201; C

Sonata; Williams; SMC; 1011; C
There is an alternate oboe part to replace flute.

Sonata in D Major; Coopersmith; PRC; 0020/1; A

Trio #2 in D Minor; KAL; 0201; C/D
This work was originally for two oboes and bassoon.

Trios; ESM; flexible instrumentation; B
Any three instruments of equal pitch may be used.

Hanmer, Ronald   1917-1995
Woodwind Trios; ESM; 1020; B/C

Hanna, James   American   1922-
Trio; c1956; SPR; 5 mins; 1011; B

Hansell, P.
A Short Walk on the Downs; ESM; 1020; C

Three Friends; ESM; 0102; C

Harbinson, William G.
Three Movements for Woodwind Trio; ALE; 0111; D
This is a Neo-Classical work in three movements composed of standard forms with modal themes and harmonies, suitable for recitals and concerts.

Harbison, John   American   1938-
Four Preludes from Dec Music; 1967; MMM; 6 mins; flexible instrumentation; D/E
Harbison studied at Harvard and Princeton; his primary teachers were Roger Sessions, Earl Kim and Boris Blacher. He has received numerous grants and awards for his music. He writes in an elegant, lucid style that embraces musical interests ranging from Bach to jazz and pop. The instrumentation is somewhat flexible and could use various combinations of flute, oboe, clarinet, violin.

Harris, Arthur   American   1927-
Four Pieces for Three Instruments; c1957; RON; 6 mins; flexible instrumentation; C
This dissonant and unpretentious work may be performed by various combinations of the following treble instruments: flute, oboe, English horn, clarinet in B-flat, violin, viola.

Harris
Trio; ESM; 1110; D/E

Hartley, Geoffrey
Jack and Jill; PRC; 0111; C/D
English horn is required and a second bassoon could replace the clarinet.

Harvey
Rocking Reeds; ESM; 1101; B/C

Haus
Auf Dem Holzweg; BBM; 0111; D/E

Hauta-Aho, Teppo   Finnish   1941-
Konserttitango; 1992; FMC; 0012

Trio #1; FMC; 13 mins; 1101
Doubling on alto flute and English horn is required.

Haydn, Joseph   Austrian   1732-1809
Dance in F Major; Benyas; INT; 1011 or 0111
Haydn is considered the creator of the classical form of the symphony and string quartet. He played an historic role in the evolution of harmony by adopting four-part writing as the compositional foundation. A prolific composer, Haydn wrote music for orchestra, chamber ensembles, concertos, dramatic works, masses and oratories. In this charming minuet, each of the three instruments has an opportunity to play the melody.

Divertimento; SMC; 0021; C

Divertimento, Op. 100; Merriman; ESM; 5 mins; 0011/1; C

Four London Trios; Moyse, Stewart; SMC, TRI; 1011; C
This set of trios was originally written for two flutes and cello, but can easily be performed on flute, oboe and bassoon or two flutes and bassoon.

Four Minuets; Sutton; NOV; 0021; B/C

Scherzando; Schaeffer; CPP; flexible instrumentation; B/C

Trio; Winkler; DBM; 0111; B/C

Hecker, Zeke   20th C.
Trio; 1990; TRI; 10 mins; 0111

Hedin, Staffan   Swedish   1954-
Trio; 1976-78; SMI; 5.5 mins; 0201
This work requires English horn.

Hedwall, Lennart   Swedish   1932-
Trio; 1962; SMI; 16 mins; 1011
Hedwall studied composition with Back and Blomdahl.

Heininen, Paavo   Finnish   1938-
Suite; FMC; 1110
Heininen studied with Kokkonen and Persichetti. His early music uses twelve-tone composition and later works explore aleatory and improvisational styles.

Hekster, Walter   Dutch   1937-
Echoes of Summer; 1975; DNA; 0111
After graduation from the Amsterdam Conservatory, Hekster was a clarinetist with the Connecticut Symphony Orchestra and later taught clarinet and composition at Brandon University (Canada), the Utrecht Conservatory and the Arnhem Conservatory. This work requires doubling on English horn and bass clarinet.

Reedmusic; 1970 DNA; 8 mins; 0111

Hemberg, Eskil   Swedish   1938-
Ten Variations; 1960; SMI; 0111
After studies at the Royal College of Music in Stockholm, Hemberg conducted the Stockholm University chorus and wrote music primarily for vocal groups. His choral music follows the structure of polyphonic

sacred music while his instrumental works incorporate more contemporary ideas.

Hemel, Oscar Van   Dutch   1892-1981
Pavanne en Gigue; DNA; 6 mins; 1101
Hemel studied with Mortelmans and Pijper. He wrote in a late Romantic style and composed works for stage, orchestra, concertos, voice and chamber ensembles. This work requires English horn.

Trio; 1959; DNA; 1101

Henneberg, Albert   Swedish   1901-1991
Liten Kvartett, Op. 36; SMI; 12 mins; 1101/1
After studies in Stockholm, Vienna and Paris, Henneberg returned to Stockholm and became a well-known conductor. He wrote operas, symphonies and chamber music.

Hennessy, Swan   American   1866-1929
Trio, Op. 54; EME; 0021; D
Hennessy wrote more than seventy works in an impressionistic style for chamber groups and piano.

Hermans, Nico   Dutch   1919-1988
Divertimento Piccolo, Op. 2; 1958; DNA; 6 mins; 0111; C/D
These two short movements have a diversity of style ranging from poignant and chromatically dissonant to cheerful and tonal.   Ensemble precision and intonation are a challenge.

Hess, Willy   Swiss   1906-1997
Trio, Op. 136; ESM; 0021
Basset horn is required.

Hetu
Quatre Miniatures; ESM; 0111; E

Heussenstamm, George   American   1926-
Canonograph 1; SEE; flexible instrumentation; B
Heussenstamm was a recipient of a 1976 National Endowment for the Arts grant and is on the faculty of California State College at Dominguez Hills. This work may be played on any three wind instruments.

Seven Etudes, Op. 17; 1968; WIM; 0111; B
This uncomplicated work, dedicated to Bernard Rosen, is written in seven movements.

Hiatt
Simurgh; ESM; 0111

Hildemann, Wolfgang   1925-
Diletto Musicale; 1978; BKH; 8 mins; 0111; D
This multimeter work will be difficult for the individual players as well
as the ensemble.

Hoch, Peter   1937-
Divertimento; MFS; flexible instrumentation; B/C

Hoffer, Paul   German   1895-1949
Kleine Suite; 1944; SIK; 0111; C
Hoffer studied composition with Franz Schreker in Berlin and later
taught piano and served as Director of the Hochschule for Musik. His
music uses many modern techniques including atonality and polytonality while modeling the formal unity of the Romantic style. This
work is a good example of German school music particularly good for
ensemble training, especially for balance and projection.

Theme with Variations; 1944; SIK; 6 mins; 0111; C
This short work, good for young ensembles, emphasizes melodic,
legato writing for all three instruments. Multimeters are found in the
last movement, but technical and range demands are minimal.

Holborne, Anthony   English   1584-1602
Two Fantasias; 1597; NPR; 3 mins; 1101; C

Holst, Gustav   English   1874-1934
Terzetto; 1925; CHE; 9.5 mins; 1110; D
This work, the only original chamber music by Holst, is actually written with viola, but it works well with clarinet. The work consists of
two short movements, the first lyrical and the second in the manner of a
scherzo with contrasting fugato and meno mosso sections.

Hongisto, Mauri   Finnish   20th C.
Trio; FMC; 1011

Horvit, Michael   American   1932-
Little Suite; 1964 SHA; 1011; B
Horvit holds degrees from Yale University and Boston University. He
studied composition with Copland, Foss, Piston, Porter and Read.
Little Suite is a statement and six variations that the composer ex-
tracted from his background music to the documentary film *How to
Choose Your College Career*. The *Prelude* contains two themes, one
of which is the basis for each of the following movements.

Hovey, Howard
Seven Pieces for Three Woodwinds; c1954; BHI; 1110; B/C

Hubbard, Brad   American   20th C.
Wildacres Suite; c1999; ALE; 1011; C

Hummel, Bertold   1925-
Five Moments Musicaux, Op. 48; 1978; PRC; 0111
The first movement has very difficult parts for all instruments, but the remainder of the work should present only moderate difficulty for the ensemble.

Husa, Karel   Czech/American   1921-
Deux Preludes; 1966; LDA, PRC; 11 mins; 1011; D/E
Husa studied at the Prague Conservatory and later in Paris with Boulanger. He uses primarily a Classical structure, while employing serial techniques, aleatory and microtonal writing. His many honors include a Guggenheim fellowship and an award from the American Academy and Institute of Arts and Letters. This two-movement work will present many challenges for the players and ensemble.

Ibert, Jacques   French   1890-1962
Cinq Pieces en Trio; 1935; EOL; 7 mins; 0111; C/D
Ibert studied at the Paris Conservatory with Paul Vidal for composition, and won several prizes there in 1914. He won the Prix de Rome in 1919, after serving in WWI. He made important contributions in all musical genres except oratorio. He used Classical forms as a foundation, but made them flexible, always with a strong sense of balance and restraint. Very similar to his wind quintet, *Trois Pieces Breve*, this work abounds in energy, charming melodies and modal harmonies. All three parts offer challenges to the players, particularly for the clarinet.

Ikonomow, Boyan Georgiev   Bulgarian   1900-1973
Trio in E Major; 1937; EOL; 12 mins; 0111; D
A student of d'Indy, Boulanger and Roussel, Ikonomow's compositions include works for opera, ballet, oratorios, orchestra and chamber music. This three-movement work shows his interest in folk themes and irregular rhythms with the last movement written in 7/8 meter. Its harmonies are tonal, though highly chromatic.

Isaacson, Michael   American   20th C.
A Jewish Wedding Suite; c1996; ALE; 1101; B
This collection of five traditional Jewish songs, perfect for weddings, includes *My Beloved, A Woman of Valor, The Messenger of Good Tidings, An Evening of Roses* and *Congratulations.*

Jacob, Gordon   English   1895-1984
Aubade; ESM; 2010; C
Jacob studied at Dulwich College and with Stanford and Howells at the Royal Academy of Music, later joining the faculty of the Royal Academy of Music. His works are deeply rooted in tradition and display fine craftsmanship. Piccolo is required and alto flute may be used in place of the clarinet.

Introduction and Fugue; ESM; 2010; C

Trio; c1993; MRI; 10 mins; 0111; C
There are no significant ensemble challenges in this light-hearted work.

Jalava, Lasse   Finnish   20th C.
Keikkeja; 1992; FMC; 5 mins; 2010

James, O.J.   American   20th C.
Fugue #1 in E-Flat Major; SHA; 1 1/2 mins; 1011; B/C
James attended Manhattan School of Music. This uncomplicated piece would be a good opportunity to teach the fugue style to student groups. Oboe may substitute for flute.

Jansson, Leif A.   Swedish   1939-
Harom kis Darab; 1994; LMA; 7 mins; 0111

Jelinek, Hanns   Austrian   1901-1969
Six Aphorisms, Op. 9 #3; 1923-30 KAL; 0021
Jelinek, a student of Schoenberg and Schmidt, composed music for film under the name of Hanns Elin and became a lecturer and professor at the Vienna Academy of Music. He wrote music for opera, orchestra, chamber ensembles and piano.

Sonata a Tre, Op. 15 #7; KAL; 0201
This twelve-tone work requires English horn.

Jemnitz, Alexander Sandor   Hungarian   1890-1963
Trio, Op. 70; 1958; EMB; 1110
A student of Reger and Koessler, Jemnitz wrote instrumental music in a style which combined the contrapuntal style of Reger and Schoenberg's atonality.

Johannes, John   Dutch   1915-
Introductie en fuga; 1968; DNA; 2.5 mins; 0111; C/D
This two movement work is atonal and contrapuntal with clarinet solos
beginning each movement. Multimeter passages and rapid tempi could
affect ensemble precision.

Johanson, Sven-Eric   Swedish   1919-1997
Lyrisk Svit; 1953; SMI; 5 mins; 0111
After studies with Melchers and Rosenberg in Stockholm, Johanson
adopted a compositional style influenced by Reger and Hindemith with
later use of occasional atonality.

Johnson
Narayanas Cows; ESM; flexible instrumentation; E
Narrator is required.

Joly, Denis   French   1906-1979
Trio; c1972; TRA; 0111; D/E

Jones, Robert
Three by Three; SHA; flexible instrumentation
This work may be played on any three like instruments.

Jones, Sister Ida   1898-
Scherzo; 1961; OPM; 3 mins; 1011
Jones studied at the Cincinnati Conservatory with Leighton and
Grimm. This single movement work was the winner of the 1961
Composers Press Publication Award Contest.

Jong, Marinus de   Belgian   1891-1984
Trio, Op. 126; 1961; 17 mins; 0111; D
Jong, a student of Mortelmans, writes in a Neo-Impressionistic style
with polytonal counterpoint. This work features a lyrical and charming
melody with technical difficulty well balanced among the three parts.

Jongen, Leon   Belgian   1884-1969
Trio; 1937; SMC; 16 mins; 0111; D/E
Leon Jongen, brother of Joseph, studied at the Liège Conservatory and
later taught at the Brussels Conservatory. This Neo-Romantic, three-
movement work offers technical challenges for all three players with
some possible endurance demands. Clarinet in A is required.

Joplin, Scott   African American   1868-1917
Bethena; Holcombe; MPI; 1101; C/D
Named the "King of Ragtime," Joplin was largely self-taught though
he briefly attended the Smith College for Negroes in 1895 to gain technical skills in composition. There are at least three versions available
that use various combinations of woodwinds. Flute could replace oboe.

Easy Winners; Holcombe; MPI; 1101; C/D
Flute could replace oboe.

Elite Syncopations; Holcombe; MPI; 1101; C/D
Flute could replace oboe.

Maple Leaf Rag; Holcombe; MPI; 1101; C/D
Flute could replace oboe.

Pineapple Rag; Holcombe; MPI; 1101; C/D
Flute could replace oboe.

Ragtime Dance; Holcombe; MPI; 1101; C/D
Flute could replace oboe.

Scott Joplin Suite; Holcombe; MPI; 1101; B
·Flute could replace oboe.

The Chrysanthemum; Holcombe; MPI; 1101; C/D
Flute could replace oboe.

The Entertainer; 1902; KED, MPI; 1110; C/D

Josten, Werner   German/American   1885-1963
Trio; 1941; BHI; 1011; C/D
Josten studied theory in Munich and Geneva, moving to America in
1920 where he taught at Smith College. His music is written in the
lyrical manner of the German Romantic style with some Impressionistic devices used in his later works.

Juon, Paul   Russian/German   1872-1940
Arabesken, Op. 73; 1940; PTE; 17 mins; 0111; C/D
Juon studied composition with Arensky and Taneyev at the Imperial
Conservatory. His major works, written for orchestra and chamber
music, show the influence of Tchaikovsky and Dvorák with a style that
remained Romantic throughout his career. This work is perhaps one of
the most flashy for the reed trio. It is harmonically tonal and often
chordal, and fully explores the range for the bassoon and oboe.

Kaderavek, Milan   American   1924-
Fantasia; 1981; DNP; 1110; D/E
Kaderavek, a student of Sowerby at the American Conservatory, has
written music for orchestra, chorus and chamber music. Dedicated to

Carol Wincenc and Ronald Dennis, this is a difficult single-movement work.

Kallstenius, Edvin   Swedish   1881-1967
Piccolo Trio Seriale, Op. 47; 1956; SMI; 10.5 mins; 1110
Kallstenius studied at the Leipzig Conservatory. His early music follows late Romantic style while later works use advanced modern techniques. This work requires English horn.

Kaplan, Elliott   20th C.
Suite; 1980; PRC; 7.5 mins; 1011; C/D
Kaplan studied composition with Porter, Hindemith and   Boulanger.

Karg-Elert, Sigfrid   German   1877-1933
Trio, Op. 49 #1 in D Minor; 1902; HOF; 0110/1; D
Karg-Elert studied with Homeger and Reinecke at the Leipzig Conservatory. Later Grieg championed his work and many of Karg-Elert's early works show this influence. He developed a compositional style inspired by the Baroque but with Impressionistic devices. He is best known for his harmonium and organ compositions. English horn could replace French horn.

Karkoff, Maurice   Swedish   1927-
Divertimento, Op. 29; 1957/93; SMI; 1101/1
Karkoff's teachers included Blomdahl, Larsson, Koch, Holmboe, Jolivet and Vogel. His music reflects his interest in many cultures.

Terzetto, Op. 139; 1978; SMI; 9 mins; 0011/1

Trio Piccolo, Op. 55; 1961; SMI; 9 mins; 1011

Kauder, Hugo   Austrian/American   1888-1972
Trio #1; 1936; SEE; 1100/1
Kauder's music is contrapuntal, with canonic devices and conservative harmonies. He wrote music for orchestra and chamber groups.

Trio #2; 1936; SEE; 1100/1
Viola could be used in place of horn.

Kauffman, Georg Friedrich   German   1679-1735
Chorale Prelude; Marx; MMM; 0111
Kauffman ranks among the best of Bach's contemporaries. His music shows inventiveness and solid craftsmanship.

Keldorfer, Robert   Austrian   1901-1980
Trio; DBM; 1011
Keldorfer studied with Prohaska, Springer and Stohr at the Vienna Academy of Music. He wrote music for opera, concertos, chorus and chamber music.

Kelkel, Manfred   German   1929-
Divertimento; c1958; RIC; 10.5 mins; 0111; D
Written in five movements, this dissonant, chromatic work features a particularly difficult bassoon part.

Kelterborn, Rudolf   Swiss   1931-
Trio; 1980; BBM; 10 mins; 1101; D/E
Kelterborn studied with Guldenstein and Geiser at the Basel Academy. His music uses strict serialism.

Ketting, Piet   Dutch   1905-1984
Trio; 1929; DNA 6 mins; 1011
Ketting, a student of Averkamp and Pijper, wrote in a modern Baroque style with some dissonance.

Kibbe, Michael   American   1945-
Divertimento; c1981; SHA; 8 mins; 0201; D
Kibbe studied at San Diego State University, New Mexico State University and California State University at Northridge. He has written music for orchestra, band, chamber ensemble, choral and solo pieces. Part two is for English horn, but could be done on saxophone.

Greensleeves Variations; SHA; 2010; C

Trio; SEE; 6 mins; 1011

Trio, Op. 46; c1980; SHA, SCI; 9 mins; 1110; D

Kinyon
Ensembles for Young Performers; ESM; 2010; A

Knight, Morris   American   1933-
Selfish Giant Suite by Oscar Wilde; 1967; PRC; 1011; C
Written in seven short movements, this piece is good for student groups. Trombone could replace bassoon. Knight has composed more than eighty serious pieces including three symphonies, an opera, a violin concerto and numerous chamber pieces.

Koch-Raphael, Erwin   20th C.
Jahreszeiten, Op. 15; 1979/85; BBM; 0111; E

Kochan, Gunter   German   1930-
Divertimento; 1956; PTE; 1011
Kochan studied composition with Blacher, Noetel and Wunsch. His music emphasizes the formal design with main subjects stated repeatedly and tonal dissonance.

Kocsar, Miklos   Hungarian   1933-
Divertimento; 1956; EMB; 7.5 mins; 0111; C/D
Kocsar studied with Farkas at the Budapest Academy. Kocsar uses atonality, multimeters and diverse textures in this three-movement work. The high register passages for all players, along with some awkward technical passages, make this a challenging work.

Koechlin, Charles   French   1867-1950
Trio d'Anches; c1957; 13 mins; 0111; E
A student of Faure, Koechlin is considered a revolutionary classicist and has gained a place for himself alongside the greatest innovators of his time by his harmonious synthesis of numerous musical trends. This tonal, chromatic work pushes the virtuosic range of the three instruments with frequent use of the extreme upper register.

Trio, Op. 92; 1924; SAL; 6 mins; 1011; D
The flute part could also be done on oboe.

Koepke, Paul   1918-
Badinage; c1959; ESM; 2.5 mins; 1110; C
This is a single-movement, moderately easy work. The oboe part could be performed on flute.

Koetsier, Jan   Dutch   1911-
Six Bagatellen, op. 16 #2; 1937; DNA; 6 mins; 0111; C/D
A pianist and conductor now living in Munich, Koetsier writes in the Neo-Classic tradition of northern Europe. His music is influenced by Hindemith and is characterized by solid craftsmanship and invention. This six-movement piece features mild dissonance and multimeters. Some occasional passages require fast articulation and technical agility, particularly for oboe.

Konietzny, Heinrich   1910-
Kleine Kammermusik #2; c1953; BHI; 10 mins; 0111

Koper, Karl-Heinz   1927-
Trio; 11 mins; 0011/1
Bass clarinet and contrabassoon are required.

Koporc, Srecko   Slovenian   1900-1965
Epizode; GER; 9 mins; 1011

Kosma, Joseph   Hungarian/French   1905-1969
Divertissement; EME; 1011
Kosma studied at the Budapest Academy, then later with Eisler in Berlin. He wrote music for ballet, opera, piano and oratorio.

Kostiainen, Pekka   Finnish   20th C.
Divertimento; 1984; FMC; 17 mins; 0021

Kotschau, Joachim   1905-
Divertimento in B-Flat, Op. 12A; Voxman; PTE; 8 mins; 1011; C/D

Koumans, Rudolf   1929-
Trio, Op. 30; DNA; 13 mins; 0111

Kowalski, Julius   Slovakian   1912-
Divertimento; 1966; SHF; 1101
A student of Karel and Haba at the Prague Conservatory, Kowalski's early works are often microtonal, but his later music is more traditional.

Kraft, Leo   American   1922-
Short Suite for Flute, Clarinet, Bassoon; 1969; GMP, SER; 4 mins; 1011; B/C
A student of Boulanger and a Fulbright fellow, Kraft studied at Queens College and Princeton University. This pieces includes four movements titled *Morning Song, Little Fugue, Interlude* and *Finale*.

Kratochvil, Jiri   1924-
Trios Tschechischer Klassiker; SUP; flexible instrumentation
This work may be performed on any three woodwind instruments.

Kreisler, Alexander von   American   1894-1969
Little Trio; c1969; SMC; 4 mins; 1110; C
Kreisler graduated from the Paris Conservatory at the age of twelve, taking the Grand Prix. He wrote music for theatre, orchestra, chamber ensem-ble and songs. This three-movement work is a good training piece for students.

Three Pastels; c1964; SMC; 5 mins; 1110; C
This moderately easy work could also be performed by two flutes and clarinet.

Trio; c1964; SMC; 0111

Krejci, Isa   Czech   1904-1968
Trio: Divertimento; 1935; PAN; 8 mins; 0111
Krejci studied composition with Jirak and Novak. His musical style is Neo-Classical and shows the influence of Czech Nationalism. This work contains four movements titled *Introduction, Chorale, Scherzino* and *Rondino.*

Kreutzer, Rodolphe   French   1766-1831
Trio; Wienandt; 1803; CPP; 0111
Brother of Jean Nicolas Kreutzer, Rodolphe was a student of Stamitz. He wrote music for stage, orchestra and chamber ensembles. There is an alternate flute part in place of oboe.

Kriens, Christian   Dutch/American   1881-1934
Ronde des Lutins; c1928; CFI; 1110
Kriens is best known as a violinist and performed with the New York Philharmonic and Metropolitan Opera.

Kubik, Gail   American   1914-1984
Little Suite; 1947; HAR; 1020; D
Kubik studied composition with Rogers and Royce at Eastman School. While basically tonal, he uses many modern techniques.

Kubizek, Augustin   Austrian   1918-
Four Pieces; c1953; BKH; 1011
Kubizek wrote more than 200 works including music for orchestra, concerti, opera, ensembles and sacred works. Oboe could replace the flute in this piece.

Kleine Tanzsuite fur Three Melodie Instruments; DBM; flexible instrumentation

Kuhlau, Friedrich   German/Danish   1786-1832
Allegro, Op. 20 #2; ESM; 1011; C
Kuhlau studied composition with Schwenke and wrote music for stage, keyboard and chamber ensembles. Best known for his piano music, his influence on later Danish music was considerable. Kuhlau writes music that is full of genuine invention and imagination. Bass clarinet may replace bassoon.

Sonatina, Op. 20 #1; Tustin; c1944; ESM; 1110; C
This work, appropriate for students, is written in standard sonata form.

Kummer, Kaspar   German   1795-1870
Trio in F Major, Op. 32; ESM; 2.5 mins; 1011; C
Kummer is best known as a flutist and composer of music for flute.
This single-movement work is appropriate for advanced student groups.

Kunert, Kurt   1911-
Trio in C Minor ,Op. 7; Adams; BKH; 1011

Kupferman, Meyer   American   1926-
Cabaletta; 1989; SMC, SSP; 1110
Kupferman studied at Queens College of the City University of New
York and later taught at Sarah Lawrence College. He received awards
from Guggenheim and the American Academy and Institute of Arts and
Letters. His works make use of Neo-Classicism, serialism, jazz and
electronics.

Trio Musketeers; 1989; SMC, SSP; 1110

Laburda, Jiri   Czech   1931-
Trio; 1989; SMC; 0111; C/D
Laburda studied composition with Karel Haba and Zdenek Hula and
later taught at Charles University in Prague. His musical style is considered fairly traditional with some elements of aleatory and dodecaphonic techniques.

Langley, James W.   1927-
Green Belt Suite; c1969; ESM; 1110; C

Trio; ESM; flexible instrumentation; B/C
This work may be performed on any three equal pitch instruments.

Larson
Valse; TMP; flexible instrumentation

Lassus, Orlando di   French/Flemish   1530-1594
Motet Cantate Domino; Schmidt; WIM; 0011/1; B/C
One of the most prolific and versatile of sixteenth century composers,
Lassus wrote over 2000 works in almost every genre.

Lauer, Elizabeth   American   20th C.
Five Miniatures; 1990; ARP; 8 mins; 0110/1
The composer states that this piece is about "three wind instruments,
each of strong personality, speaking both individually and collectively,
such that, at the conclusion, each knows whereof the other is speaking,
and can finish the thought."

Lawrance
Sonata for Wind Instruments; ESM; 0011/1; C/D

Lazarof, Henri   Bulgarian/American   1932-
Trio; c1982; PRC; 13 mins; 1110; D/E
After studying at the Sofia Academy, the New Conservatory in
Jerusalem, Academia di St. Cecilia and Brandeis University, Lazarof
joined the faculty of the University of California in Los Angeles. His
music is atonal and frequently serial. This work requires alto flute,
English horn and bass clarinet.

Lee, William R.   American   20th C.
Chamber Music for Three Winds; SHA; 4 mins; flexible instrumentation
Written in a contemporary style, this work uses the Baroque tradition
of instrumental pieces with contrasting movements for small ensembles.

Leef, Yinam   Israeli   1953-1978
Gilgulim; 1978; PRC; 0111

Lefevre, Jean Xavier   Swish/French   1763-1829
Trio in B-Flat; c1974; ESM; 0021; C
A well-known clarinetist of his time, Lefevre wrote music primarily for
chamber ensembles as well as seven clarinet concertos.

Legley, Victor   Belgian   1915-
Trio, Op. 11; c1961; ESM; 0111; E

Legrenzi, Giovanni   Italian   1626-1690
Bonacossa, Op. 8; CON; 1011
Legrenzi was a highly regarded violinist, composer and conductor of
his time. His sonatas served as models of the Baroque forms later used
by Vivaldi and Bach. He wrote operas, oratorios and chamber music.

La Bevilague, Op. 8 #8; CON; 1011

La Boiarda, Op. 8 #10; CON; 1011

La Fini, Op. 4 #5; CON; 1011

La Secca Soarda, Op. 4 #2; CON; 1011

Lehmann, Hans Ulrich   Swiss   1937-
Tractus; 1971; EAM; 8.5 mins; 1110; E
Lehmann studied with Paul Muller, Stockhausen and Boulez. This
work is clearly avant garde, using numerous twentieth-century devices.

Lemaire, Felix
Mini Trio; BIL; 0111; C/D

Lemeland, Aubert   French   1932-
Pastorale; c1977; BIL; 0111
Lemeland's works comprise more than a hundred pieces of chamber, instrumental and orchestral music.

Lessard, John   American   1920-
Trios of Consanguinity; 1973; SER, SCI; 6 mins; 1011
Lessard studied with Boulanger and has received many distinguished awards including Guggenheim Fellowships. His music includes many works for winds, orchestra, vocal and chamber music. These three movements (*Budding Fork, Middle Stem* and *Flowering Shoot*) are part of an eight movement work that uses strings with winds in the other five movements.

Levy, Frank Ezra   French/American   1930-
Trio; 1961; COR; 9 mins; 0011/1; D/E
Levy, son of Ernst Levy, holds degrees from the Juilliard School of Music and the University of Chicago. He was a cello student of Rose and Starker.

Lewin, Gordon   English   20th C.
Scherzola; c1959; BHI; 3.5 mins; 0111; C/D
This brief, single-movement work uses humor, jazz and a lively rhythmic tempo in a tonal style. A good encore piece, the parts require facile technique and rapid tonguing capabilities.

Lickl, Ferdinand Carlo
Three Trios; PTE; 0011/1; C/D

Lickl, Johann Gerog   Austrian   1769-1843
Trio in E-Flat Major; ESM; 0011/1; C/D
Lickl, a student of Haydn, was a conductor and composer of music for piano, singspiels and chamber groups.

Lilja, Bernhard   Swedish   1895-1984
Tre Sma Pianostycken; 1964/80; SMI; 5 mins; 0111

Limmert, Erich   1909-
Serenade; 1962; BKH; 6 mins; 1101; D

Lockwood, Normand   American   1906-
Three; AMC; 1110
Lockwood studied with Respighi and Boulanger and later taught at the
Oberlin Conservatory, Columbia University, University of Oregon and
University of Denver. He wrote music for opera, orchestra, voice and
chamber groups.

Lorenzo, Leonardo   Italian/American   1875-1962
Trio Eccentrico, Op. 76; PTE; 1011
Lorenzo studied with Nascimento and Braga. Many of his works are
based on traditional native Brazilian music and he is best known for his
songs.

Trio Romantico, Op. 78; PTE; 11 mins; 1110; C/D
Many tempo changes and technically challenging sections are found in
this single-movement work.

Loucheur, Raymond   French   1899-1979
Portraits; 1947; BIL; 9.5 mins; 0111
A pupil of d'Indy and Boulanger, Loucheur won the Prix de Rome and
the Georges Bizet Prize. His work is characterized by clarity and solid
technique.

Luening, Otto   American   1900-1996
Prelude and Fugue; 1974; 1011
Luening has been an influential musical force for most of the twentieth
century. His diverse musical activities have included composition,
conducting, writing and teaching.

Short Suite; GLM; 1011

Lunde, Ivar   Norwegian   1944-
Drawings, Op. 34; c1979; NOR; 2010
Lunde, an oboist, has served on the faculties of the University of Mary-
land and the University of Wisconsin. Piccolo is required.

Lutyens, Elisabeth   English   1906-1983
Trio, Op. 52; 1963; EAM; 1011
Lutyens attended the Royal College of Music where she studied with
Darke. Her music incorporates twelve tone technique and other twen-
tieth-century devices.

Lybbert, Donald   American   1923-1981
Trio for Winds; 1956; PTE; 14.5 mins; 0011/1
Lybbert attended the University of Iowa, the Juilliard School and Colum-bia University. He studied with Carter, Luening and Boulanger. His style is a fusion of Classical and serial elements.

Maasz, Gerhard   German   1906-1984
Divertimento; c1957; SIK; 1011; C
This light five-movement, burlesque-like work should present no significant technical difficulties.

Machaut, Guillaume de   French   1300-1377
Double Hoquet; EOL; 1110
Machaut was an important composer of his time, writing ballads, vir-elais, motets, rondeaux and one of the earliest polyphonic settings of the Mass.

Madsen, Trygve   Norwegian   1940-
Serenata Monellesca, Op. 26; HUS; 0111; D
Madsen studied with Norwegian composer Egil Hovland and later at the Academy of Music and Fine Arts in Vienna. Among his compositions there are works for piano, chamber ensembles, orchestra and theatre.

Maessen, Antoon   Dutch   1919-
Cassation; 1958; DNA; 10 mins; 0111; C/D
This seven movement work uses chromatic pitches quite freely. While there are some ensemble precision challenges in the third movement, the range and technical requirements are within the reach of advanced high school players.

Trio; DNA; 10 mins; 1011

Maganini, Quinto   American   1897-1974
Ars Contrapunctus; ESM; 1011; C
A composer, conductor and flutist, Maganini studied with Boulanger and performed with the New York Philharmonic. He wrote an opera and many orchestral and chamber music works.

Havana (Rhumba Danzon); CFI; 1011
Oboe may substitute for flute.

Three Little Kittens; ESM; 1110; B/C

Marais, Marin   French   1656-1728
Three Old French Dances; East; c1962; ESM; 5 mins; 0111: C
Marais was the leading figure in the French school of composers in
Paris during the late seventeenth and early eighteenth centuries.

Margola, Franco   Italian   1908-1992
Trio per Fiata; c1968; 0111
After studies at the Parma Conservatory and the Academia di Santa
Cecilia, he taught at conservatories in Cagliari, Bologna, Milan, Rome
and Parma. He wrote music for opera, orchestra and chamber groups.

Mariassy, Istvan
Chamber Music for Beginners; ESM; flexible instrumentation; A/B
A variety of woodwind instruments may be used in performing this
work.

Chamber Music II; Vigh; ESM; 1011; C/D

Maros, Rudolf   Hungarian   1917-
Serenata Part I; 1951; EMB; 9 mins; 0111; D
Maros was a student of Kodaly and Alois Haba. His works show the
integration of traditional elements with twentieth century techniques.
This three-movement work features multimeters and sometimes heavy
technical demands for the players.

Martelli, Henri   French   1895-1980
Trio, Op. 45; 1938; BIL; 15 mins; 0111; D/E
Featuring the bassoon, this piece is harmonically chromatic with lively
rhythms throughout. Advanced technical facility is required, though
there is little use of extreme ranges for the instruments which makes
this work somewhat easier than many works by other French composers of this period.

Martini
Pastorale e Rondeau and Due Sonate; ESM; 2001; C

Martinon, Jean Francis   French   1910-1976
Sonatine #4, Op. 26 #1; 1940; COS; 7 mins; 0111; D/E
Martinon, undoubtedly best remembered in America for his directorship
of the Chicago Symphony from 1963 to 1968, has written music for
orchestra and chamber music. A student of Albert Roussel, this
cheerful work clearly shows that influence with its clear sense of form
and color. High technical demands are made on the oboist and
clarinetist.

Martinu, Bohuslav   Czech   1890-1959
Quatre Madrigaux; 1938; PRC, EME ;13 mins; 0111; D/E
Martinu, a gifted and professional craftsman, was greatly influenced by Czech Nationalism and used folk music as the frequent basis for his melodies.

Mason, Daniel Gregory   American   1873-1953
Canonic Device; OPM; flexible instrumentation; B
Mason, a student of Paine and Chadwick, wrote in a traditional style with expansive melodies, conservative harmonies and calculated dialogue between instrumental voices.

Maxwell, Charles   20th C.
Trio; c1969; WIM; 9 mins; 1011; C/D
This work is written in three movements titled *In a Playful Mood, In a Serious Mood* and *In a Cheerful Mood.*

Mayr, Anton   1900-
Little Suite; DBM; 1101

Mayr, Johann Simon   German   1763-1845
Twelve Bagatelles; c1971; EKB; 1011; C/D
Mayr's astonishing ability to write for wind instruments which we find in his opera scores is also displayed in the *Twelve Bagatelles*. Apart from typical Italian passages, we find in the last movement the initial theme of the *Scherzo* of Beethoven's *Sixth Symphony*. The clarinet part was originally for basset horn.

McBride, Robert   American   1911-
Fugue; ACA; 0120
A prolific composer of more than 1,000 works in various genres, McBride frequently used American or Mexican themes with a jazz influence.

Variations on Various Popularisms; ACA; 0111
English horn required instead of oboe.

McGuire, Edward   Scottish   1948-
Trio; 1971; SMP; 10 mins; 1101
McGuire studied at the Royal Academy of Music and State Academy of Music in Stockholm.

McKay, Francis Howard   American   1901-
At the Puppet Show; BHM; flexible; B/C
A native of Washington State, McKay studied at the Eastman School and the University of Washington. He taught in the music departments

of the University of Oregon, Oregon College, Washington State University and the University of Southern California. McKay composed numerous instrumental solos and ensembles in addition to concert band works.

Blue Tapestry; BHM; flexible instrumentation; B/C

Trail to Sunny Point; BHM; flexible instrumentation; B/C

Mechem, Kirke　　　　　　American　　　　　　1925-
Trio, Op. 8; 1955; SCI; 6 mins; 0111; C/D
Mechem is a student of Walter Piston and Randall Thompson. He has written music for opera, chamber ensembles, orchestra, chorus and piano. His music is basically tonal with resolvable dissonance.

Melartin, Erkki　　　　　　Finnish　　　　　　1875-1937
Trio; 1929; FMC; 1011
Melartin studied with Wegelius and Fuchs, then taught theory at the Helsinki Music Institute. His lyrical works often use Finnish folk themes.

Melkich, Dimitri　　　　　　Russian　　　　　　1885-1943
Trio, Op. 17; c1928; UNE; 0111
Melkich's music, written in archaic Russian modes, shows the influence of his teacher, Yavorsky. He wrote music for orchestra and chamber groups.

Mellnas, Arne　　　　　　Swedish　　　　　　1933-
Divertimento; 1955; SMI; 7 mins; 1011
Mellnas studied with Larsson, Blomdahl and Wallner at the Stockholm Musikhogskolan. Privately he worked with Deutsch, Ligeti and Koenig. He is considered one of Sweden's most innovative avant-garde composers. This work requires piccolo and bass clarinet.

Mendelssohn, Felix　　　　　　German　　　　　　1809-1847
Lift Thine Eyes and Cast Thy Burden; Buchtel; c1963; KMC; 1110; B
Mendelssohn's music emphasizes clarity and adherence to the Classical tradition.

Wedding March from Midsummer Night's Dream; Stewart; 1842; TRI, ESM; 10 mins; 0111 or 1011

Mersson
Pieces Provencales, Op. 11; ESM; 0021; D
Bassoon could be replaced with bass clarinet.

Mertens, Hardy   Netherlands   1960-
Trio; DNA; 7 mins; 1110

Meulemans, Arthur   Belgian   1884-1966
Trio #2; 1960; 15 mins; 0111
After studies with Edgar Tinel in Mechelen, Meulemans founded the
Liburg School for organ at Haselt and later conducted the Brussels
radio orchestra. A prolific composer, he has written works for all
genres.

Meyer, Jean   1910-
Variations sur un Theme Classique; c1966; LDA; 0120
Flute may replace oboe.

Michalsky, Donal Ray   American   1928-1975
Trio Concertino; 1961; WIM; 5 mins; 1100/1; C
Michalsky studied with Dahl and Halsey Stevens at the University of
Southern California and did postgraduate work in Germany with Wolfgang Fortner on a Fulbright grant. His music is characterized by lyrical
melodic lines, effective use of counterpoint and generally conservative
harmonies and phrasing. His forms paraphrase traditional styles.

Migot, Georges   French   1891-1976
Trio; 1944; LDA; 18.5 mins; 0111; E
Migot was an accomplished composer, poet and visual artist. His music uses diatonic melodies but avoids any suggestion of definite tonality. The flowing quality of Migot's music is in the tradition of Debussy and Couperin. This *Trio* features five movements: *Prelude, Pastorale, Chorale, Fanfare and March, Conclusion.* It is harmonically
chromatic, with intricate rhythms and modal melodies. There are
considerable technical challenges for all players and the oboe part ex-
tends to the extreme high register.

Mihalvoci, Marcel   Rumanian/French   1898-
Trio; 1955; PRC; 12 mins; 0111; D/E
Mihalvoci studied with d'Indy, Martinu, Bech and Harsanyi. Within
an atonal style, this complex work is remarkably tuneful. Multimeters
and lively rhythms characterize the style and the three parts are well
balanced.   Ensemble precision is a substantial challenge.

Milhaud, Darius   French   1892-1974
Pastorale, Op. 147; 1935; MMP, ESM; 4 mins; 0111; C/D
Milhaud studied at the Paris Conservatory with Dukas, Widor and
Leroux. This brief, single-movement work is written in ternary form
and uses a highly chromatic and dissonant harmonic style. At the

tempo markings indicated, this work would be extremely difficult and endurance is a real consideration for the oboist.

Suite d'Apres Corrette; 1937; EOL; 9 mins; 0111; C/D
Written in eight movements in eighteenth-century style, this work is light and charming, with some dissonance. There are significant endurance demands on the oboist which is featured throughout the movements. This edition is published by EOL in an album of trios.

Mirandolle, Ludovicus   1904-
Mouvements por Trio d'Anches Cinq; BVP; 0111

Miscellaneous
Adagio and Fuga; Maros; EMB; 5 mins; 0111; C
This set includes music by Mozart and Bach. Flute may replace oboe.

Carols for Christmas; Dale; PIP; 1011; A/B
Oboe or clarinet may substitute for flute.

Christmas Carol Suite #1; Holcombe/Nagle; MPI; flexible instrumentation; B/C
This set of arrangements includes *The First Noel, Hark the Herald Angels Sing, Joy to the World* and *God Rest Ye Merry Gentlemen.* There are interchangeable parts for flute, oboe, clarinet, bass clarinet and bassoon.

Christmas Carol Suite #2; Holcombe/Wade; MPI ;flexible; B/C
This set includes *O Come All Ye Faithful, We Three Kings, Angels We Have Heard on High* and *Bring A Torch.* There are interchangeable parts for flute, oboe, clarinet, bass clarinet and bassoon.

Christmas Medley; Kile; ALE; 1101; B/C
This set includes seven familiar Christmas carols arranged in a delightful medley. It is scored for any two treble instruments and one bass instrument.

Christmas on the Mall; Holcombe/Nagle; MPI; flexible instrumentation; B/C
Arrangements in this set include *Deck the Halls, O Tannenbaum, Up on the Rooftop and We Wish You a Merry Christmas.* There are interchangeable parts for flute, oboe, clarinet, bass clarinet and bassoon.

Deck the Halls; Lombardo; ALE; 1101; B/C
This arrangement is scored for any two treble instruments and one bass instrument.

Eighteen Trios; Andraud; SMC; 1110; C

Ensembles for Everyone; Ostling; BEL; flexible instrumentation; A
These are three part arrangements of very easy material. There are part books for flute, oboe, clarinet, bassoon, horn, trumpet, trombone and tuba which may be used together in any combination.

Evergreens; Holcombe; MPI; flexible instrumentation; C

Fifteen Trios from Classic Masters; Andraud; SMC; 1110
Easy arrangements of music by Mozart, Bach, Haydn and others, suitable for student groups.

First Program Ensembles; Ostling; BEL; flexible instrumentation; A
These are three part arrangements of very easy material. There are part books for flute, oboe, clarinet, bassoon, horn, trumpet, trombone and tuba which may be used together in any combination.

Five Classic Rags; North; TRI; 1011
This collection includes rags by Joplin and Charles Johnson. Oboe may replace flute.

Folk Song Movements; Wennig; BBL; 1011
Alternate oboe part for flute.

Four Christmas Vignettes; Halferty; KED; 4.5 mins; 1110; C
Clarinet may substitute for oboe. Selections include *Pat-a-Pan, Infant Holy, Infant Lowly, Silent Night, Joy to the World.*

Grant Us Peace; Schaeffer; c1967; 2 mins; 1110; B

Jingle Bells and We Wish You a Merry Christmas; Kile; ALE; 1101; A/B
Two of the most popular Christmas carols, these arrangements may be played by any two treble instrument and one bass instrument.

Jolly Old St. Nicholas; Lombardo; ALE; 1011; B
The clarinet part could also be played on flute.

March of the Toys; Lombardo; ALE; 1011; B/C
The clarinet part could be played on flute.

More Christmas Vignettes; Halferty; KED; 1110; B/C
This set includes arrangements of *God Rest Ye Merry Gentlemen; Joseph Dearest, Joseph Mine; We Three Kings;* and *Ding Dong! Merrily On High.*

Music for Weddings, Vol. 1, 2 and 3; Holcombe; MPI; flexible instrumentation; B/C
There are interchangeable parts for flute, oboe, clarinet, bass clarinet and bassoon.

Renaissance Wind Trios; Carp; PRC; 0111; B/C
These easy arrangements of music by Bruolo, Senfl, Tomkins and Gibbons are good for student ensembles. The oboe part may be played on flute.

Russian Suite; Schmidt; WIM; 1110; B/C
This arrangement includes music by Barvinsky and Kabalevsky.

Seven Pieces for Three Woodwinds; Hovey; 1954; BHI; 16 mins; 1110; B/C
Appropriate for student groups, the collection includes music by Clementi, Schumann, Mozart and others.

Short Arrangements for Wood Wind Trio; Phillips; OUP; 8 mins; 0111; B/C
This book contains arrangements of music by Tchaikovsky, Mozart, Purcell, Beethoven, Bach and Corelli that are good training pieces for young players.

Simple Gifts; Stewart; 1850; TRI, ESM; 5 mins; 1011

Six Short Classics; Thorpe; ESM; 0021

Ten Woodwind Trios; Schaeffer; ESM; 1-3 mins each; 1110; B
This set includes arrangements of music by Purcell, Haydn, Mozart, Beethoven, Prokofiev, Stravinsky, Bartok and Kabalevsky.

The Virgin Mary Had a Baby Boy; Isaacson; ALE; 1101; B
This arrangement may be played by any two treble instruments and any bass instrument.

Three Pieces for Woodwind Trio; Camden; PRC; 6 mins; 0111; C/D
This set includes easy arrangements of music by J.S. Bach, Couperin and Dandrieu. Camden, a bassoonist, had a long and distinguished career as a teacher and bassoonist in England.

Three Woodwinds: Vol. 1; Voxman; c1958; Rubank; 1110; B/C
These are easy to medium arrangements of music by Mozart, Handel, Haydn, Beethoven and more.

Three Woodwinds: Vol. 2; Voxman; Rubank; 1011; B/C
Composers range from Corelli through Beethoven and all three parts are interesting.

Time Out for Ensembles; Ostling; BEL; flexible instrumentation; A
These are three part arrangements of very easy material. There are part books for flute, oboe, clarinet, bassoon, horn, trumpet, trombone and tuba which may be used together in any combination.

Tis a Gift to Be Simple; Weller; 1850; ALE; 1101; B/C
This old Shaker hymn tune is perhaps best known today from Copland's treatment of it in *Appalachian Spring.* This arrangement

showcases each member of the trio and may be performed by any two treble instruments and one bass instrument.

Tune Up and Play; Ostling; BEL; flexible instrumentation; A
These are three part arrangements of very easy material. There are part books for flute, oboe, clarinet, bassoon, horn, trumpet, trombone and tuba which may be used together in any combination.

Twelve Days of Christmas; Isaacson; ALE; flexible instrumentation; B
This arrangement may be played by any two treble instruments and any bass instrument.

Twelve Trios for Woodwinds; Schaeffer; 1110; B/C
These trios may also be done with two flutes and clarinet.

Twenty-One Christmas Carols; James; SHA; 1011; B
Arranger O.J. James was born in Portland, Maine. He received the BM degree from Manhattan School and taught vocal, instrumental and general music classes in New Jersey. Oboe or clarinet may substitute for flute and bass clarinet may replace bassoon.

Twenty-One Masterworks; James; SHA; 1011
These are arrangements of music by Mozart, Haydn, Schumann, Beethoven, Bach, Greig, Schubert and Chopin.

Moeschinger, Albert   Swiss   1897-1985
Divertimento; 1952; ESM; 0111; D/E

Mollicone, Henry   American   1946-
Trio; AMC; 1011

Mozart, Wolfgang A.   Austrian   1756-1791
Adagio and Canonic Adagio; ESM; 0021; C
Two basset horns are required.

Allegro Brillante from *Divertimento #6*; Halferty; KED, ESM; 1110; C/D

Canon; Marx; MMM; 0111 or 0201

Canonic Adagio, K.484a; Marx; 1785; MRI; 0021; C
This trio was originally written for two clarinets and basset horn.

Contredance and Minuet; Morsch; UNE, KAL; 1011; B/C

Die Zauberflote, Vol. 1; ESM; flexible instrumentation; C/D
Various combinations of woodwinds may be used.

Divertimenti #1-#6, K. 439b; Meyer, Glazer; 1783; ESM, OUP; 7 mins; 0021; B/C
Divertimento from Don Giovanni; ESM; 0021; C/D

Divertimento from La Clemenza di Tito; ESM; 0021; C/D

Divertimento from The Magic Flute; ESM; 0021; C/D

Divertimento from The Marriage of Figaro; ESM; 0021; C/D

Divertimento #1 in B-Flat Major, K.439a; Dorian; IMC; 7 mins; 1011; B/C

Divertimento #3, K.439b; Wienandt, Dorian; 1783; KAL, IMC; 11 mins; 0111 or 1011; B/C
This arrangement, originally for two clarinets and bassoon, is from a set of divertimenti written for his friends.

Divertimento in C Major #5, K.439b; Kraber; 1783; IMC; 11 mins; 1011; C
This arrangement, originally for two clarinets and bassoon, is from a set of divertimenti written for his friends.

Don Giovanni; ESM; 2001; C/D

Duet #7 "Bei Mannem" from The Magic Flute; Stewart; 1791; RIC; 3 mins; 1011; C/D

Five Divertimenti; Oubradous; LKM, KAL, EOL; 0021
These five *Divertimenti* are characteristic of the genial and fun-loving Mozart when he was writing music for "diversion."

Four Arias from *Don Giovanni;* 1787; INT; 1011
This set features arrangements of *Eh Via Buffone, Or sai Chi l'onore, Ah Taci Inguisto Core* and *Il Mio Tesoro.* Oboe may replace flute.

From the London Notebook; ESM; 0021; B/C

German Dance; PTE; 1101

The Marriage of Figaro Overture; Benyas; INT; 1011
This is a challenging version of the complete overture for advanced trios. Oboe may replace flute.

Pantomime from *Le Petit Rien;* 1778; INT; 1011
From Mozart's rarely performed ballet, this delightful dance is well suited for woodwind trio. Oboe may replace flute.

Piano Sonata #VII, K.333; Schweitzer; MSM; 20 mins; 1011
This work was originally for piano.

Piano Sonata #XIIII, K.547a; Schweitzer; MSM; 20 mins; 1011
This work was originally for piano.

Serenade #1-#5; 1783; BAR, BKH; 6-11 mins each; flexible instrumentation; C
Originally for two basset horns and clarinet or bassoon, there are versions of these serenades for flute/oboe/bassoon, flute/clarinet/bassoon and two clarinets/bassoon.

Six Piccoli Pezzi; 1000/2; C

Three Arias from *Cosi fan Tutte*; Benyas; 1790; INT; 1011
This set features *Una bella serenate, Fra gli amplessi* and *Come scoglio*. Oboe may replace flute.

Twelve Variations; Hacquard; PRC, ESM; 0111; D

Two Trios; MMM; 0111; C/D

Viennese Sonata; Kenny; CMU; 1101; B/C
Flute and oboe parts may be played on oboe and clarinet respectively.

Muczynski, Robert   American   1929-
Fragments; 1958 SHA; 6 mins; 1011; C/D
Muczynski studied with Alexander Tcherepnin at DePaul University. He has won fourteen ASCAP awards and two Ford Foundation grants. Muczynski received both Bachelor and Masters degrees from DePaul University in piano and composition. This work is written in five movements: *Waltz, Solitude, Holiday, Reverie* and *Exit*.

Mulder, Ernest W.   Dutch   1898-1959
Fuga #7: Ars Contrapunctica; DNA; 1011
Mulder studied and later taught at the Toonkunst Conservatory in Amsterdam. He specialized in sacred music.

Mulder, Herman   Dutch   1894-1989
Trio, Op. 117; 1960; DNA; 1101
Mulder, who had a brief career as a concert singer, wrote music for orchestra and chamber groups. English horn is required.

Muller, Ladislaus   Swedish   1934-
Divertimento #1; 1972; SMI; 1110

Sonata a Tre; 1977; SMI; 0021

Musgrave, Thea   Scottish/American   1928-
Impromptu #2; 1970; CHE, SCI; 9 mins; 1110; D/E
Musgrave studied with Boulanger and Copland. Her numerous awards include the Koussevitzky and a Guggenheim fellowship. The composer described her writing style as "dramatic-abstract: that is dramatic in the sense of presentation, but at the same time abstract because there is no programmatic content." This work was commissioned by the Depart-

ment of Music, University College, Cardiff, in association with the Welsh Arts Council.

Navarre, Randy   American   20th C.
Trio No. 3 (The Jazz Trio); 1982; ALE; 3 mins; 1011; D
Navarre studied saxophone, theory and composition at Austin State University and Temple University. This is an upbeat, swing style piece which will be a welcome addition to the trio repertoire.

Nemiroff, Isaac   American   1912-1977
Perspectives; c1973; MMM; 5 mins; 1101; C/D
Nemiroff studied at the Cincinnati Conservatory and with Stefan Wolpe at the New York College of Music. The composer recommends all three players perform from a score in order to accommodate the complexity of the scoring.

Variations to a Theme; 1961; MMM; 3 mins; 1101; C
This is a single-movement, multimeter work of only moderate difficulty.

Neumann, H.
Rondo Brillante; Taylor; c1945; MCA; 2 mins; 1101; C
The oboe part could be played on flute

Nilsson, Bo   Swedish   1937-
Zwanzig Gruppen; 1958; UNE; 4.5 mins; 1110; D/E
Nilsson is considered one of the most gifted Swedish composers of postwar years. His works are built on precise quasi-mathematical, serial principles. This challenging work uses many twentieth-century devices. Piccolo is required.

Noon, David
Motets and Monodies, Op. 31; c1974; CFI; 0201
English horn is required.

Nordgren, Erik   Swedish   1913-1992
Serenata a Tre, Op. 77; 1966; SMI; 9 mins; 1011

Nowak, Lionel   American   1911-1995
Soundscape; 1973; ACA; 1011
Nowak studied with Elwell, Sessions and Porter at the Cleveland Institute of Music, and later taught at Converse College, Syracuse University and Bennington College.

Olivadoti, Joseph   1893-1977
Divertimento; c1958; Rubank; 3 mins; 1110; B/C
This multi-section, single-movement work would be good for young
ensembles.

Olsen, Sparre   Norwegian   1903-
Suite, Op. 10; 1946; LYC; 5 mins; 1110; C/D
Olsen studied music with Percy Grainger and Fartein Valen. He represents the continuation of the Grieg tradition and Norwegian nationalism. He is particularly known for his vocal works. The third movement of this work has some intricate rhythms that would challenge
young players.

Olsson, Sture   Swedish   1919-1987
Trio; 1981; SMI; 15 mins; 0111

Orland, Henry   American   1918-
Fughetta; SEE; 1011

Orrego-Salas, Juan A.   Chilean   1919-
Divertimento #1, Op. 43; 1956; PIC; 1101; D
After studies with Randall Thompson and Copland, Orrego-Salas
taught at the University of Chile and Indiana University. His works
demonstrate his mastery of the Neo-Classical style.

Osterc, Slavko   Yugoslavian   1895-1941
Trio; 1934; BKH; 1011

Ostransky, Leroy   American   20th C.
Trio in G Minor; c1959; Rubank; 5 mins; 1110; C/D
This three-movement work which incorporates some interesting rhythmic patterns and a wide range of dynamics and tempo would be appropriate for advanced students. Ostransky wrote several books about jazz.

Otten, Ludwig   Netherlands   1924-
Divertimento #2; DNA; 1001/1

Trio; DNA; 12 mins; 1011

Owen, Blythe   American   1898-
Trio #1, Op. 18; 1950; Hall-Orion; 0111
Owen studied with Howard Hanson and Boulanger. She has won numerous awards and grants and has served on the faculties of Northwestern University, Chicago Teachers College and Andrews University.

Two Part Inventions; Orion; 0111

Pachelbel, Johann   German   1653-1706
Canon; Stewart; TRI; 4 mins; 1011; C
Though a busy organist throughout his life, Pachelbel was also a prolific composer. He wrote for keyboard, chamber ensembles and various
vocal groups in a clear, uncomplicated style.

Pachernegg, Alois   1892-1964
Hirtemusik; MFS; 1020; B

Paciorkiewicz, Tadeusz   Polish   1916-1998
Trio Stroikowe; c1967; PWM; 10 mins; 0111; D
Paciorkiewicz studied with Sikorski and later taught in various music
schools including the Warsaw State College of Music. This atonal,
five-movement work uses varying tempi and texture to maintain interest. Ensemble precision may be challenging due to the independent
nature of the three parts.

Paganini, Niccolo   Italian   1782-1840
Moto Perpetuo; 1110; C/D
Paganini, legendary violinist, wrote a number of works for orchestra,
chamber ensembles and violin concertos.

Parfrey, Raymond   English   1928-
Fair Shares for Three; ESM; 1110; C
Parfrey was a choirboy for five years before being drafted into the army
where he learned to play the standard popular tunes of the day from his
fellow servicemen. After leaving the military, he studied with Alan
Bush and began writing music for wind ensembles, choir, piano, organ
and string orchestra.

Runaround; ESM; 1020; C

Three's Company; ESM; 1110; B/C

Trio; c1973; ESM; 4 mins; 0111; B/C
The four movements of this work are titled *Italian Madrigal, Indian
Lament, Chorale* and *Irish Jig*.

Parik, Ivan   Yugoslavian   1936-
Music for Three; 1964; SHF; 1110
After graduating from the Batislava Academy of Music, Parik was appointed to its faculty. His music incorporates serialism and pointillistic
minimalism.

Parker
Rag Bag for Wind Trio; ESM; 0111; C
There is another version for brass trio.

Parris, Robert   American   1924-
Five Easy Canons and a Fugue; AMC; flexible instrumentation; B/C
Parris studied composition with Mennin at the Juilliard School and
later with Ibert, Copland and Honegger. His music shows tonal
cohesion and strong formal structure while incorporating serialism.
This work could be performed on any two treble instruments and a bass
instrument.

Four Pieces; AMC; 0011/1

Pasquini, Bernardo   Italian   1637-1710
Sonata (Fuga); Rocereto; Volkwein; 0021
Pasquini, a highly regarded keyboard player, is primarily known for his
keyboard studies and variations.

Patterson, Paul   English   1947-
Wind Trio; 1968; ESM; 8 mins; 1011; C/D
Patterson studied with Stoker and Bennett. His music uses serial
procedures with strong rhythmic elements. This work was first
performed by the Royal Academy of Music's New Music Group at
Conway Hall on October 16, 1968.

Paubon, Pierre   French   1910-
Colloque a Trois; PRC, BIL; 1110; C/D

Prelude et Scherzo; ESM; 1101; C/D
Flute part could be played on oboe, oboe part could be played on alto
flute and the bassoon part could be played on bass flute.

Peeters, Flor   Belgian   1903-1974
Trio, Op. 80; 1955; PTE; 10 mins; 1011; C/D
Peeters gained international reputation as a concert organist. He is a
prolific composer of works mainly for organ. Written in Neo-Classic
style, this energetic work is a good recital piece for college or advanced
high school players.

Perceval, Julio   Argentinean   1903-1934
Serenata; 1934; PIC; 6 mins; 1011; C/D

Pettersson, Allan   Swedish   1911-1980
Fuga in E Major; 1948; NMS; 0111
Pettersson's music shows the influence of Mahler in its passion and
grandiose design. He wrote music for orchestra, voice and chamber
groups.

Pezel, Johann Christoph   German   1639-1694
Eighteen Pieces; ESM; 0201; B

Pfeiffer, Georges Jean   French   1835-1908
Musette; Andraud; c1964; SMC; 1011

Phillips, Burrill   American   1907-1988
Huntindon Twos and Threes; 1975; GLM; 10 mins; 1101
Phillips studied with Howard Hanson and Bernard Rogers at the
Eastman School and received numerous awards and grants. His works
show a clarity of line and texture that reflects his appreciation of
Scarlatti and Purcell. However, his style has evolved from a con-
sciously "American" style in his early works to free serial techniques
later. This work is written in six movements, originally with cello
instead of bassoon.

Phillips
Pastorale; PTE; 1110

Phillips, Mark   1952-
Shadow Play; 1992; MMB; 1101

Pierne, Paul   French   1874-1952
Bucolique Variee; 1947; BIL; 8 mins; 0111; D
Pierne studied at the Paris Conservatory. He wrote music for opera,
ballet, chorus, piano and chamber ensembles. This is a light-hearted
single-movement, multi-section, chromatic work requiring advanced
technical abilities from all three players.

Pietrzak, Bernard   Polish   1924-1978
Trio; c1972; PWM; 0111

Pijper, Willem   Dutch   1894-1947
Trio; 1926; DNA, PRC; 5 mins; 1011; D
Pijper was the most important Dutch composer and teacher of the early
twentieth-century. His early music shows the influence of Brahms,
Mahler, Faure and Debussy. Later works use his "germ-cell" principle
where the growth of a work develops from a simple motif or chord. The
Trio is a difficult and intense work.

Pisk, Paul Amadeus   Austrian/American   1893-1990
Trio, Op. 100; 1960; AMC; 16.5 mins; 0111; D
Pisk describes his style in this work as "linear, not atonal but free in tonal centers and using the traditional structures and motivic development." Written in a contrapuntal style, this multimeter work uses all three players almost constantly which could present endurance problems.

Piston, Walter   American   1894-1976
Three Pieces; 1926; BBM, AMP, SCI; 10 mins; 1011; D
Piston studied at Harvard and with Nadia Boulanger in Paris, later teaching at Harvard and authoring several books on composition. He uses a witty and sophisticated compositional style which shows the influence of Faure, Roussel, Bach and jazz. This moderately difficult work is written in three movements. The first and third of these are marked with vigorous activity reined by ostinato rhythmic figures and giving way to slower lyric sections. The second piece has a nostalgic quality maintained by both closely and widely spaced sonorities. This work is one of the earliest for this instrumentation and has enjoyed a steady popularity since its composition.

Platti, Giovanni B.   Italian   1690-1763
Trio; COR; 0011/1
Platti writes in a style similar to Vivaldi's, but with sparkling, graceful melodic lines more common with the pre-Classical style Galant so popular during the mid-century.

Trio Sonata in G Major; MRI; 8 mins; 1101

Pleyel, Ignaz   Austrian   1757-1831
Three Trios; 1805; MRI; 1011; C
Pleyel studied with Haydn but is perhaps best known for his manufacturing of pianos. A prolific composer, he composed symphonies, symphonie concertantes, concertos and chamber music. All three instruments are given equal thematic and virtuosic treatment. The clarinet part was originally notated in C, but is presented here in B-flat.

Trios, Op. 20 #1 and #2; PTE, MRI; 0021; C

Polin, Claire   American   1926-1995
Tower Sonata; 1974; SEE; 1011
Polin studied flute with Kincaid and composition with Persichetti in Philadelphia. Her music uses various modern techniques with occasional modal elements.

Pollet, L.
Three Transcriptions; SHA; flexible instrumentation; C/D

Ponse, Luctor   Swiss/Dutch   1914-
Trio; DNA; 10 mins; 1011
Ponse won the Prix d'Excellence for theory at the Conservatory in Valenciennes, France.

Poot, Marcel   Belgian   1901-1988
Ballade; 1954; PRC; 5 mins; 0111; D/E
Poot studied piano with Arthur De Greef, a close friend of Grieg, and composition with Mortelmans, Gilson and Dukas. Poot's music is strongly rhythmic and basically tonal, brilliant and vigorous. He wrote several important orchestral works and many compositions for piano. This energetic, single-movement work presents significant technical demands on all three players, particularly the oboist. It is highly chromatic, though lacking a tonal center.

Divertimento; 1942; PRC; 5 mins; 0111; C/D
While not as difficult as the *Ballade* listed above, this work will still prove to be challenging for all the players, particularly the final movement. It is short and written in a sharply dissonant idiom.

Pospisil, Juraj   Slovak   1931-
Three Inventions, Op. 15; SHF; 1011
Pospisil studied with Petzelka, Moyzes and Cikker.

Presser, William Henry   American   1916-
Trio; c1975; PRC; 4 mins; 0111; C/D
Presser studied with Bernard Rogers, Burrill Phillips, Roy Harris and Gardner Read at the Eastman School. He has won numerous awards and grants and has served on the faculties of Florida State University, West Texas State College and the University of Southern Mississippi. Although he didn't start composing until age twenty-five, Presser has written well over 200 works, of which more than 120 have been published. This work is written in three movements titled *Fantasia, Minuet and Fugue* and *Capriccio*.

Trio; 1987; PRC ; 0201

Prokofiev, Sergei   Russian   1891-1953
Three Pieces, Op. 65; Schmidt; WIM; 0011/1; C/D
One of Russia's most famous composers, Prokofiev wrote many works for ballet, opera, orchestra, chamber ensembles, piano and voice.

Puccini, Giacomo   Italian   1858-1924
Two Arias; 1896-1904; INT; 1011 C
These arrangements of *Un bel di* from *Madame Butterfly* and *Quando me'n vo' soletta* (*Musette's Waltz*) from *La Boheme* will be popular selections for jobs or recitals. Oboe may replace flute.

Purcell, Henry   English   1659-1695
Fantasia #1; Davis; WIM; 2.5 mins; 0011/1; C
Purcell was one of the greatest composers of the Baroque period. This is a good training piece on fantasia form for students.

Querat, Marcel
Magie; BIL; 6.5 mins; 1011; C
The bassoon part could be done by tenor saxophone.

Quinet, Marcel   Belgian   1915-1986
Polyphonies; 1971; 1110
Written in a manner typical of the twentieth-century French school, Quinet's music shows the influence of his teachers Absil, Jongen and Maas. This work requires doubling on multiple instruments.

Trio; 1967; 9 mins; 0111; D
This work combines angular melodic material, a varied rhythmic style and an interesting contrast of textures both within and between movements. The oboe part has frequent high register passages and advanced technique is required by all three players.

Rausch, Carlos   American   1924-
Trio; AMC; 1020
Bass clarinet is required.

Razzi, Fausto   Italian   1932-
Invenzione A Tre; c1964; EAM; 7 mins; 0120
Razzi studied composition with Goffredo Petrassi at the Santa Cecilia Academy in Rome, then devoted himself to teaching. He wrote music for orchestra and chamber groups. Soprano clarinet and bass clarinet are required.

Read, Thomas L.   1938-
Corrente; 1980; PTE; 11 mins; 0111; C/D
While the individual parts are not overly difficult, putting this together
will require an advanced group.

Reger, Max   German   1873-1916
Canon in D Minor; Schwadron; c1969; KED; 2 mins; 1011; B/C
Reger was a student of Hugo Riemann at the Sondershausen Conser-
vatory and later studied at the Wiesbaden Conservatory. His prolific
output includes music for orchestra, voice, chamber, organ and piano.
The bassoon part could be played on bass clarinet.

Regner, Hermann   1928-
Divertimento; PTE; 1020

Regt, Hendrik de   Dutch   1950-
Musica, Op. 5; DNA; 6 mins; 0111
After studies with Otto Ketting in The Hague, Regt wrote music
primarily for chamber groups.

Musica, Op. 25 #2; DNA; 9 mins; 0111

Musica, Op. 27; DNA; 12 mins; 1110

Reicha, Anton   Czech   1770-1836
Twelve Trios, Vols. 1 and 2; ESM; 0001/2; C

Reiche
Varianten; ESM; 1011; E

Reinhardt, Bruno   Israeli   1929-
Four Scherzi; PRC; 0111

Reizenstein, Franz   German/English   1911-1968
Trio; ESM; 1011; D
Reizenstiein's output of Neo-Romantic music for wind instruments was
large. His clarity of style, melodic invention and underlying wit,
together with a natural understanding of the instruments, produced a
number of works that have become part of the standard repertoire.

Rheinberger, Josef   German   1839-1901
Ten Trios; Opel; TRI; 20 mins; 0111
After studies at the Munich Conservatory, Rheinberger was an organist,
teacher and conductor. He wrote in traditional polyphonic and formal
styles and was not influenced by modern ideas.

Ribari, Antal   Hungarian   1924-
Five Miniatures for Wind Trio; 1969; EMB; 1011
Ribari studied composition at the Budapest Academy of Music and
later took lessons with Ferenc Szabo.

Riegger, Wallingford   American   1885-1961
Duos for Three Woodwinds, Op. 35; 1944; PRC; 1110; D
Riegger won numerous awards and grants including the Koussevitzky
and New York Music Critics' Circle. He studied at the Institute of
Musical Arts (now the Juilliard School) and then pursued postgraduate
work at Berlin's Hochschule für Musik. His compositional style
includes twelve-tone techniques and atonality within more traditional
Neo-Classic structures. The *Duos* are composed in the twelve-tone
system. No transposition of a given tone series is employed, although
there is the customary use of inversion and retrogression. The three
duos are intended to be played as a group, but they also may be used
singly. Each movement involves only two of the players.

Rieti, Vittorio   Italian/American   1898-1994
Prelude for Flute, Clarinet and Bassoon; c1966; GMP, SER; 1 min;
1011; B/C
Rieti studied with Frugatta and Respighi. His music is generally Neo-
Classical in style and demonstrates an elegant charm and technical
mastery.

Riisager, Knudage   Danish   1897-1974
Conversazione; 1932; PTE; 8 mins; 0111; C/D
After studies with Peter Gram, Peter Moller and Otto Malling, Riisager then moved to Paris to study with Roussel and Le Flem and later
Hermann Grabner in Leipzig. A prolific composer, he wrote music for
stage, orchestra, voice and chamber groups. Unexpected rhythmic syncopations and cross rhythms make this work a real ensemble challenge,
though the individual technical demands are not extreme. Clarinet in A
is required.

Divertimento; 1944; PTE; 1101/1; C

Rimsky-Korsakov, Nikolai   Russian   1844-1908
Flight of the Bumblebee; Ruggiero PTE, ZAN; 3 mins; 1011
One of the great masters of Russian music, Rimsky-Korsakov wrote
music for opera, stage, voice, piano and chamber ensembles.

Rivier, Jean   French   1896-1987
Petite Suite; 1934; EPF; 9 mins; 0111; D/E
Rivier won the premier prix in counterpoint and fugue in 1926 at the
Paris Conservatory. He wrote in a traditional Impressionistic style.

Using robust counterpoint and vigorous rhythms and concentrating on the development of a small number of thematic ideas, Rivier's music shows the influence of Roussel. This lively work is written in four movements titled *Humoresque, Idylle, Valse, Depart.* Technical demands include fast articulations and intricate rhythms.

Roberts, Wilfred   20th C.
A Day in the Country; 1963; COR; 6 mins; 0111 or 0011/1; B
The top part is actually for English horn rather than oboe, but it may also be played on flute. Written in five movements (*The Frog Pond, Cloud Pictures, Old Indian Trail, The Pine Wood,* and *Wading in the Brook*), this easy work is appropriate for student groups.

Miniatures for Three Winds; 1960; COR; 2.5 mins; 0011/1; B/C
The three movements are titled *Slip of the Tongue, Ivory Tower* and *Child's Play.* There are alternate parts for brass trio (trumpet, horn and trombone).

Rodriguez
Plaisir D'Amour, After the song by Padre Martini; 1982; SCI; 5 mins; 1011
This work is based on a song by eighteenth-century composer Johann Paul Martini.

Roentgen, Julius   Dutch   1855-1932
Trio, Op. 86; PTE; 1101
Roentgen was a prolific composer of the late Romantic school.

Roger, Denise   French   20th C.
Pieces En Trio; 1979; 7 mins; 0111; C

Roos, Robert de   Dutch   1907-1976
Four Pezzi for Wind Trio; 1970-71; DNA; 12 mins; 0111
Roos studied composition with Koechlin, Roland-Manuel and Milhaud. His music includes works for orchestra, ballet, incidental music for dramas and chamber pieces.

Ropartz, Joseph Guy   French   1864-1955
Entrata e Scherzetto; c1948; SAL, ESM; 6 mins; 0111; D
Ropartz writes in a chromatic and sharply dissonant style. Played at the tempo markings indicated, this work would present significant technical demands on all three players.

Roper, Harrison   American   20th C.
A Little Suite; SHA; 5 mins; 0111; C
This piece was written for a music composition class. Its four movements demonstrate such devices as imitation, thematic unity, sequence, repetition and modulation. Roper, a native of Atlanta, GA, received BA and MA degrees from Haverford College and Catholic University.

Rosenberg, Hilding   Swedish   1892-1985
Trio; 1927; SMI; 0111
After studies with Ellberg and Stenhammar at the Royal Academy of Music in Stockholm, he became a conductor with the Stockholm Opera (1932-34) and later visited the United States where he conducted the first American performance of his fourth symphony. His music shows the traditional style of Scandinavian Romanticism with clear elements of Neo-Classical polyphony.

Rosseau, Norbert   Belgian   1907-1975
Trois Jouets, Op. 53; 1954; 11 mins; 0111; D
Rosseau studied with Respighi after his family emigrated to Italy in 1921. His music is in the style of traditional European modernism. The melodic lines in this work range from tonal to chromatic with unusual scale patterns and arpeggios. With few rests, endurance could be a factor for all three players.

Rossi, Salomone   Italian   1570-1630
Three Sinfonias; Ephros; c1971; SMC; 3 mins; 1110; B
Rossi's music is in a conservative style and his four instrumental collections contributed to the development of the Baroque trio sonata texture. This simple, three-movement work would be good training material for students.

Rossini, Gioachino   Italian   1792-1868
Largo al factotum from *The Barber of Seville*; Benyas, Buck; 1816; INT, ESM; 1011; C
Recognized as one of the greatest Italian composers of his time, he is best known for his operas. This is Figaro's famous virtuoso aria in a challenging and humorous transcription that will leave the audience and players breathless!

Rozmann, Akos   Hungarian   1939-
Cinque Pezzi; 1963/75; SMI; 10.5 mins; 1011

Rueff, Jeanine   French   1922-
Three Pieces; c1959; LDA; 11.5 mins; 0111; D/E
Rueff, a student of Busser at the Paris Conservatoire, writes in the style
typical of twentieth-century Paris composers with an emphasis upon
technical display, intricate rhythms and chromaticism. This work
places considerable technical demands upon all three players.

Sabatini, Guglielmo   1877-1949
Puppet Waltz; COR; 0101/1

Salieri, Antonio   Italian   1750-1825
Three Trios; UNE; 5 mins each; 0201; C
Only in our time has the life of the Imperial Court Kapellmeister Salieri
begun to be seen in a new light and his work to be reassessed. Not a
great deal of Salieri's work was published during his lifetime. Many of
his successes were short-lived, and much of his music reflects the taste
of his public, the aristocracy, and the members of the imperial court.
Salieri's importance as a teacher is, however, uncontestable.
Composers such as Beethoven, Mozart and Schubert quite rightly
spoke proudly of having studied with him.

Salomon, Karel   Israeli   1897-1974
Elegy and Dance; PRC; 2100

Sauguet, Henri   French   1901-1989
Trio; 1946; EOL; 12 mins; 0111; C
A pupil of Canteloube and Koechlin, Sauguet's music emphasizes
melody, harmony and rhythm in a clear and simple style. This four-
movement work is published in a set with works by Milhaud and
Canteloube. While the individual parts are somewhat challenging, there
should be no serious problem for the ensemble.

Trois Chants de Contemplations; LDA; 1101/1

Scarlatti, Domenico   Italian   1685-1757
Baroque Allegro; KED; 1101; C
A prolific composer, Scarlatti composed over 500 works for solo
keyboard.

Scarmolin, Anthony Louis   Italian/American   1890-1969
A Ghostly Tale; c1963; BHM; 4.5 mins; 0111; B/C
After studies at the New York College of Music and serving in the U.S.
Army in WW I, Scarmolin wrote more than 200 works for opera,
orchestra and chamber groups. The composer describes this piece as:
"Style—Misterioso, Descriptive." A minor mode is used throughout
most of this short work. Oboe and clarinet are written in thirds with the

bassoon mostly an accompanying part. This piece will present few technical or ensemble problems and could be played by middle school students.

Barcarolle and Petite Humoresque; BHM; 0021

Schenker, Friedrich   German   1942-
Frammenti de "Orfeo"; 1978; BKH; 1101

Schickele, Peter   American   1935-
Commedia; c1979; EVI; 0201; C/D
Schickele, bassoonist, studied composition with Persichetti, Bergsma Roy Harris and Milhaud.

Dances for Three; 1980; PRC, EVI; 14 mins; 0021; C/D
The six movements are titled *Prologue, Minuet, Tango, Bossa Nova, Gigue, Sarabande* and *Finale.*

Diversions: Bath, Billiards, Bar; 1963; EVI, PRC; 9 mins; 0111; C/D
Written as an anniversary gift for a friend, this three-movement work is composed in a witty, jocular style.

Divertimento; 1984; EVI; 9 mins; 0021; C/D

Schiff, Helmut   German   1918-
Divertimento; c1966; DBM; 8 mins; 0111; C/D
This five-movement work shows the melodic and harmonic influence of Hindemith. The fast movements are generally rhythmic and cheerful while the slow movements are somber and lyrical. Rapid articulation is required by all players and the oboe has frequent passages in the low register.

Schimi, Iraj   Swedish   1936-
Triglotte; SMI; 13 mins; 0111

Schiske, Karl   Austrian   1916-1969
Trio Sonata, Op. 41; DBM; 0111
Schiske studied with Ernst Kanitz in Vienna and was later appointed to the faculty of Vienna Academy of Music and served as a visiting professor at the University of California, Riverside. His music uses elements of medieval counterpoint and serial methods.

Schlemm, Gustav Adolf   1902-
Trio; c1963; TBM; 0111; B/C

Schmid, Henrich Kasper   German   1874-1953
Trio, Op. 99; MVH; 1110
Schmid was a student of Ludwig Thuille at the Munich Academy of
Music where he later taught. He belonged to the "Munich School" and
his compositions are clearly Romantic and reminiscent of Brahms.

Schmidt, William   American   1926-
Prelude and Fugue; c1966; WIM; 3 mins; 1011; C
Schmidt, best known as a saxophonist and music publisher, writes in a
compositional style influenced by Halsey Stevens and Ingolf Dahl.

Sinfonia; WIM; 1011; C

Schmit, Camille   Belgian   1908-1976
Trio; 1945; Belge; 10 mins; 0111; D
This work features atonality, textural variety and rhythmical variety.
Extended high register passages and endurance demands make this
particularly difficult for the bassoonist, though advanced technical
facility is required of all three players.

Schmitt, Florent   French   1870-1958
A Tour d'Anches; PRC; 0111
Schmitt was an influential composer who wrote music for ballet, sym-
phonies and chorus.

Schneider, Willy   1907-1983
Blaserwerk, Das, Heft 6: Triospiel Nach Alten Meistern; c1974; MOS;
1110

Spielbuch fur Blaser; c1974; MOS; 0021
A second version for flute, oboe and clarinet is also available.

Schoemaker, Maurice   Belgian   1890-1964
Suite Champetre; 1940; 12.5 mins; 0111; C/D
A student of Theo Ysaye, Martin Lunssens and Paul Gilson, Schoemaker was one of the "Groupe des Synthetistes," whose purpose was to
promote modern music. This seven-movement suite is fairly straightforward except for some occasional harmonic dissonance. The clarinet is
featured in two movements. Fast articulation and high register passages
for the oboe are the main technical problems.

Schubert, Franz   Austrian   1797-1828
Two Songs; Carp; 1817 and1823; PRC; 0111; C
Schubert produced great masterpieces in virtually every field of
composition. His music is rich in melody and expressive harmony.

The two songs featured here are *Die Forelle* (D550) and *Auf dem Wasser zu singen* (D774).

Schulhoff, Erwin   Czech/Russian   1894-1942
Divertissement; 1926; EAM; 15 mins; 0111; D/E
Schulhoff was a versatile composer who responded to the trends of the day. He died in a Nazi concentration camp in World War II. This is an interesting and charming work in seven movements titled *Overture, Burlesca, Romanzero, Charleston, Tema con variazioni e fugato, Florida* and *Rondino-Finale*. Due to the rhythmic complexity and extended range requirements, this work requires advanced players.

Schumann, Robert   German   1810-1856
Suite; Oubradous; SEL; 5 mins; 0111; B/C
Schumann was a central figure of the Romantic period. These four familiar songs by Schumann should present no difficulty for student groups and could also serve as filler on concerts by professional players.

Suite; Seay; SPR; 1011; B

Schwadron, Abraham A.   1925-
Trio; c1966; PMP; 0111

Sclater, James   American   1943-
Trio; 1968; WIM; 11 mins; 1011; D
Sclater, clarinetist, studied composition with William Presser and Hunter Johnson. This four-movement, multimeter work uses many twentieth-century devices.

Scott, Stuart J.   English   20th C.
Conversations; 1979; ESM; 15 mins; 1110; D

Sehlbach, Oswald Erich   German   1898-1985
Bagatellen, Op. 119; c1973; MOS; 1101

Selmer-Collery, Jules   French   1902-
Divertissement; c1953; EDP; 11 mins; 0111; D/E
This is one of the few pieces of program music for this genre. The composer writes this description of his three-movement work: "Three young fellows are walking cheerfully and enjoying the spring weather, far from the student's life. There came on three lovely girls who, in spite of their indifference, disturb the merry boys' chatter, making them dreamy and sentimental. But philosophy prevails and our three careless youngsters prefer to go on walking, telling jokes and thinking gaily of the hopeful future." The bassoonist has few rests in the second

movement, low note passages are frequent for the oboe and there are technical challenges for all three players.

Serebrier, Jose   Uruguayan/American 1938-
Canine Suite; 1957; SMC, PIC; 10 mins; 0111; D/E
Serebrier studied with Giannini and Copland. This interesting work features movements titled *Elegy to My Dead Dog, Dance of the Fleas* and *Transformation and Toccata*. Rapid articulation and awkward twills are among the technical requirements that will be challenging to the players.

Serini, Giovanni Battista   Italian   1715-1765
Aria and Gigue; Pilgrim; ESM; 1020; B/C

Shapero, Harold Samuel   American   1920-
Three Pieces for Three Pieces; 1938; PIC, SMC; 1011; C/D
Shapero studied with Slonimsky, Krenek, Piston, Hindemith and Boulanger. He received the American Prix de Rome in 1941 and had Guggenheim fellowships in 1946 and 1947. His music uses a Classical form with contrapuntal techniques. The three movements in this work are titled *Classical, Oriental* and *Contrapuntal.*

Shawn, Allen   American   20th C.
Jete; c1983; GLM; 0011/1

Sherard, James   English   1666-1738
Adagio and Allegro, Op. 2 #4; CON; 1011

Shostakovich, Dmitry   Russian   1906-1975
Preludes; Maganini; ESM; 1011; B/C
Shostakovich is widely regarded as the greatest symphonic composer of the mid-twentieth-century.

Shur, Laura
Gentle into the Night; ESM; 2100; D

Sichler, Jean   French   20th C.
Trio D'Anches; CON; 2 mins; 0111; B/C

Siebert
Eight Rounds; ESM; flexible instrumentation; A/B
These rounds may be played on any three equal instruments.

Siennicki, Edmund John American 1920-
Pony Ride; LMP; 1011
Siennicki, author of four educational books for woodwinds, studied at
Kent State University and Columbia University. He received numerous
fellowships and commissions and has written music for orchestra, band
and chamber ensembles.

Population Zero; LMP; 1011

Vicarswood, Choral and Fugue; Hite; c1963; SMC; 2 mins; 1011; B

Simeonov, Blago 20th C.
Little Overture from *Max and Moritz*; c1982; SMC; 2.5 mins; 0111; C
This charming overture is appropriate for advanced high school players.

Sims
Partita; ESM; 0201; C/D
English horn is required.

Skolnik, Walter American 1934-
Three Canonic Tunes; c1962; ESM; 2 mins; 1110; B/C
Skolnik, a student of Bernard Heiden, has a strong preference for the
melodic intervals of the second and fourth supported by a tertian
harmonic structure. This is an easy training piece for canon style.

Slavicky, Klement Czech 1910-1999
Trio; 1937; SUP; 14 mins; 0111; E
Slavicky studied composition with Jirak and Suk. On the score, the
composer writes the following description: "It is based on the contrasting juxtaposition of the four movements with respect to the
technical and virtuosic possibilities of the respective instruments. The
spirit, influenced by Moravian folk melodies, is but slightly felt in the
first three movements, but in the last movement it becomes more
authentic and expressive." The influence of Bartok is clear in this
interesting piece. Multimeters and advanced technical requirements are
found throughout the work.

Smirnova, Dmitri Russian 1948-
Little Triptych; BHI; 1011; D

Smith, Leland C. American 1925-
Trio; 1960; AMC, SAP; 14 mins; 0111; E
Smith studied with Milhaud, Messiaen and Sessions, and has taught at
the University of California (Berkeley), Mills College, the University of
Chicago and Stanford. He writes in a modern and eclectic com-
positional style. This multimeter work is dissonant and rhythmically

complex. Ensemble precision may be a challenge and the individual parts require virtuoso players.

Smith-Masters, Anthony   English
Clowns; PIP; 0111

Smyth, Ethel   English   1858-1944
Two Interlinked French Folk Melodies; 1929; OUP; 1110
Smyth, an important composer in the renaissance of English music, wrote in an eclectic style with an overall impression of power and grandeur. This work, from the opera *Entente Cordiale*, was originally written for orchestra.

Snyder, Randall   American   20th C.
Dragonfly; 1968; DNP; 6 mins; 1011; D/E

Soderholm, Valdemar   Swedish   1909-1990
Preludium Och Fuga; 1970; SMI; 3.5 mins; 1101

Sorenson, Torsten Napoleon   Swedish   1908-
Trio #1, Op. 19; 1949; SMI; 7.5 mins; 1110
A graduate of the Royal College of Music in Stockholm, Sorenson later studied composition with Hilding Rosenberg and Orff. English horn is required.

Trio #2, Op. 33; 1959; SMI; 11 mins; 1011

Spannheimer, Franz Erasmus   1946-
Sonate Fantastique; 1983; ZIM; 3 mins; 1110; C/D
Spannheimer studied composition, church music and conducting, and soon became known through radio, television and recordings.

Spisak, Michal   Polish   1914-1965
Sonatina; 1946; PRC; 10 mins; 0111; D
Spisak was one of the most outstanding Polish composers of his generation. His music was heavily influenced by Boulanger and Stravinsky. This work is widely chromatic and includes significant technical demands on all three players.

Spoljaric, Vlado   1926-
Chaconne; CMI; 0111

Spratt, Jack   American   1915-
Three Miniatures for Three Woodwinds; 1945; SPR; 4.5 mins; 0111; C

With occasional dissonance and moderate technical requirements, this work is a good introduction to twentieth-century music for young players. Flute may be used in place of oboe.

Sramek, Vladimir   Slovak   1923-
Im Kreis; SUP; 1011
Sramek graduated from the Prague Conservatory and was active in the music department of the National Museum. He wrote primarily chamber music.

Srebotnjak, Alojz F.   Slovenian   1931-
Serenata; 1961; GER; 13 mins; 1011
Srebotnjak studied composition with Skerjanc at the Ljubljana Music Academy and later served on its faculty. He wrote music for orchestra and chamber ensembles.

Srom, Karel   Czech   1904-1981
Trios Tschechischer Klassiker; SUP; flexible instrumentation
Srom studied composition with Jan Zelinka and Karel Haba, later working as a music critic and head of the music department of the Czech Radio. Three different instrumentations of this set, using two treble voices and bassoon, are available.

Stallaert, Alphonse   Dutch   1920-
Epitaphes et Bagatelles; 1967; DNA; 11 mins; 0111; D
This abstract five-movement work is dissonant and atonal. Ostinato rhythms are found in two movements. Low register passages are frequently written for oboe and high register passages for bassoon. There are occasional technically difficult passages for all players.

Standford, Patric   English   1939-
Four Cartoons; 1984; ESM; 0111; D/E
Standford studied with Rubbra, Malipiero and Lutoslawski. His music is marked by solid craftsmanship and creative intuition.

Stark
Sonata in G Minor, Op. 49; SCH; 0021; D

Stearns, Peter Pindar   American   1931-
Five Short Pieces; 1961; AMC; 3 mins; 0111; D
The composer writes: "The work is simply in what I call a paraphrase form. That is the second and third, fourth and fifth are all based on the material, note for note and in the same order of the first piece. You might call it a sort of serial procedure that encompasses as its 'set' an

entire body of music, rather than an order of twelve notes. I have used this method often."

Steffen, Wolfgang   German   1923-1993
Trio, Op. 2; 1947; BBM; 0111
After studies at the Berlin Conservatory and the Hochschule für Musik in Tiessen, Steffen devoted himself to the promotion of new music.

Steiner, Gitta Hana   American   1932-
Suite; 1958; SEE ; 1011
Steiner received both BA and MM from The Juilliard and is currently on the faculty at Brooklyn Conservatory.

Stent
Tunes for Three; ESM; flexible instrumentation; B
There are versions for various woodwind and brass trios.

Stewart, Don   American   1935-
Blues Masters, Op. 38; TRI; 1011; D
Stewart, a member of the Boehm Quintette, studied with Harris, Heiden and Schuller.

Voluntary Fantasy, Op. 33; 1991; TRI; 6 mins; 0111
A review in the *New York School Music News* described this piece as: "A sophisticated and very interesting short showpiece well conceived and deserving of serious attention."

Stieber, Hans   German   1886-1969
Spielmusik #1; c1953; HOF; 8 mins; 0201; C
One oboe part could be played on flute.

Spielmusik #2; HOF; 2010

Trio; HOF; 1110

Stock, David Frederick   American   1939-
Icicles; 1976; AMC; 6 mins; 1110
Stock studied with Berger and Shapero and played trumpet in various orchestras. His works include music for orchestra and chamber groups. This work requires piccolo and E-flat clarinet.

Stranz, Ulrich   German   1946-
Trio D'Anches; 1979; BAR; 10 mins; 0111

Stratton, Donald   20th C.
Rt. K284 to Bangor; 1983; DNP; 5 mins; 1110
This is a theme and nine variations based on the hymn *Bangor* and in celebration of that city's 150th birthday.

Strauss, Johann   Austrian   1825-1899
Champagne Polka; Kenny; 1858; UNE; flexible instrumentation; C/D
Johann Strauss, the most famous of the Strauss musical family, is known for his inspired melodic invention and wide, sweeping melodies in dance music. Various combinations of flute, clarinet, oboe, bassoon and bass clarinet may be used.

Stravinsky, Igor   Russian/American   1882-1971
Pastorale; Maganini; 1933; ESM; 1 min; 1011; B/C
Stravinsky's music went through several changes, often startling and sometimes disturbing to the public. His early years show the Russian influence, then Neo-Classical which eventually moved to serial techniques in his later years. The *Pastorale* was originally a vocal work and was arranged by the composer for voice with winds and violin with winds.

Street
Pocketful o'Jingle; ESM; flexible instrumentation; C/D

Strietman, Willem   Netherlands   1918-
Divertissement D'Anches; DNA; 9 mins; 0111

Stringfield, Lamar   American   1897-1959
Chipmunks; ESM; 1011; B/C
Stringfield was a composer, flutist and conductor. His music is dominated by folk tunes based on traditional harmonies.

Strutt, C.
Music; ESM; 0101/1; D

Sung, Stella   American   20th C.
Paris 1987; c1988; SMC; 6 mins; 1011; C/D

Suter, Robert   Swiss   1919-
Divertimento; 1955; BHI; 16 mins; 0111; E
Suter studied with Hans Huber, Faisst and Reinecke. He settled in Basel where he is active as a conductor and teacher and served as director of the Basel Conservatory from 1918 to 1921. This complex, five-movement work features atonality and diverse textures. All three parts

require players of the highest level due to challenges in range, rhythmic precision and technical agility.

Suthoff-Gross, Rudolf   1930-
Fetzen; c1975; MOS; 1110

Svara, Danilo   Yugoslavian   1902-1981
Pihalni Trio; Durstva; 15 mins; 1011

Swindale
Arran Sketches; ESM; 0301; C
There is an optional English horn part in place of one oboe or the bassoon.

Sonatina Giocosa; ESM; 1110; C
Alternate instrumentation could include oboe, clarinet and bassoon.

Sydeman, William J.   American   1928-
Trio for Treble Instruments; SEE; 1110; D/E
Sydeman studied with Felix Salzer and Sessions and he later joined the faculty of Mannes College in New York. His compositions, which show the influence of Mahler and Berg, are atonal, linear, motivic and use complicated rhythms. Any three treble instruments could be used.

Szalowski, Antoni   French   1907-1973
Divertimento; c1956; CHE; 0111

Trio; c1943; CHE; 0111
Szalowski studied with Sikorski at the Warsaw Conservatory and with Boulanger in Paris. He wrote in an elegant Neo-Classical style, mostly orchestral and chamber pieces.

Szekely, Endre   Hungarian   1912-1989
Divertimento; 1958; EMB; 8 mins; 0111; C/D
Szekely studied with Siklos at the Budapest Academy of Music, later becoming active as a conductor. This interesting work features a modal, melodic style with folk influences. Except for occasional rhythmic precision challenges and high register bassoon passages, this appealing work should be accessible to high school players.

Szonyi, Erzsebet (Elizabeth)   Hungarian   1924-
Five Old Dances; c1968; BHI; 7 mins; 0111; C/D
Szonyi studied with Janos Viski at the Academy of Music in Budapest and later with Aubin, Messiaen and Boulanger in Paris. She played an important part in implementing the Kodaly teaching methods in

Hungarian schools. This work includes five movements titled *Gavotte, Sarabande, Menuet, Gigue, Allemande.*

Trio; 1958; BHI; 0111

Tallgren, Johan   Finnish   20th C.
Asteria; 1994; FMC; 4 mins; 1110

Tansman, Alexandre   Polish/French/Amer. 1897-1986
Suite pour Trio D'Anches; 1949; PRC; 10.5 mins; 0111; C/D
Tansman's early music shows the influence of Chopin, Stravinsky and Ravel. Later works may be compared to Milhaud in the use of folk themes and of different instrumental combinations. The *Suite* is written in four movements titled *Dialogue, Scherzino, Aria, Finale.* While there are only moderate technical demands on the individual players, there are some ensemble challenges due to intricate rhythms.

Tapkoff, Dimitri   Bulgarian   1929-
The Conceited Frog; c1967; LDA; 5 mins; 1110; D/E
Tapkoff's witty music makes use of new techniques. This work is a musical tale with optional narration, good for children's programs. It requires piccolo, English horn and bass clarinet.

Taylor, Paul Arden   English   1954-
Carry On, Bach!; c1978; ESM; 0111; C
These are Bach imitations written by Taylor while still a student at the Royal Academy of Music. They include *Bach Goes to Sea, Bach Goes East* and *Bach Goes North.* English horn may replace clarinet.

Telemann, George Philip   German   1681-1767
Trio Sonata in A Minor; Stewart; TRI; 15 mins; 1011; D
Telemann was the most prolific composer of the Baroque period and is widely regarded as Germany's leading composer in the early to middle eighteenth-century.

Thiriet, Maurice   French   1906-1972
Lais et Virelais; c1956; Meridian; 13 mins; 0111; D
Thiriet studied with Koechlin and Roland-Manuel. According to a brief note on the score, these five pieces are musical settings of lais and virelais taken from the *Manusrit de Bayeux.* Stylistic similarities to the fourteenth and fifthteenth centuries are found throughout. There are some awkward passages in the last movement, high bassoon range and low oboe range.

Thurner
Trio, Op. 56; TBM; 0200/1

Toch, Ernst   Austrian/American   1887-1964
Sonatinetta, Op. 84; 1959; CPP; 14 mins; 1011; C/D
Toch's musical style is generally Neo-Classical, though occasionally
he experimented with chromatic and atonal ideas. A good recital piece
for college or advanced high school groups, this work has a vigorous,
rhythmic style.

Tomasi, Henri   French   1901-1971
Concert Champetre; 1939; PRC; 9 mins; 0111; D/E
Tomasi is best known for his stage works. His music shows the
influence of his French contemporaries such as Ravel. This modal piece
is written in five movements (*Overture, Minuetto, Bourree, Nocturne,
Tambourin*) which have a decidedly pre-Baroque style. Rapid articulation and expanded registers make this work challenging.

Topliff, Roger   20th C.
Reflections for Woodwind Trio; PRC; 4.5 mins; 0021; D/E

Torke, Michael   American   1961-
Two Pieces; c1980; DNP; 3 mins; 1011; C/D
Torke's quirkily irreverent music belies its formidable technical under-
pinnings. Several of his works have been commissioned by the New
York City Ballet.

Torrenga, Benno   1953-
Trio; 1978; DNA; 16 mins; 0021
Bass clarinet could substitute for bassoon.

Tscherepnin, Nikolay   Russian   1873-1945
Divertimento, Op. Posthumus; PTE; 1101; C/D
A student of Rimsky-Korsakov and later on the faculty of the St.
Petersburg Conservatory, Tcherepnin's music embodies the Russian
Nationalist style with lyrical melodies and lush harmonies.

Tustin, Whitney   1907-
Pastorale Moderne; c1954; BHM; 1110; C

Scherzo; c1939; BHM; 1110; B/C

Tarantella; c1939; BHM; 1110; B/C

Waltzing Woodwinds; c1954; BHM; 1110; A/B

Uber, David   American   1921-
Serenade; c1995; ALE; 1110; C
Uber's career ranges from award-winning composer to trombonist,
college professor to band director. He was professor of music at Trenton

State College for more than three decades. He received both a masters and doctoral degrees from Columbia University. This is written in a lyrical, Neo-Romantic style with considerable interplay in the voicing.

Suite for Wind Trio, Op. 46; 1987; KED; 7.5 mins; 1110; D
This moderately difficult work is written in six movements.

Urbanner, Erich   Austrian   1936-
Aphorisms; 1966; DBM; 1011
Urbanner studied composition with Karl Schiske and Hanns Jelinek at the Vienna Academy, then devoted himself to teaching and composition.

Vachey, Henri   French   1353-1355
Quartre Instantanes; c1968; LDA; 7.5 mins; 0111; C
While there are some challenging passages for individual players, generally this would not be difficult for the ensemble.

Valkare, Gunnar   Swedish   1943-
Fuga pa ettmaterial av Jorge Alcaide; 1995; SMI; 1011

Vallier, Jacques   French   1922-
Trio D'arches; CHO; 0111

Van de Woestijne, David   Belgian   1915-1979
Divertimento; 13 mins; 0111

Vanhal, Johann Baptist   Bohemian   1739-1813
Two Trios; ESM ; 0012; C

Velden, Renier van der   Belgian   1910-1993
Divertimento; 1957; 11 mins; 0111; E
Written in an atonal melodic style, this work explores the full range of each instrument and demands virtuoso technical abilities.

Verdi, Giuseppe   Italian   1813-1901
Three Arias; Drapkin; ESM; 0021; C/D
Included in these arrangements by one of the great opera composers are *La Donna e Mobile; Un di Felice, Eterea;* and *Parigi o Cara.*

Veress, Sandor   Hungarian/Swiss   1907-1992
Sonatina; 1931; EAM; 8.5 mins; 0111; E
Veress studied with Kodaly and Lajtha, worked with Bartok on the folklore collection at the Academy of Sciences in Budapest and taught at the State Academy of Music in Budapest, Bern University, Peabody Conservatory and the University of Oregon. This work shows the

influence of Bartok, both in a similar shifting modality and rhythmic drive as well as its use of Hungarian folk materials.

Verhaar, Ary   Netherlands   1900-1994
Trio, Op. 38; DNA; 11 mins; 1110

Verrall, John   American   1908-2001
Divertimento for Clarinet, Horn and Bassoon; 1941/1971; ACA; 0011/1
Verrall studied with Donald Ferguon and Kodaly, later teaching at Hamline University, Mt. Holyoke College and the University of Washington. This work, originally written in 1941, was completely revised in 1971 including new second and fourth movements.

Viecenz, Herbert   1893-1959
Terzett; 1955; BBL; 0200/1

Viitala, Mauri   Finnish   20th C.
Kolme Joululaulufantasiaa; 1977; FMC; 13 mins; 1011

Villa-Lobos, Heitor   Brazilian   1887-1959
Trio; 1921; PRC; 22 mins; 0111; D/E
Villa-Lobos, one of the most original composers of the twentieth century, had a remarkable ability to recreate native melodies and rhythms in large instrumental and choral forms. This three-movement work presents extreme challenges for the individual players as well as the ensemble, but should be well worth the effort. Primarily motivated by various rhythmic ostinati, it retains a great deal of academic formal structure.

Vivaldi, Antonio   Italian   1678-1741
Sonata #1 Op. 1, Gigue; CON; 1011
Vivaldi is considered the most original and influential Italian composer of his time.

Concerto in G Minor, P. 402 (RV.103); Rampal; MRI; 8 mins; 1101; C
This is a work of pastoral feeling, pleasant and relaxed, striving for mood and tone color and attaining its goals with good humor and easily communicated charm. Clarinet may substitute for flute and there is an optional piano part.

Trio in G Minor; BMC; 0201; C/D
There are alternate parts for oboe d'amore and English horn.

Vogel, Vladimir   Russian/German   1896-1984
Terzett; 1975; EUL; 1011
Vogel, a student of Heinz Tiessen and Busoni, taught at the Klind-worth-Scharwenka Conservatory in Berlin and later moved to Switzer-land. Much of his music is written in Neo-Classical format, but with some elements of serialism. This work requires piccolo.

Voorn, Joop   Dutch   1932-
Trio; DNA; 7 mins; 0111
Voorn studied at the Brabant Conservatory and later taught there.

Vredenburg, Max   Dutch   1904-1976
Trio; 1965; DNA; 7 mins; 0111; E
Vredenburg studied with Paul Dukas in Paris, later returning to the Netherlands where he established the National Youth Orchestra. This three-movement work is atonal and rhythmically complex. Virtuoso technical skills are required of all players and ensemble precision may be extremely challenging.

Wailly, Paul de   French   1854-1933
Aubade Trio; Kirkbride; SMC, IMC; 2.5 mins; 1110; C
Wailly was a student of Franck and his music shows this influence. He wrote a limited amount of music for orchestra, oratorio and chamber ensembles. This is a tonal, single-movement work that presents no ensemble difficulties.

Waitzman, Daniel   American   20th C.
Trio in B Major; 1997; DWP; 26 mins; 1101; D
Written as a memorial to Samuel Baron, this work uses many twentieth-century devices and requires oboe d'amore.

Walckiers, Eugene   French   1793-1866
Trio, Op. 12 #1-3; ESM; 1011; C/D

Walentynowicz, Wladyslaw   Polish   1902-
Trio for Reeds; c1980; PWM, PRC; 7 mins; 0111
This is an interesting work with four movements titled *All in Har-mony, In Waltz Time, Conversation* and *Merry March*.

Walker, Richard   American   1912-
Air and Dance; 1959; KED, BHM; 2 mins; 0111; C
This lively, lyrical work requires minimal technical facility and is perfect for middle and high school players.

Bagatelle; c1951; AMP; 1110

Ballet Dance; 1958; AMP; 1110; B

Rococo; 1961; KED; 1.5 mins; 0111; C/D
This work is more rhythmically lively and dissonant than *Air and Dance*. The parts are well balanced and it should be appropriate for high school players.

Spring Dance; KED; 1020; A/B
Oboe may replace one clarinet part.

Wallner, Alarich
Funf Bagatellen; MFS; 0020/1

In Modo Classico; MFS; 0020/1

Walshe, Michael   1932-
Trio Pastorale; c1979; ESM; 1110; C

Walthew, Richard   English   1872-1951
Prelude and Fugue   ; ESM; 0021
Walthew studied with Parry and later taught at the Guildhall School of Music and Queens College.

Triolet in E-Flat Major; c1934; BHI; 10 mins; 0111; C/D
This Post-Romantic style piece is tonal and features all three instruments equally.

Warfield, Gerald Alexander   1940-
Two for Three; c1967; CPP; 1110
There are optional parts for flute and two clarinets.

Warren, Elinor Remick   American   1900-1991
Trio; ESM; 0011/1; C/D

Washburn, Robert   American   1928-
Three Pieces for Three Woodwinds; 1962; OUP; 5 mins; 1011; C/D
Washburn studied with Bernard Rogers, Hovhaness, Milhaud and Boulanger. He has written music for orchestra, band and ensembles. This lively, syncopated work is written in three movements titled *Prelude and Fugue, Passacagia* and *Invention*. The bassoon part could be performed on bass clarinet.

Waters, Charles   English   1895-
Serenade; c1966; PTE; 6.5 mins; 0111; C/D
Using a homophonic texture, this piece features lyrical melodic lines and chromatic harmony. High register passages are found for the oboe and intonation could be a challenge in some sections.

Waxman, Donald   American   1928-
Trio; 1967; GLM; 22 mins; 0111; D/E
One of the longest works for the reed trio, this piece features intricate rhythms with jazz influence and tuneful melodies. The individual parts are as challenging as the ensemble aspects.

Weait
Ten by Three; ESM; 0111; C/D

Weber, Alain   French   1930-
Trio D'Anches; 1959; LDA; 8 mins; 0111; D/E
Weber was a student of Aubin and Messiaen at the Paris Conservatory and won the Prix de Rome in 1952. This is a three-movement, atonal work with chromatic melodic material. It is challenging to the individual players and the ensemble.

Weber, Carl Maria   German   1786-1826
Die Freischutz; 1817-21; SMC; 0011/1
Weber is an important founder of the Romantic movement in Germany and one of its leading composers.

Weegenhuise, Johan   Netherlands   1910-
Trio D'Anches; DNA; 8 mins; 0111

Weigl, Vally   Austrian/American   1889-1982
Brief Encounters; AMC; 0110/1
Weigl studied with Karl Weigl who later became her husband. After moving to the United States, she taught music therapy at the New York Medical College. Doubling on English horn is required.

Weir, Judith   Scottish   1954-
Mountain Airs; 1988; SCI, CHE; 5 mins; 1110
Weir studied with Tavener.

Weis, Flemming   Danish   1898-1981
Music for Flute, Clarinet and Bassoon; 1928; PTE; 4 mins; 1011; C/D
Weis studied composition with Nielsen and Helsted at the Royal Danish Conservatory in Copenhagen. His music, typical of the Danish School, shows a Romantic intensity with elements of gentle humor.

Welander, Svea   Swedish   1898-1985
Divertimento; SMI; 0111

Preludium efter ett synagogalt tema; 1955; SMI; 1 min; 1011

Weller, David
The Ash Grove; ALE; 1101; B
A folk song from the British Isles with an elegant, dance-like quality.

Werner, Jean-Jacques   French   1935-
Trio D'Anches; c1962; BIL; 14 mins; 0111; C/D
Written ·in four movements, this work prominently features the
bassoon. Technical agility and endurance are the primary performance
challenges in this work.

Westering, Paul Chr. van   Netherlands   1911-
Sonatina; DNA; 1101
English horn is used in place of oboe.

Whittaker, William Gillies   English   1876-1944
Miniature Suite; SMP; 1011
Whittaker taught at the University of Glasgow, edited a variety of
music for chorus and wrote a small quantity of music for piano, voice
and chorus.

Wiederkehr, Jacques   French   1759-1823
Trio #1 in F Major; 1820; ESM; 1001/1; D
Wiederkehr is best known for his symphonie concertantes for wind
instruments. His music is melodious, well designed and light hearted.
The French horn part could be played on English horn.

Trio #2 in G Minor; ESM; 1001/1; D
The French horn part could be played on English horn.

Trio #3 in E-Flat Major; ESM; 1001/1; D
Optional English horn part in place of French horn.

Wiener, Karl   1891-1942
Drei Stucke, Op. 20; c1931; UNE; 1110
English horn is required.

Wijdeveld, Wolfgang   Dutch   1910-
Trio; 1958; DNA; 12 mins; 1101
Wijdeveld studied theory with Sem Dresden and composition with
Willem Pijper, subsequently serving as director of the Conservatory of
Zwolle, piano instructor at the Utrecht Conservatory and music critic
for an Amsterdam newspaper. English horn is used in place of oboe.

Wildberger, Jacques   Swiss   1922-
Trio; 1953; BHI; 13 mins; 0111; E
Wildberger studied with Vladimir Vogel and later taught music in Karlsruhe and Basel. While observing formal traditions, he writes in a serialistic style. This work has a homophonic texture and shows a jazz influence. Rapid tempi make some sections technically challenging and endurance is a factor.

Wilder, Alec   American   1907-1980
Moosacaglia for Charles Lunde; MAR; 3 mins; 0101/1; B
Wilder studied with Herbert Inch and Edward Royce at the Eastman School. He has won numerous awards and has written music for theatre, opera, orchestra and chamber ensembles. This is a single movement work of modest difficulty.

Suite; MAR; 0111

Wildgans, Friedrich   Austrian   1913-1965
Kleines Trio; c1961; DBM; 1011; C/D
Wildgans wrote in all musical genres, in an ultramodern style including twelve tone technique. This work is a florid showpiece of dissonant passages.

Wilson, Donald M.   American   20th C.
Stabile II; AMC; 1101; B/C
This could be played on any two treble and one bass instrument.

Wilson, Richard   American   1941-
Gnomics; 1981; SMC, PIC; 1110
Gnomic verse is poetry containing maxims or aphorisms. It is associated with a school of Greek poets in the sixth century BC. The composer states on the score: "I am afraid they are somewhat whimsical pieces, the first two especially. They lack individual titles, but the first could be thought of as a prelude, the second a scherzo, and the third a madrigal, in which passages of homophony and polyphony alternate. With the exception of solos for the flute near the end of the first piece and at the start of the third, the texture remains fairly consistent in its three voices as I am particularly taken with the blended sound of flute, oboe and clarinet." *Gnomics* was given its premiere in 1982 by Bertha Frank, flute, Margaret Helfer, oboe, and Meyer Kupferman, clarinet.

Wiseman, Carlo
Trio; PRC, ESM; 2001; C

Wissmer, Pierre   Swiss   1915-1992
Serenade; 1938; COS; 7 mins; 0111; C/D
Wissmer studied with Roger-Ducasse and Daniel-Lesur. He writes in a
Neo-Classical style and this work features homophonic texture,
multimeters and modal melodies. The oboe part explores a wide
range, and the multimeter nature of the last movement may present
some ensemble challenges. This work should be accessible to advanced
high school trios.

Wolfl, Joseph   Austrian   1773-1812
Trio in B Major; c1974; ESM; 0021; C
Wolfl, a piano virtuoso, was a student of Mozart and Michael Haydn.

Trio in E-Flat Major; ESM; 0021; C

Worth, Ernest H.
The Music Box; A Miniature Song Tustin; c1939; BHM; 1110

Wuorinen, Charles   American   1938-
Turetzky Pieces; AMC; 1110
Wuorinen began playing piano and composing at age five and received
the Young Composers Award from the New York Philharmonic at age
sixteen. He taught at Columbia University and the Manhattan School
of Music. He won the Pulitzer Prize in 1970 for a work using
synthesized sound. His music is serialistic and shows the influence of
Schoenberg, Stravinsky and Varese.

Yavelow, Christopher Johnson American   1950-
Moments; AMC; 0111
Yavelow wrote a book titled *Macworld Music and Sound Bible* about
computer sound processing.

Yost, Michael   French   1754-1786
Three Trios; MRI; 0021
Best known as a clarinetist, Yost wrote concertos and chamber music.

Trio in F Major; Voxman; c1968; EAM; 4 mins; 0021; C

Yun, Isang   Korean/German   1917-1995
Rondell 1975; 1975; BBM; 14 mins; 0111; D/E
Yun studied Western music in Korea and Japan, later teaching in South
Korean schools. He moved to Berlin in 1956 where he produced several
successful theatrical works and taught at the Hochschule für Musik.
Yun incorporates Asian musical ideas with Western techniques. He is a
student of Revel, Blacher, Rufer and Schwarz-Schilling. This is a diffi-
cult, single-movement work.

Trio; 1992; BBM; 8 mins; 0011/1; D

Zagwijn, Henri   Dutch   1878-1954
Trio #1; 1944; DNA; 15 mins; 1110
While he had no formal music education, Zagwijn wrote music in a
French Impressionistic style. He taught at the Rotterdam School of
Music and the Rotterdam Conservatory, founded the Society of Modern
Composers in the Netherlands and published a biography of Debussy.

Zamecnik, Evzen Czech   1939-
Serenata; ESM; 9 mins; 1110
Zamecnik, a violinist, studied at the Janacek Academy and the Aca-
demy of Musical Arts in Prague.

Zanaboni, Giuseppe   Italian   1927-
Piccola Suite; c1967; PTE, ZAN; 10.5 mins; 0111; C/D
This atonal trio is one of the few written by an Italian composer. Written in four movements, this work requires only moderate technical ability.

Zaninelli, Luigi   American   1932-
Christmas for Three-Like; SHA; flexible instrumentation; B
Zaninelli is a graduate of the Curtis Institute where he studied with
Menotti and Martinu. He has over 200 published works.

Music for Three Woodwinds, Vol. 2; SHA; flexible instrumentation
Parts are interchangeable within the woodwind family.

Rome Suite; SHA; 11 mins; 1011; D
According to the composer, this work, written in four movements, is
autobiographical in a musical sense. "They contain memories, dreams
and experiences, all mine and uniquely Roman."

Zbinden, Julien-François   Swiss   1917-
Trio D'Anches, Op. 12; 1949; ESM; 14 mins; 0111; D
Zbinden writes in a Neo-Classical style influenced by Stravinsky,
Honegger and Ravel. This work is written in three movements:
Ricercare, Divertimento, Tema con Variazioni. Multimeters, intricate
rhythms and expanded range are the primary technical challenges of
this work.

Zelenka, Istvan   Hungarian   1936-
Ritournelles; TON; 1101
Zelenka writes in an experimental style with elements of serialism and electronic techniques.

Zieritz, Grete von   Austrian   1899-
Trio; REM ; 0111
Zieritz taught at the Stern Conservatory in Berlin and toured extensively as a pianist. Her compositions are perhaps better known in Europe than in the United States.

Zipoli, Domenico   Italian   1688-1726
Italian Airs and Dances; BHI; 0111; B/C
Zipoli was an organist at various Jesuit churches in Rome and South America.

Zipp, Friedrich   German   1914-1997
Maienmusik; 1987; MBV; 5 mins; 1101; B/C
Zipp's music is influenced by his interest in German folksong and church music. He wrote more than 900 works.

Zulawski, Wawrzyniec   Polish   1874-1915
Aria con Variazioni; 1950; PWM, PRC; 10.5 mins; 1011; B/C
Zulawski was a student of Sikorski and Boulanger.

Adolphus, Milton   American   1913-
Quartet, Op. 20; AMC; 1111
Adolphus studied with Rosario Scalero in Philadelphia and wrote music for orchestra and chamber ensembles.

Albéniz, Isaac   Spanish   1860-1909
Three Selections from Espana; Lesnick; 1890; INT; 1111; C/D
Albeniz, one of the most important figures in Spain's musical history, helped create a national idiom and an indigenous school of piano music. Virtually all his music written for piano is inspired by Spanish folklore and he is credited with establishing the modern school of Spanish piano literature which is derived from original rhythms and melodic patterns, rather than imitating the Spanish music written by French and Russian composers. He studied with Reinecke, Dukas and d'Indy. This work features three contrasting Spanish dance movements very effectively arranged for quartet titled *Tango, Capricho Catalan* and *Zortzico*, a lively and difficult 5/8 Basque dance.

Alemann, Eduardo A.   Argentine   1922-
Tres Micropoemas; c1965; PIC; 8 mins; 1111; D
Alemann studied composition, piano and clarinet. The majority of his music are chamber works with well-defined melodic lines, clear handling of the different voices and a solid musical structure.

Allgen, Claude Loyala   Swedish   1920-1990
Fuga for Trablasare; SMl; 1111

Ames, William T.   American   1901-
Quartet; AMC; 1111

Amos, Keith   English   20th C.
Catland; 1982; ESM; 8 mins; 2020; C

Sir Robert Walpole in Richmond Park; ESM; 2020; C/D

Apostel, Hans Erich   Austrian   1901-1972
Quartet, Op. 14; 1947-49; KAL, UNE; 1011/1
Apostel studied with Schoenberg and Berg. His early works were written in a dissonant, expressionistic style with later works using a twelve-tone system.

Arrieu, Claude   French   1903-1990
Suite en Quatre; 1979; BIL; 6 mins; 1111; C/D
Arrieu studied at the Paris Conservatoire with Caussade, Long, Roger-Ducasse and Dukas, taking a Premier Prix for composition in 1932. Her subsequent career was in teaching and in work of various kinds for French radio, which she joined in 1946. *Suite en Quatre* is a moderately difficult work in four movements. Her music shows the ease and elegance typical in the Parisian Neo-Classical style.

Augenblick, Leopold   Austrian   18th C.
Scherzo in C Major; Auslender; c1970; WIM; 2 mins; 1111; C
Augenblick's background remains vague. Research has revealed very little about him, but analysis of his music leads one to believe that he was a contemporary of the young Beethoven in the late 1700s. This work shows much grace and charm.

Babbitt, Milton Byron   American   1916-
Quartet for Woodwinds; 1953; AMP; 12 mins; 1111
Babbitt studied with Bauer and Philip James at New York University and later with Sessions at Princeton. He is best known for works in the twelve-tone compositional method and extended the concept of serialism to include register, dynamics, duration and timbre.

Bach, Erik   Danish   1946-
Wood Music; 1970; MRI; 9 mins; 1111

Bach, Johann Christian   German   1642-1703
Blaserinfonien I and II; HOF; 0021/1

Bach, Johann Sebastian   German   1685-1750
Air from Suite #3; Schmidt; WIM; 1111; B/C

Aria et Douze Variations, BWV 988; Chardon; EME; 0121
The most famous of the Bach family, Johann wrote primarily sacred music and works for keyboard. He also was a master organist and instructor. This traditional melody with a counter-melody and harmony, arranged for woodwind quartet, is suitable for contests or light programs. Bass clarinet is required.

Bouree; Rice-Young, Dahm; c1936; ALE, CFI; 1111; B
This traditional melody with a counter-melody and harmony, arranged for woodwind quartet, is suitable for contests or light programs.

Chorale and Prelude; Banquer; CFI; 1030
The flute part may be played on oboe.

Contrapunctus; PTE; 0111/1

Four Pieces from the Anna Magdalena Book; Wilkinson; c1961; NOV; 1111

Fuga #1, Art of the Fugue; Schmidt; WIM; 0111/1; C/D

Fughetta; Cafarella; c1933; Volkwein; 1111

Fugue in C Minor; Seay; SPR; 1111; C
Oboe may replace flute.

Fugue in E-Flat Major; Hirsch; CFI; 1011/1
Oboe may replace flute.

Fugue in G Minor; Hahn; CFI; 1111
Clarinet may replace oboe.

Fugue #2; CON; 1111; C

Fugue #4; McKay; BHM; 1111; B/C

Fugue #23; CON ; 1111

Gavotte; Cox; c1950; BHI; 1111; B
This work, from the fifth French Suite, uses simple rhythms, a limited melodic range and is good material for young students.

Menuet in G Minor; Guenther; 1111

Prelude #14; Kessler; c1934; SMC; 1111; C

Quartetto #1-#5; Crozzoli; PRC; 0301; C

Sarabande and Double; Reed; KED; 0121; B/C

Wake Up Bach; Griffiths; PRC; flexible instrumentation
Any four woodwinds may be used.

Well-Tempered Wind Quartet; Verral; PRC; 1111; C
Featuring arrangements of six movements from the *Well Tempered Klavier* and other works by Bach, this work is appropriate for formal concerts as well as training material in the Baroque style.

Bacon, Ernst   American   1898-1990
The Cockfight; BBL; 1.5 mins; 0220
Among his many teachers were Franz Schmidt and Ernest Bloch. A former member of the faculties of Converse College in South Carolina and Syracuse University, he was primarily known for his lyric songs.

Bainbridge, Simon   English   1952-
Wind Quartet; 1974; PRC; 15 mins; 1111

Baird, Tadeusz   Polish   1928-1981
Divertimento; 1956; PWM, IMC, CHE; 6 mins; 1111
Baird studied with Woytowicz, Sikorski, Rytel and Perkowski. His early music is Neo-Classic and his later works are in a late Romantic, tonal style with some twentieth-century elements.

Bartók, Béla   Hungarian   1881-1945
Five Easy Pieces; Schmidt; WIM; 0111/1; B/C
Bartók, a student of Koessler, began collecting folk songs in 1906 from Hungary, Romania, Slovak, Bulgaria and Croatia. He used these in much of his music in either substance or spirit.

Bartolozzi, Bruno   Italian   1911-1980
Concertazioni a Quattro; 1968; EAM; 1111; E
Bartolozzi studied at the Florence Conservatory and the Academia Chigiana in Siena. He is perhaps best known for a treatise on woodwind techniques that describes the production of chords and pitches outside the tempered scale. His compositions use serialism, quarter tones and new techniques for most instruments.

Bartos, Jan Zdenek   Czech   1908-1981
Divertimento #15; MFS; 1011/1
Bartos studied with Jirak and Kricka in Prague. He has written opera, ballet, choral works and chamber music.

Beckerath, Alfred von   1901-1978
Heiteres Spiel fur Holzblaser; c1972; MOS; 1111

Beethoven, Ludwig van   German   1770-1827
Menuetto, Op. 10; Tarlow; WBP; 1021
Beethoven's early achievements show him to be extending the Viennese Classical tradition. Later he began to compose in an increasingly individual musical style, and at the end of his life he wrote his most sublime and profound works.

Minuet; Cafarella; c1951; Volkwein; 1111
This arrangement is from the *Piano Sonata, Op. 22*.

Two German Dances; Erickson; ESM; 1111; B
There are alternate parts for clarinet and bass clarinet in place of oboe and bassoon respectively.

Bennett, Richard Rodney   English   1936-
Travel Notes 2; 1976; NOV; 6 mins; 1111; C
Bennett, considered one of the most brilliant and versatile of English
composers, attended the Royal Academy of Music in London where he
studied with Berkeley and Ferguson. Written as a sort of musical travel
log, the movements include *In an Air Balloon, In a Helicopter, In a
Bath-chair,* and *Car Chase.*

Benton, Daniel Joseph   1945-
Woodwind Quartet; SEE; 1111

Berbiguier, Benoit Tranquille   French   1782-1838
Theme and Variations; Wienandt; CPP; 1030
Best known as a flutist, Berbiguier wrote a great variety of music for
chamber ensembles.

Berger, Arthur   American   1912-
Quartet in C Major; 1941; PTE; 10 mins; 1111; D
Berger studied with Piston and Milhaud. Heavily influenced by Stravinsky, Berger's music is usually classified as Neo-Classical. This
witty and challenging piece is one of the best written for wind quartet.

Berlinski, Herman   German/American   1910-
Quadrille; 1952; SMC; 8 mins; 1111; D
Berlinski was an instructor at Hebrew Union College, then later became
organist and music director at Washington Hebrew Congregation, in
D.C. The five movements are *Entree, Tempo di Menuetto, Gavotte,
Sarabande* and *Gigue.*

Bernet, Dietfried   Austrian   1940-
Caprices; c1967; UNE; 1021
Bernet, a student of Swarowsky and Mitropoulos, has conducted at
many major opera houses and has been a guest conductor with leading
orchestras since 1962. The flute part here may be performed on oboe.

Bishof, Rainer   Austrian   1947-
Blaserquartett, Op. 5; DBM; 1011/1
Bischof studied composition at the Vienna Academy of Music and
privately with Apostel. His music shows the influence of Schoenberg,
Berg and Webern.

Bitsch, Marcel   French   1921-
Divertissement; 1947; LDA; 11 mins; 1111; D
Bitsch studied composition with Busser and won the 2nd Prix de Rome in 1943 and 1st Prix de Rome in 1945. This three-movement work (*Prelude, Pastorale, Fugues*) is somewhat difficult technically, but written well for the instruments. The oboe part goes to high F.

Bizet, Georges   French   1838-1875
Selections from Carmen; 1875; Sparl; flexible instrumentation; B/C
Bizet is primarily known for his French operas, but he also composed music for piano and orchestra. This set includes arrangements of the *Toreador Song, Habanera* and *Canzonetta*.

Bjelinski, Bruno   Croatian   1909-
Scherzi di Notte; c1971; GER; 1111
Bjelinski studied at the Zagreb Conservatory and later joined the faculty there. His music has Romantic coloring and is often related to literary subjects.

Blacher, Boris   German   1903-1975
Divertimento, Op. 38; 1951; BBM; 6 mins; 1111; D
Blacher's music is playful, with a sparse, transparent instrumentation of delicately traced and colored ornamental lines. *Divertimento* is a theme and variations, single-movement work that uses a multimeter pattern.

Blinov, Ypnu   Russian
Russian Scherzo; c1960; SCI; 1111

Boccherini, Luigi   Italian   1743-1805
Menuet; LDA; 1111; C
Boccherini's style was very similar to Haydn's and almost all his works are for instrumental chamber ensembles. This arrangement includes multiple parts in C, B-flat and E-flat.

Serenade for Don Luis; Kenny; ESM; 1111; C

Bochsa, Charles   French   1789-1856
Suite: Petit Airs en Quatuor, Op. 31; ESM; 10 mins; 1101/1; C/D
This is a suite of fifteen short movements, primarily dance styles including two boleros, two marches, two waltzes and others simply titled romance, andante or allegro.

Boeringer, James   American   1930-
Dance Suite; c1968; AMP; 7.5 mins; 1111; C/D
Boeringer was a student of Seth Bingham and Douglas Moore. The
four dance movements in this work are titled *Allemande, Courante,
Sarabande* and *Gigue*.

Bottje, Will Gay   American   1925-
Threesome for Four; AMC; 2011
Bottje studied composition with Giannini at the Juilliard School, then
later with Badings and Boulanger. His music is very experimental with
much dissonance. He has written music for opera, orchestra and chamber ensembles.

Boustead, Alan   English   20th C.
Three Bagatelles; ESM; 1011/1

Three Madrigals; ESM; 1011/1

Boyce, William   English   1711-1779
Allegro; CON; 1111
Boyce's style has a fresh energy which is apparent in this work. He
uses middle movements that are quick, light and soft rather than slow.
In the nineteenth century, Boyce's reputation depended mainly on his
Cathedral Music, a three-volume collection of sacred music by English
masters of the sixteenth through eighteenth centuries. However, in the
early twentieth century, interest in his music was revived when a
number of Boyce's overtures were published by Constant Lambert.
This is an arrangement of the first movement from the *Symphony in E-
Flat, K. 18*.

Marcato; CON; 1111
This is an arrangement of the first movement from Boyce's *Symphony
#7*.

Vivace; CON; 1111
This is an arrangement of the third movement from his *Symphony #1*.

Bozza, Eugene   French   1905-1991
Serenade; c1969; LDA; 1111; D
Bozza studied with Busser, Rabaud, Capet and Nadaud at the Paris
Conservatory where he won the Premiers Prix for the violin (1924),
conducting (1930) and composition (1934), and also the Prix de Rome
in 1934. Though his larger works have been successfully performed in
France, his international reputation rests on his large output of chamber
music for winds. His works display at a consistently high level the

characteristic qualities found in mid-twentieth century French chamber music: elegant structure, melodic fluency and an awareness of the capabilities of the instruments for which he writes.

Sonatine; c1971; LDA; 8 mins; 1111; D
There is another arrangement of this for four clarinets.

Trois Pieces; 1954; LDA; 4 mins; 1111; C/D
This light and lively work is enjoyable for performers and audience alike.

Brahms, Johannes   German   1833-1897
Three Easy Quartets; Hunter; c1961; EAM, ESM; 1111; B/C
One of the greatest masters of music, Brahms composed works for orchestra, voice, piano, chorus and chamber music. This is an arrangement from *Four Scotch Songs*.

Intermezzo; Schmidt; WIM; 0111/1; C

Braun, Carl Anton Philipp   German   1788-1835
Quartet #2; BKH; 1101/1
Braun, an oboist and composer, was a member of the well-known Braun family of German musicians. Though primarily known as a virtuoso, he also composed light pieces for a variety of combinations.

Bridge, Frank   English   1879-1941
Divertimenti; 1934-38; BHI; 7 mins; 1111; D/E
Bridge studied violin and composition at the Royal College of Music. He quickly made a reputation for himself as an outstanding conductor and chamber musician. His music evolved greatly over time with clear influences ranging from Brahms to Berg. *Divertimenti* has four movements titled *Prelude, Nocturne, Scherzetto, Bagatelle*.

Buchtel, Forrest L.   American   1899-1996
Enchanted Forest; c1960; KMC; 2 mins; 1111; B/C
Known to his friends as "Frosty", Buchtel received degrees from Simpson College, Northwestern University and VanderCook College of Music. He taught high school and college and wrote more than 800 works for band, ensembles and instrumental solos. This single-movement work is written in waltz style and would be appropriate for young ensembles.

Burgon, Geoffrey   English   1941-
Little Missenden Variation; 1984; CHE; 0111/1
English horn is required.

Butt, James   1929-
Winsome's Folly; c1956; BHI; 0111/1; C/D
This work features three movements titled *Ostinato, Pastorale* and
Tarantelle.

Carter, Elliott   American   1908-
Eight Etudes and a Fantasy; 1950; AMP; 23 mins; 1111; E
Carter's reputation is derived mainly from a few large-scale works. He
studied with Piston, Hill and Boulanger. Carter has been the recipient
of the highest honors that a composer can receive and has honorary
degrees from many universities. His best music has an energy of
invention that is unmatched in contemporary compositions.

Castillo, Ricardo   Guatemalan   1891-1966
Contrastes; 1946; PRC; 1111

Castle, Alfred   20th C.
Summer Sketches; c1961; KED; 2020; B

Cazden, Norman   American   1914-1980
Insistence, Op. 40 #5; SPR; 0202
Cazden studied at the Musical Arts in New York and the Juilliard
School, later studying with Piston and Copland at Harvard. He wrote
contrapuntal, rhythmic music that often reflected his interest in folk
music of the Catskills.

Waltz #1, Op. 40 ; c1960; SPR; 2 mins; 1111; B

Cervantes, Ignacio   Cuban   1847-1905
Six Cuban Dances; Lesnick; c1995 INT; 1111
One of the pioneers of native Cuban music, Cervantes employs lively
Cuban rhythms in this set of six short dances. These salon pieces,
originally for piano, work well as a set or individually, and are perfect
for recitals, jobs and educational concerts.

Cervetti, Sergio   Uruguayan   1940-
Divertimento; c1966; PIC; 7 mins; 0121; D/E
Cervetti studied piano and composition in Uruguay, then at the Pea-
body Conservatory in Baltimore, MD. Bass clarinet is required.

Chabrier, Emmanuel   French   1841-1894
Danse Villageoise; Schmidt; WIM; 1011/1 or 0111/1; D
Trained first as a lawyer, Chabrier later became a well-known composer and pianist. His music is written with a free treatment of dissonance, modality, bold harmonic contrasts, rhythmic energy and striking
originality which inspired many subsequent French composers such as
Ravel.

Chagrin, Francis   English   1905-1972
Renaissance Suite; NOV; 1111
This is an arrangement for either string or woodwind quartet with four
movements titled *Intrada Marziale, Pavana e Gagliarda, Canzona
Lamentevole* and *Rondo Gioioso.*

Serenade: Jottings for Jeremy; c1968; NOV, SHA; 1111

Chailley, Jacques   French   1910-1999
Suite sans Pretention pour Monsieur de Moliere; c1982; PRC;12
mins; 1111; D
Chailley studied composition with Boulanger, Delvincourt and Busser,
and later taught at the Paris Conservatory. His compositions include
two operas, a ballet, orchestral works and chamber music. This
delightful and challenging work has four movements titled *Prologue,
Angelique, Diafoirus Pere et Fils* and *Ballet-Divertissement.*

Suite du XV Siecle; LDA; 1101/1; B/C

Chaminade, Cecile   French   1857-1944
Scarf Dance; Guenther; c1965; 1.5 mins; 1111; B
Chaminade wrote primarily light music for opera, orchestra, vocal and
piano.

Chandler
Pas de Quatre; ESM; 1111; C/D

Chopin, Frederic   Polish   1810-1849
Nocturne Op. 15, #1; WIM; 1011/1; C/D
Oboe may replace the flute.

Prelude #6, Op. 28; Stratton; SER; 0031; B/C
This short, pensive piece is in the original key of B-minor.

Christensen
Turkey in the Straw; ESM; 2020; C

Clementi, Aldo   Italian   1925-
Duetto; 1983; SUV; 2020
Clementi studied composition with Sangiorgi and Petrassi at the Santa
Cecilia Conservatory in Rome. His music incorporates many twentieth-
century devices.

Cohan, George M.   American   1878-1942
George M. Cohan Medley; Nagle; MPI; 5 mins; C/D
Like the version for wind quintet, this popular arrangement is sure to
please both the audience and musicians.

Connolly, Edmund
Swingin' the Blues; PRC; flexible instrumentation
This work has an optional percussion part.

Corelli, Arcangelo   Italian   1653-1713
Allemanda; Maganini; c1954; ESM; 1111; B/C
Corelli's greatest achievement was the creation of the concerto grosso
form. He was also known as a virtuoso violinist and is regarded as the
founder of modern violin technique. Despite a small output of music,
Corelli greatly influenced form, style and instrumental technique during
his lifetime. While his music may seem rather predictable today, his
music was considered very original by his contemporaries.

Gavotte and Gigue; Maganini; c1950; ESM; 1111; B/C

Gigue; Goldsmith; PRC; flexible instrumentation; B/C
This piece has an optional piano part.

Couperin, François   French   1668-1733
Cantus Firmus; Morris; c1974; CPP; 1111; A/B
Couperin is considered one of the greatest French composers of his time
with music written for voice, chamber ensembles and harpsichord.

Cowles
Twin-Sets; ESM; 2020; B/C

Cox, Noel   20th C.
Minuet; c1951; BHI; 2 mins; 1111; B/C

Croft, William   English   1678-1727
Aires in the Comedy; ESM; 0301; C/D
English horn is required.

Csonka, Paul   1905-
French Suite; c1968; PIC; 1030 or 0121
Flute part may be played on oboe.

Curtis, Mike   20th C.
A Klezmer Wedding; ESM; 1111 or 0301; D

Tango La Invitacion; MSS; 1111 or 0301

Datshkovsky, Yasha
Lullaby for Alexandra; Campoy; c1986; SMC; 1111; C/D
This work was originally for piano.

De Lamarter, Eric   American   1880-1953
Sketch Book in Eire; c1949; SMC; 6 mins; 1111
De Lamarter studied with Guilman and Widor in Paris. Describing
scenes, this work includes five movements titled *Terns...Dun Laog-
haire, Aonarach, Chase Me Charlie, Gab at th' Hedge* and *Bridgid 'n'
Andy's Jig.*

Debras, Louis   American   20th C.
Rotationen; c1968; SEE; 4 mins; 1111; E

Debussy, Claude   French   1862-1918
Clair de Lune; 1890-1905; BIG; 1111
Debussy studied with Chopin and later at the Paris Conservatory with
Durand. He wrote music for opera, ballet, orchestra, piano and chamber
ensembles. This work was originally part of a suite for solo piano.

Golliwog's Cakewalk; Blyth; 1908 ESM; 1111; D
This work was originally written for piano.

La Plus Que Lente; Schmidt; WIM; 1111; C/D

Dedrick, Christopher
Sensitivity; KED; 0111/1; C

Delibes, Leo   French   1836-1891
Music from the Ballet; 1870; ESM; 1111; C
Nearly all of Delibes' works were composed for the theater. He had a
natural gift for harmonic dexterity and a good sense of orchestral color.
His music shows a clear feeling for the seventeenth-century French
Classicism. Included in this appealing arrangement are three dances
from *Sylvia* and *Coppelia.*

Diemer, Emma Lou   American   1927-
Music for Woodwind Quartet; 1972; OUP; 1111; D
Diemer studied with Hindemith, Sessions, Rogers and Hanson. She
was composer-in-residence for the Ford Foundation Young Composers
Project and on the faculties of the University of Maryland and the Uni-
versity of California at Santa Barbara.

Dionisi, Renato   Italian   1910-
Quartet, D. 335; PTE, ZAN; 4.5 mins; 1111

Donovan, Richard   American   1891-1970
Quartet for Woodwinds; 1953; VMP; 13.5 mins; 1111; C/D
Donovan studied at Yale and the Institute of Musical Arts in New York
City. After an early Post-Impressionist phase his compositional style
became polyphonic with frequent use of modal themes, sometimes even
folk tunes.

Doppelbauer, Josef Friedrich   1918-1989
Quartet; c1967; DBM; 1111

Dubois, Pierre Max   French   1930-
Trois Mousquetaires; LDA; 0121; D
Dubois studied at the Paris Conservatoire and won the Prix de Rome
in 1955. His music has been influenced by Milhaud, Francaix and
Prokofiev and he has written music for orchestra, dance and chamber
ensembles. He writes in a light, humorous style, with chromatic scales,
unusual harmonies and lively rhythms.

Duck
Cats Cradle; ESM; 1111; C
There are alternate parts for bass clarinet and clarinet.

Partita; ESM; 1111; C/D

Durand, Auguste   French   1830-1909
Pomponette; Leonard; c1978; 2 mins; 1111; B/C
Alternate clarinet parts are available to replace oboe and bassoon.

Dussek   Bohemian   18th-19th C.
Rondo; Erickson; BEL; 1111; B
There are alternate clarinet and bass clarinet parts for the oboe and bas-
soon respectively.

Dvořák, Antonín   Czech   1841-1904
Humoreske; 1884; INT; 1111
Dvořák's musical style is diverse with his early works reflecting the influence of Beethoven and Schubert, then Wagner and later Brahms. This arrangement of his popular parlor piece features the flute.

Ehrenberg, Carl Emil Theodor   German   1878-1962
Quartet, Op. 40; c1965; Schauer, Simrock; 0111/1
Ehrenberg studied with Draeseke at the Dresden Conservatory and later became a conductor with various orchestras, eventually devoting himself to teaching in Cologne and Munich. He wrote two operas, two symphonies, several overtures and chamber music.

Ekstrom, Lars   Swedish   1956-
Teroni; 1986; SMI; 10 mins; 0022

Eler, Andre Frederic   French   1764-1821
Quartet in F Major, Op. 11, #1-#3; Dienstbier; pre-1806; LKM; 1011/1; C
Schooled in German Classicism, Eler's music demonstrates a solid technique with pure harmonies, Classical melodies and strong counterpoint. He wrote many interesting chamber music works at a time when the genre was largely ignored in France.

Quartet, Op. 6 #1; EUL; 1011/1

Elliott, Willard   American   1926-
Noggin the Nog, Northlands Suite ; ESM; 1111; C
Elliott, a renowned bassoonist, studied at North Texas State University and the Eastman School.

Erbse, Heimo   German   1924-
Quartet, Op. 20; 1961; PTE; 1111
Erbse, a student of Blacher in Berlin, wrote dramatic music for stage, orchestra and chamber ensembles.

Erdmann, Dietrich   German   1917-
Improvisation; GER; 1111
Erdmann studied with Hindemith and Paul Hoffer. Committed to the cause of contemporary music, he has written solo concerto, orchestral music, chamber music and vocal music.

Erickson, Frank
Scherzino; c1964; 1111; A/B
This uncomplicated work would be good for young players.

Eriksson, Nils   Swedish   1902-1978
Quartetto a Fiati di Legno Trablasarkvartett; 1957; SMI; 12 mins;
1111

Rondino alla Marcia; 1962; SMI; 2.5 mins; 1111

Erixon, Per Anders   Swedish   1930-
Rondo, Op. 2; 1963; SMI; 4 mins; 1111
This work requires clarinet in A.

Erod, Ivan   Hungarian   1936-
Ricercare et Aria S.C.H.E.; DBM; 1110/1
Bass clarinet is required.

Etler, Alvin   American   1913-1973
Fragments; c1974; EAM; 1111
Etler studied with Hindemith while teaching woodwinds and conducting the band at Yale. He used serialism, but usually with a tonal center
and jazz is sometimes evident in his music. He wrote music for orchestra, chamber ensembles and chorus.

Eyser, Eberhard   Polish/Swedish   1932-
El Fuego de Oro; 1978; SMI; 10 mins; 0022
Eyser studied at the Music Academy in Hannover and later became a
violist with the Royal Opera House Orchestra in Stockholm.

Kvartino; 1981; SMI; 1111
Oboe d'amore is required.

Serenata II; 1976; SMI; 12 mins; 0022

Fairhead
Jazz Gavotte; ESM; 2020; C

Fasch, Johan Friedrich   German   1688-1758
Sonata in F Major; ESM; 0202; C
Though none of his music was published during his lifetime, Fasch's
early works show the influence of Telemann. He is best known today
for his overtures, symphonies, concertos and chamber music and musical scholars view him as an important link between the Baroque and
Classical styles.

Finger, Gottfried   Austrian   1660-1732
Ayers in the Comedy of Sir Harry Wild Hair; Nex; ESM; 0301; C/D
English horn is required.

Fischer, Johann Christian   German   1733-1800
Banquet Music; Andraud; SMC; 1111
Fischer was one of the most popular oboists of his time, and his oboe concertos were famous, inspiring many composers, including Mozart, to make arrangements of his music.

Fongaard, Bjorn   Norwegian   1919-1980
Quartets #1-#3; 1975; NOR; 1111
Fongaard, a guitar virtuoso, teacher and prolific composer, wrote microtonal music for stage, orchestra and chamber groups.

Fontyn, Jacqueline   Belgian   1930-
Five Mosaics; 1965; SCI; 5 mins; 1111; C/D
Fontyn, awarded the Prix de Rome and Prix Oscar Espla, studied composition in Paris and Vienna. Her earlier works are very traditional, but since 1959 she has written in a modern idiom.

Frackenpohl, Arthur   American   1924-
Toccata for Woodwind Quartet; c1969; SCI; 3 mins; 1111; D/E
Frackenpohl studied with Milhaud and Boulanger. His melodic style is distinctive in his numerous works, many having been inspired by his university teaching and his work as an organist/choir director.

Françaix, Jean   French   1912-
Quartet; 1933; EAM; 10 mins; 1111; D/E
A brilliant piano virtuoso, Francaix's music shows an innate gift for invention and an ability to express the freshness and wonder of childhood.

Frank, Marcel   1909-
Canon and Fugue; KED; 1111

Frescobaldi, Girolamo   Italian   1583-1643
Canzona; Klauss; TMP; 1111
An important keyboard player and composer of his time, Frescobaldi primarily wrote music for keyboard and voice.

Fricker, Peter Racine   English   1920-1990
Five Canons; 1966; ESM; 2200
Fricker studied at the Royal College of Music and was later a student of
Seiber and Tippett. His musical style begins with the influence of
Bartok and Hindemith, occasionally using twelve-tone and serialism.
There are two optional clarinet parts.

Fuchs, Franz D. J.
Serenade; MFS; 1111

Furst, Paul Walter   Austrian   1926-
Blaserquartett, Op. 40; c1967; DBM; 1111
Furst, a viola player, studied at the Vienna Academy with Boskovsky
and Marx. His style is freely tonal, sometimes featuring jazz elements
and contemporary techniques.

Futterer, Carl   1873-1927
Quartet in F Major; EKB; 1011/1; C/D

Gabrielsky, Johann Wilhelm   German   1791-1846
Adagio, Op. 53 #2; c1965; KMC; 1111

Finaletto; c1965; KMC; 1111

Gambaro, Giovanni Battista   Italian   1785-1828
Quartet #1 in F Major; BVP, KAL; 1011/1; C/D

Quartet #2 in D Minor; BVP, KAL; 1011/1; C/D

Quartet #3 in G Major; Balassa; BVP, KAL; 1011/1; C/D

Garlick, Anthony   1927-
Quartet; SEE; 1111

Gattermayer, Heinrich   1923-
Quartet, Op. 81 #2; 1965; DBM, ESM; 0111/1; C/D

Gebauer, François Rene   French   1773-1844
Quartette #5; SIE; 1111
Gebauer, son of a German military bandsman, studied bassoon at the
Paris Conservatory where he later served as professor of bassoon from
1796 to 1802 and later from 1826 on. Between 1801 and 1826 Gebauer
played bassoon at the Grande Opera in Pairs. In his numerous compositions he concentrated especially on woodwind instruments.

Quartette, Op. 41; EUL; 1011/1

Three Quartets, Op. 20; SIE; 1101/1 or 1011/1

Three Quartets, Op. 27; SIE; 1101/1 or 0021/1

Gerber, Steven R.			American			1948-
Quartet; 1967; AMC, MOB; 8 mins; 1111

Ghent, Emmanuel			Canadian/American	1925-
Quartet; c1963; OUP; 1111; D
While influenced by Shapey and Varese, Ghent concentrates on the harmonic and melodic exploration of fixed interval groups. The flute part could be done on oboe.

Gibbons, Orlando			English			1583-1625
Two Corantos; Cruft; c1968; BHI; 2.5 mins; 1111; B/C
Gibbons was one of the outstanding organists of his time. He wrote music for organ, chorus, keyboard and voice.

Gladkovsky, Alexander
Miniature Procession; Schmidt; WIM; 1111; B/C

Glaser, Werner Wolf			Swedish			1910-
Capriccio e Canzone; 1978; SMI; 12 mins; 0022
Glaser studied composition with Jarnach and Hindemith, and later became a choral conductor. His compositions for opera, orchestra and chamber groups is in a Neo-Classical style.

Goepfart, Karl			German			1859-1942
Quartet, Op. 93; c1963; SMC; 7 mins; 1111; C/D
With three movements titled *Allegro, Scherzo* and *Fuga*, this work is unusual in that there is no true slow movement.

Greaves, Terence			English			1933-
Four Bagatelles; PRC; 2020; C

Grechaninov
En Route!; ESM; 2020; C

Grieg, Edvard Hagerup		Norwegian		1843-1907
Elfin Dance; ESM; 1110/1
One of Norway's most important musical figures, Grieg is perhaps best known for *Peer Gynt* on which he collaborated with Ibsen.

Norwegian Dance, Op. 47; Carafella; Volkwein; 1110/1

Solveig's Song; Ralston; ESM; 1021; B
There is an alternate bass clarinet part to replace bassoon.

Three Chansons d'Enfants en Quatour; Voirpy; PRC; flexible instrumentation
Any combination of woodwinds may be used.

Two Lyric Pieces; Ralston; ESM; 1021; B
There is an alternate bass clarinet part to replace bassoon.

Grunauer, Ingomar   1938-
Blaserquartett; c1966; DBM; 1111

Guenther, Ralph R.   20th C.
Serenade for Heidi; 1111; B/C

Song for Manana; c1982; 1.5 mins; 1111; B/C

Hallauer, Dankwart   1936-
Kleine Suite; c1971; EAM; 5 mins; 1111
This work, written in seven short movements, requires piccolo doubling.

Hancock, Paul   English   1952-2001
With the Mermaids, Op. 18; 1985; ESM; 18 mins; 1111; E

Handel, George F.   German/English   1685-1759
Alexander in Serveus: Overture; CON; 1111
Handel's music featured grand design, lush harmonies and a certain eloquence. He wrote music for opera, oratorios, chamber ensembles and orchestra.

Allegro; CON; 1111

Almirena's Aria; Schmidt; WIM; 1111; B

Bouree and Hornpipe; LDA; flexible; B
Written with flexible instrumentation in mind, there are parts for instruments in C, B-Flat and E-Flat.

Concerto; CON; 1111

Faramondo: Overture; CON; 1111

Parnasso in Festa: Overture; CON; 1111

Petite Fugue; Ostling; c1937; CPP; 1111; B

Sarabande from Suite XI; Sutton; MidSx; flexible instrumentation; B
There are parts for flute, oboe and clarinet on each of the four voices.

Three Movements; Cox; c1962; NOV; 1111
This may also be played with two flutes, oboe and clarinet.

Hanmer, Ronald   1917-1995
Cuckoo Quartet; ESM; 2020; B/C

Woodwind Quartets; ESM; 1120; B/C
The oboe part may be played on flute.

Hansell, P.
Four Antique Dances; ESM; 0202 C

Harper   20th C.
Atarah's Elastic Band: Four Fun Pieces; ESM; 3010; A/B

Harris, Arthur   American   1927-
Diversion; 1955; BBL; 8.5 mins; 1111; C

Hartley, Walter Sinclair   American   1927-
Woodwind Quartet; c1958; FMP; 1111; C/D
Hartley studied with Bernard Rogers and Howard Hanson at Eastman.
He wrote music for band and chamber music specifically for brass and
woodwinds.

Hasquenoph, Pierre   French   1922-1982
Sonata q Quatre; EME; 1111

Haydn, Franz Joseph   Austrian   1732-1809
Allegro con Brio; Hahn; c1938; CFI; 1111; C
Haydn is considered the creator of the classical form of the symphony
and string quartet. He played an historic role in the evolution of
harmony by adopting four-part writing as the compositional foundation.
A prolific composer, Haydn wrote music for orchestra, chamber ensembles, concertos, dramatic works, masses and oratories. This movement
from the *String Quartet #4* would be a good training piece for young
ensembles.

Andante from Surprise Symphony; Ostling; 1791; CPP; 2 mins; 1111; B

Divertimento; Reichenbach; HAN; 0020/2

Divertimento #4 in C Major; KAL; 0020/1; C/D

Divertimento Hob. II:14 or #30; Cuninghame, Landon; 1761; ESM, DBM; 1111 or 0020/2; C

Menuetto and Scherzando; von Kreisler, Loffler; SMC, ESM; 1111 or 1021; B

Minuet; Seay; SPR; 1111

Presto Scherzando from Op. 20 #4; Banquer; 1781; MCA; 1111

Quartet #18, Op. 3 #5; Nakagawa; AMP; 1011/1; C/D

Theme and Variations; Hahn; c1948; CFI; 1111; C
These are variations on a theme from the *Emperor String Quartet*.

Twelve Nocturnes in D Major; BBL; 2000/2; C/D

Haydn, Johann Michael   Austrian   1737-1806
Divertimento in D Major, Op. 100; 1796; HOF; 17 mins; 1101/1; C/D
John Michael Haydn, younger brother of Joseph, was best known in his lifetime as a master of church music. He was, however, a respected and prolific composer of instrumental works also. This six-movement .work, written in standard Classic style, is appropriate for professionals or students. Two manuscripts of this work are preserved in two collections in Vienna. This edition is based on a comparison of the two manuscripts.

Hekster, Walter   Dutch   1937-
Relief #1; DNA; 1111
After graduation from the Amsterdam Conservatory, Hekster was a clarinetist with the Connecticut Symphony Orchestra and later taught clarinet and composition at Brandon University (Canada), Utrecht Conservatory and Arnhem Conservatory.

Helm, Everett   American   1913-1999
Quartet for Woodwinds; c1962; Schauer; 1111
Helm graduated from Harvard, then studied composition and musicology in Europe. He wrote music for opera, piano, orchestra, voice and chamber ensembles.

Henning, Ervin Arthur   American   1910-
Badinage; 1946; PRC; 1111; C/D
Henning graduated from the New England Conservatory with honors.
He writes primarily for chamber music; his later works use the twelve-
tone technique.

Hermann, Friederich   German   1828-1907
Zur Ubung im Zusammenspiel fur Blasinstrumente; BKH; 0111/1

Hertel, Johann Wilhelm   German   1727-1789
Sonata a Quattro; PTE; 0002/2
A student of Heil and Graun, Hertel composed sacred choral music,
cantatas, symphonies, concertos, chamber music and keyboard pieces.

Hessenberg, Kurt   German   1908-1994
Serenade, Op. 89; c1974; EAM; 0111/1

Hoddinott, Alun   Welsh   1929-
Divertimento, Op. 32; 1963; OUP; 16 mins; 0111/1
Hoddinott's music is characterized by a highly chromatic, late
Romantic tonal style. His huge output includes music for orchestra,
opera, chorus, concertos and chamber ensembles.

Hodges, Maurice   20th C.
Irish Tunes, Set I; c1992; 5 mins; 1111; D
This lyrical four-movement work includes *The Red Haired Boy, I
Know My Love, Lovely Mollie* and *The Mountain Lark*.

Holbrooke, Josef   English   1878-1958
Serenade in D-Flat, Op. 94; c1932; ESM; 1111; D/E
Holbrooke studied composition with Corder at the Royal Academy of
Music. He wrote operas, symphonies, concertos, chamber and piano
music. The three movements of this challenging work are titled *Moon-
light on the Water, Sad Memories* and *Scherzo Caprice.*

Holzbauer, Ignaz Jakob   Austrian   1711-1783
Divertimento; Janetzky; BBL; 0002/2; D
Holzbauer was an influential composer in Mannheim during the late
1700s. He wrote music for opera, ballet, orchestra and chamber
ensembles.

Hope
Three Miniatures; ESM; 1111; C/D

Horovitz, Joseph   Austrian/English   1926-
Jazz Suite; c1980; BHI; 2020; C
Horovitz studied at New College in Oxford and wrote music for opera, ballet, orchestra and chamber ensembles.

Hovhaness, Alan   American   1911-
Divertimento, Op. 61 #5; c1950; CFI, PTE; 12 mins; 0111/1; B/C
Although most of Hovhaness's music is instrumental, almost every work is religious in nature. His melodies are clear and modal, harmonies are consonant but progress chromatically rather than tonally, and he uses counterpoint from a variety of periods. Written in seven parts, this excellent work is in the style of a Baroque suite.

Hugues, Luigi   Italian   1836-1913
Quartett, Op. 72 in G Minor; RIC; 1111

Quartett, Op. 76 in B-Flat Major; RIC; 1111

Ibert, Jacques   French   1890-1962
Deux Mouvements; 1922; LDA; 4 mins; 2011, 1111; D
Ibert studied at the Paris Conservatory with Paul Vidal for composition, and won several prizes there in 1914. He won the Prix de Rome in 1919 after serving in WWI. He made important contributions in all musical genres except oratorio. He used classical forms as a foundation, but made them flexible, always with a strong sense of balance and restraint. This work was originally written for two flutes, clarinet and bassoon, then was revised by the composer for wind quartet.

Isaacson, Michael   American   20th C.
November Song; c1990; ALE; 1111; A/B
Originally for piano and piccolo, this bittersweet melody reflects the melancholy feeling as the crispness of October settles into winter's approach during November.

Jacob, Gordon   English   1895-1984
A Simple Serenade; c1976; ESM; 7 mins; 1111; C
Jacob studied with Stanford and Howells at the Royal Academy of Music and Dulwich College and later joined the faculty of the RAM. His works are deeply rooted in tradition and display fine craftsmanship. This appealing work includes six movements titled *Fanfare and March, Nocturne, Panpipes, Bells, Chorale* and *Adieu.*

Aubade; c1980; FML; 2020

Four Little Sketches; 1984; PRC; 3 mins; 1111; B
This delightful work, with movements titled *Water Rat, Mole, Badger* and *Toad*, is   printed in a set with music by Wright, Parfrey and Winters.

Four Old Tunes; c1975; PRC; 8.5 mins; 1111; B/C
Based on four English and Scottish songs titled *Bobby Shafto, Golden Slumbers, Tell Me Daphne, Charlie's My Darling*, this charming work is a welcome addition to the quartet literature.

Jadin, Louis Emanuel   French   1768-1853
Nocturne #2 in F Major; c1990; EKB; 1011/1; C

Nocturne #3 in G Minor; c1967; EKB; 6 mins; 1011/1; C
Jadin wrote a variety of festive music for special occasions including music for orchestra and piano. There is an alternate horn part for the bassoon.

Janacek, Leos   Czech   1854-1928
Our Evening; Schmidt; WIM; 0111/1; C
Janacek, like Smetana and Dvorak, was a composer who worked indefatigably for the advancement of the music of his native Czechoslovakia. He often made use of what he called "speech melody"—melody whose contours were inspired by the characteristic rhythm and cadence of the Czech language.

Three Moravian Dances; Munclinger; 1892-1904; IMC; 5.5 mins; 1111; C/D

Jemmett
Dish Rag; KED; 1111; B/C

Jones, Charles William   Canadian/American   1910-
Lyric Waltz Suite ; 1948; PTE; 10.5 mins; 1111; C
Jones studied at the Juilliard School with Wagenaar. His early diatonic and Neo-Classical style evolved with increasing chromaticism.

Jongen, Joseph   Belgian   1873-1953
Two Paraphrases on Walloon Christmas Carols, Op. 114; 1940; SMC; 3010, 1111; D
Brother of Leon Jongen, Joseph's early music shows the influence of Debussy and Ravel while his later works are frequently atonal. Alto flute and English horn are required. There is an alternate version for four flutes.

Joplin, Scott   American   1868-1917
Strenuous Life; 1903; 1111
Named the "King of Ragtime," Joplin was largely self-taught though
he briefly attended the Smith College for Negroes in 1895 to gain technical skills in composition.

The Ragtime Dance; INT; 1111
This is one of the most popular Joplin rags complete with foot
stomping!

Josephs, Wilfred   English   1927-1997
Five Fictitious Folksongs; c1962; BHI; 1111; C
A prolific composer in virtually every genre, Josephs studied with
Nieman and Deutsch. He describes his own music as "atonal with
tonal implications." There is an alternate clarinet part to replace the
oboe.

Kabalevsky, Dmitri   Russian   1904-1987
Children's Suite, Op. 27; Seay; 1944; ESM; 4 mins; 1111; B/C
Kabalevsky's fame within Russia rests mainly on his vocal works and
in the West on his orchestral compositions, concertos and piano music.
This easy work, originally for piano, is in four movements titled *An
Old Dance, An Old Song, Scherzo* and *Dance*.

Kammel, Antonin   Bohemian   1730-1787
Serenata in G Major; MMM; 0101/2
Kammel, writing in a style very similar to J.C. Bach, composed more
than forty sets of instrumental music, mostly for amateurs.

Karganov
Scherzino, Op. 21 #6; Parfrey; KED; 1111; C/D

Karkoff, Maurice   Swedish   1927-
Divertimento, Op. 141; 1978; SMI; 8 mins; 0022
Karkoff's teachers included Blomdahl, Larsson, Koch, Holmboe, Joli-
vet and Vogel. His music reflects his interest in many cultures.

Kauder, Hugo   Austrian/American   1888-1972
Quartet; SEE; 0111/1
Kauder's music is contrapuntal, with canonic devices and conservative
harmonies. He wrote music for orchestra and chamber groups.

Kay, Norman Forber   English   1929-
Miniature Quartet; c1959; ESM; 8.5 mins; 1011/1; D
Kay studied at the Royal Conservatory of Music and wrote music for
ensembles, chorus, television and opera. This work includes three
movements titled *Moderato e marcato, Lento* and *Fughetta.*

Keldorfer, Robert   Austrian   1901-1980
Quartet; c1978; MFS; 1111
Keldorfer studied with Prohaska, Springer and Stohr at the Vienna
Academy of Music. He wrote music for opera, concertos, chorus and
chamber ensembles.

Kelley, Edgar Stillman   American   1857-1944
He Is Born!; SHA; 1110/1; C/D
Kelley's works show good craftsmanship, inventiveness and unique or
fanciful touches that add interest to his otherwise orthodox musical
style derived from German academic concepts.

Kingman, Daniel   American   20th C.
Four Miniatures; WIM; 1111; D

Knight, Tim   English   20th C.
Short Woodwind Suite; ESM; 1111; B/C

The Frog's March; ESM; 1111; B/C

Koetsier, Jan   Dutch   1911-
Pezzi #3; DNA; 1111; C
A pianist and conductor now living in Munich, Koetsier writes in the
Neo-Classic tradition of northern Europe. His music is influenced by
Hindemith and is characterized by solid craftsmanship and invention.

Kuhnau, Johann   German   1660-1722
Allegretto Grazioso; Cafarella; Volkwein; 1111
Kuhnau studied at the Kreuzschule in Dresden. He wrote primarily
sacred cantatas and keyboard music. This is an arrangement of a movement from *Piano Sonatina, Op. 55.*

Kurka, Robert   American   1921-1957
Moravian Folk Songs Op. 18; 1951; SCI; 4 mins; 1111; B/C
Kurka studied composition with Luening and Milhaud. His music uses
Neo-Classical forms with harmonic dissonance. These six folk songs
are good for student groups.

Lajtha, Laszlo   Hungarian   1892-1963
Quatre Hommages; 1946; LDA; 1111; D
Lajtha studied with Viktor Herzfeld at the Academy of Music in Budapest. He was one of the leading figures of the folk music research movement initiated by Kodaly and Bartok. This work requires clarinet in A.

Lange, Friedrich   Norwegian   1861-1939
Pastoral Quartett; ESM; 0301; D
Lange's influence in Norway is still noticeable, since many of today's teachers had a personal relationship with Lange. English horn is required.

Lauber, Joseph   Swiss   1864-1952
Quatre Intermezzi; ESM; 13 mins; 1111
After studies with Hegar, Rheinberger, Massenet and Diemer, Lauber taught at the Zurich Conservatory. He wrote music for orchestra, opera, oratorio and chamber groups. This work requires English horn.

Leeuwen, Ary van
Turkey in the Straw; ESM; 2020; C/D

Lehar, Franz   Austrian   1870-1948
Romance from "The Merry Widow"; Stewart; 1910; TRI; 8 mins; 1111

Lemeland, Aubert   French   1932-
Idealide, Op. 111; 1981; BIL; 9.5 mins; 1111
Lemeland's works comprise more than a hundred pieces of chamber, instrumental and orchestral music. This work is based on a unique and rhythmic theme, played "cantando" in the slow sequences. These contrasts clearly define the work's form, its spontaneity and the sharpness of its development.

Leonard, Beldon   20th C.
Nightfall; c1978; 2 mins; 1111; B/C

Palm Desert Nocturne; 1111; B/C

Levi, William
Dance of the Reeds; WIL; 1021

Lewin
Petits Fours; ESM; flexible instrumentation; C

Lidarti, Christian Joseph   Austrian   1730-1793
Quartet in C Major; ESM; 3001; D

Lilja, Bernhard   Swedish   1895-1984
Liten Humoresk; SMI; 5 mins; 1111

Liljeholm, Thomas   Swedish   1944-
Texture I; 1987; SMI; 8.5 mins; 1111

Limmert, Erich   1909-
Suite en Miniature; 1962; MOS; 1111; D

Lipatti, Dinu   Romanian   1917-1950
Aubade for Woodwind Quartet; c1958; BBL; 18 mins; 1111

Lorenzo, Leonardo de   Italian/American   1875-1962
First Quattro Virtuosi, Divertimento Fantastico,   Op. 80; PTE;   12
mins; 1111; D
Lorenzo studied at the Naples Conservatory and performed on flute with
a variety of orchestras including the New York Philharmonic, Los Angeles Philharmonic and Minneapolis Symphony. He later taught at
Eastman and then settled in California in 1935.

Luening, Otto   American   1900-1996
Bass with the Delicate Air; 1940; GLM; 2 mins; 1111; C
Luening has been an influential musical force for most of the twentieth-
century. His diverse musical activities have included composition,
conducting, writing and teaching. This is a single-movement work
with an ostinato pattern throughout.

Lunden, Lennart   Swedish   1914-1966
Serenade; SMI; 15 mins; 1111
Doubling on English horn is required.

Maasz, Gerhard   German   1906-1984
Finkenschlag Variations; c1956; SIK; 1111

Majo, Ernest   German   1916-
Suite; MFS; 0021/1; C

Malipiero, Gian Francesco   Italian   1882-1973
Sonata A Quattro; 1954; UNE; 14 mins; 1111; C
Although less known than Casella and Pizzetti, Malipiero was the most original and inventive Italian composer of his generation. He wrote hundreds of works for orchestral, chorus, piano, vocal and chamber ensembles. This single-movement work is of moderate difficulty and should be accessible to advanced high school players.

Manson, Eddy Lawrence   American   1922-
Fugue for Woodwinds; c1958; AMP; 1111

Marais, Marin   French   1656-1728
Le Basque; INT; 1 min; 1111
Marais was the leading figure in the French school of composers in Paris during the late seventeenth and early eighteenth centuries. This famous one-minute encore piece was used by virtuoso Dennis Brain, who called it "a little French dance which also happens to be the shortest piece I know." Also available for wind or brass quintet, this version features the flute.

Marez Oyens, Tera de   Dutch   1932-
Suite de Petit Prince; DNA; 5 mins; 1111
Marez Oyens studied piano, violin, composition and conducting at the Amsterdam Conservatory. She wrote music for piano, chamber groups and chorus.

Marshall, Jack   1921-1973
Goldrush Suite; SHA; 1111

Marvia, Einari   Finnish   1915-
Kvartetti; FMC; 17 mins; 1111
Marvia won the Award of Honor from the Foundation for Support of Finnish Music and Finland's Cross of Freedom. He wrote music for ensembles, vocal solos and chorus.

Mascagni, Pietro   Italian   1863-1945
Intermezzo from *Cavalleria Rusticana*; 1890; 1111
Mascagni, best known for his opera *Cavalleria Rusticana*, wrote primarily for voice but did complete a number of works for orchestra, piano and chamber ensembles.

Mason, Daniel Gregory   American   1873-1953
Haul Away—Three Shanties; OPM; flexible instrumentation; B
Mason, a student of Paine and Chadwick, wrote in a traditional style with expansive melodies, conservative harmonies and calculated dialogue between instrumental voices. In this work there are various combinations possible using flute, oboe, clarinet, bassoon and horn.

Mazellier, Jules   French   1879-1959
Fugues pour Instruments a Vent Sur Des Sujets Donnes; c1954; LEM; 1111

McBride, Robert   American   1911-
Interwoven; ACA; 0022
A prolific composer of more than 1,000 works in various genres, McBride frequently used American or Mexican themes with a jazz influence.

Television Special; ACA; 0022

McClellan, Randall   American   1940-
Three Modes; WIM; 1030; D
McClellan, a student of Dahl and Huston, received music degrees from the Cincinnati College-Conservatory of Music and University of Southern California. Bass clarinet is required in this work.

McKay, Francis Howard   American   1901-
Fugue #4; BHM; 1111
A native of Washington State, McKay studied at the Eastman School and the University of Washington. He taught in the music departments of the University of Oregon, Oregon College, Washington State University and University of Southern California. McKay composed numerous instrumental solos and ensembles in addition to concert band works.

Musette; BHM; 1111; B/C

Three Nautical Characters; c1956; BHM; 2 mins; 1111; B/C
The three movements are titled *Sailor Jack, A Mermaid* and *Barnacle Bill*. There is an optional French horn part to make this a quintet and bass clarinet may replace bassoon.

Melkich, Dimitri Russian   1885-1943
Quartett, Op. 19; c1934; BHI; 1111
His music, written in archaic Russian modes, shows the influence of his teacher, Yavorsky. He wrote works for orchestra and chamber groups.

Mendelssohn, Felix   German   1809-1847
Prelude, Op. 37/2; Heim; 1837; KED; 1021; C
Mendelssohn's music emphasizes clarity and adherence to the Classical tradition.

Mercadante, Saverio   Italian   1795-1870
Quartet #1 in F Major; McAlister; MMP; 1011/1; C/D
Best known for his operas, Mercadante studied composition with Zingarelli and later became the director of the Naples Conservatory. In addition to operas, he wrote music for ballet, sacred works, orchestra and chamber ensembles.

Migot, Georges   French   1891-1976
Three Pastorales; c1972; TRA; 1111; D
Migot was an accomplished composer, poet and visual artist. His music uses diatonic melodies but avoids any suggestion of definite tonality. The flowing quality of Migot's music is in the tradition of Debussy and Couperin.

Mikiten, D.
Most Wonderful Christmas; KED; 1120; B/C
The oboe part could be played on flute. Bass clarinet is required.

Waltz for Christmas Day; KED; 1120; B/C
The oboe part could be played on flute. Bass clarinet is required.

Wonder of Christmas; KED; 1120; B/C
The oboe part could be played on flute. Bass clarinet is required.

Miletic, Miroslav   Croatian   1925-
Folk Music Designs; CMI; 1111
Miletic founded the renowned Pro Arte String Quartet which specializes in performances of modern music.

Mills, N.   English   20th C.
Cornish Pastyche; ESM; flexible instrumentation; B
This woodwind version is compatible with the brass version.

Mirandolle, Ludovicus   1904-
Quartet; BVP; 1111

Miscellaneous
American Popular Songs; EAM; 1111

Blackbird Pie; Allen; PRC; flexible instrumentation
This can be played with any three treble instruments and a bass instrument.

Christmas Carols for Woodwind Quartet; Conley; KED; 1111; C
Selections include *Joy to the World, Adeste Fideles, He Is Born, The First Noel, O Little Town of Bethlehem, Hark the Herald Angels Sing, We Wish You a Merry Christmas, Deck the Halls, The Wassail Song, Jingle Bells, Angels We Have Heard on High, Silent Night.*

Christmas Dinner; McCubbin; PRC; 1111

Christmas Jazz Medley; Niehaus; KED; 1120
This requires bass clarinet and the oboe part could be played on flute.

First Concert Book; Kenny; CMU; 1111; B/C

La Renaissance; Stone; BHI; flexible; B
This collection includes songs and dances by French and German composers of the sixteenth and seventeenth centuries. Various instrumentations are available using oboe, clarinet, bassoon, horn and bass clarinet.

Music from the Court of the Sun King; ESM; 0301; C
English horn is required.

Renaissance Works; Mariassy; ESM; 1111; B
This arrangement features music by Haussmann, Banchieri, and others from this period. There are alternate flute and clarinet parts to replace oboe.

The Minstrel's Gallery; Stone; BHI; flexible instrumentation; A/B
There are parts for oboe, clarinet and horn in varying combinations.

Turkey in the Straw; Christensen; KED; 2020; C/D

Moravec, Paul   American   1957 -
Woodwind Quartet; 1987; SUB; 8 mins; 1111
Moravec, a graduate of Harvard and Columbia University, has composed more than sixty chamber, lyric and orchestral works as well

as several film scores, music theater pieces, and electro-acoustic works. His distinguished career includes the Prix de Rome (1984-85), fellowships from the National Endowment for the Arts and Rockefeller Foundation.

Morley, Thomas   English   1557-1638
Madrigal Magic; Hicks; PRC; 1111
Morley, an influential composer, music editor, and theorist, wrote service music, anthems, psalms and Latin Motets as well as more than 100 madrigals and lighter secular works.

Mourant, Walter   American   1910-
Hallowe'en Dance; 1973; AMC; 3 mins; 1111

Mouret, Jean Joseph   French   1682-1738
Sinfonies de Fanfares; 1729; 1111
Mouret studied at the Notre Dame des Doms choir school in Avignon and served as the composer/director of the New Italian Theatre for two decades. These works are taken from *Premiere Suite* and *Second Suite*.

Moyse, Marcel   French   1889-1984
Suite in C Major; SMC; 2011
Moyse, father of Louis Moyse, is best known as a flutist and composer of flute studies.

Mozart, Wolfgang Amadeus   Austrian   1746-1791
Adagio and Allegro, K. 594 in F Minor; Munclinger; 1790; IMC; 1111; C
Mozart was a musical genius whose works in virtually every genre are unmatched in lyrical beauty and rhythmic variety. Subtitled *The Musical Clock*, this work was originally written for mechanical organ.

Adagio in B Minor, K.540; Stallman; 1788; IMC; 7 mins; 1011/1; C
The flute part could be done on oboe. This piece was originally written for piano.

Adagio in C Major, K.580A; c1959; SIK; 6 mins; 0121, 1021, 0101/2; C
This work was originally for English horn and strings.

Allegro, K.402; CON; 1111

Alleluia; Leonard; c1974; 1111; C

Andante and Menuetto from String Quartet #21; Langenus; CFI; 1111; C

Andante in F Major, K.616; Munclinger; c1963; KAL, IMC; 1111 or 2020; C
This piece was originally for mechanical organ,.

Cassazione; Andraud; SMC; 0111/1; C
This work was discovered in 1910 and revised by Albert Andraud. The oboe part could be played on flute.

Conzertantes Quartett; CFI; 0111/1

Divertimento #11 in D Major, K.251; Richter, Gee; c1951, c1971; KAL, CPP; 27 mins; 1111; C

Eine Kleine Nachtmusik, K.525; Kenny; 1787; EUL; 5.5 mins; flexible instrumentation; C/D
This is an arrangement of the first movement from this famous work originally written for strings.

Fantasia in F Minor, K.608; Munclinger; 1791; IMC; 1111; C
This single-movement work in three sections was originally for mechanical organ.

Fugue, K.546; CON; 1111

Divertimento; NOV; 1111

Non Piu Andrai; Kenny; EUL; flexible instrumentation; C
This arrangement offers multiple parts on flute, clarinet, oboe, saxophone and bassoon for each voice. There is another version for two flutes, three clarinets and one bassoon.

Quartet in A Major, K.298; Lentz; TMP; 12 mins; 1111; B/C
This was originally for flute and strings.

Quartet in G Major, K.387; Kraber; 1782; IMC; 29 mins; 2011; C/D
This was originally written for string quartet.

Toy Symphony; ESM; 1120; D
There is also an arrangement for four clarinets.

Two Pieces Arranged for Winds; UNE; Variable instrumentation

Mussorgsky, Modest   Russian   1839-1881
Mushrooms; Skolnik; ESM; 1021; B/C
Mussorgsky is considered one of the most important and influential composers of the Russian Nationalist School.

Nemiroff, Isaac   American   1912-1977
Four Treble Suite; c1958; MMM; 1120; C
Nemiroff studied at the Cincinnati Conservatory and New York College of Music. Flute could be used in place of oboe part.

Nicholes
Ril Dryslwyn a Bro Pheilffordd; ESM; 1111; B/C
The oboe and bassoon parts could be played on clarinet and bass clarinet respectively.

Niehaus, Lennie   American   1929-
Christmas Jazz Medley; ESM; 1120; C
Niehaus is best known for his music written for films including an Emmy for his score to *Lush Life*. Bass clarinet is required.

Daystar; KED; 2020; B
Bass clarinet is required.

Ladybug Blues; c1983; KED; 4 mins; 2020 or 1120; C
Bass clarinet is required.

Nielsen, Carl   Danish   1865-1931
Humorous Bagatelles, Op. 11; Mann; 1894-97; CHE; 7 mins; 1021; C/D
Nielsen studied at the Royal Conservatory in Copenhagen where he studied with Rosenhoff. While his early music shows the influence of Grieg, Brahms and Liszt, his later works have more dissonance though often utilizing a diatonic, folk song quality. Originally written for piano, there is also a wind quintet version of this work.

Nilsson, Bo   Swedish   1937-
Deja-Vu; 1967; HAN, SMI; 6 mins; 1111
Nilsson is considered one of the most gifted Swedish composers of postwar years. His works are built on precise quasi-mathematical, serial principles.

Kvartet; 1978; SMI; 1111

Nowak, Lionel   American   1911-
Suite for Four Wind Instruments; ACA; 1110/1
Nowak studied composition with Elwell, Sessions and Porter at the Cleveland Institute of Music. He later taught at Converse College, Syracuse University and Bennington College.

Orland, Henry   1918-
Fugue; SEE; 1111

Pacchioni, Giorgio   Italian   1947-
Sonata #1 in F Major; M21; 11.5 mins; 1111
Currently professor of recorder at the Conservatory of Bologna, Italy,
Pacchioni has devoted himself to musicological studies of the theory
and practice of Renaissance and Baroque music. In this Neo-Baroque
work there are three movements with a strong feel of counterpoint, but
not in the traditional fast-slow-fast form.

Padovano, Andrea   1920-
Rondo; c1966; PTE, ZAN; 7 mins; 0111/1

Paganini, Niccolo   Italian   1782-1840
Paganini Variations; Richards; PRC; 1111; D
Paganini, a legendary violinist, wrote numerous works for orchestra,
chamber ensembles and violin concertos.

Palestrina, Giovanni Pierluigi   Italian   1525-1594
Ricercare; Catelinet; PTE; 0111/1
A contemporary of Byrd and Lassus, Palestrina is considered one of
the foremost composers of his time. He wrote in a polyphonic style of
the Franco-Flemish school.

Parchman, Gen. Louis   1929-
Sonata for Woodwind Quartet; SEE; 1111

Parfrey, Raymond   English   1928-
A Couple of Moods; ESM; 1021; C
Parfrey was a choirboy for five years before being drafted into the army
where he learned to play the standard popular tunes of the day from his
fellow servicemen. After leaving the military, he studied with Alan
Bush and began writing music for wind ensembles, choir, piano, organ
and string orchestra.

Four Sketches; ESM; 1021; B/C
Bass clarinet could replace bassoon.

One Plus Three; ESM; 1030; C

Out of Doors; ESM; 2020; C

Three Short Pieces; ESM; 1021; C

Three Show Tunes; c1981; KED, ESM; 5 mins; 1111 or 2020; B/C
Woodwind Quartet; ESM; 1021; C

Pasquini, Bernardo   Italian   1637-1710
Sonata II Tempo di Ballo; Rocereto; Volkwein; 1111
Pasquini, a highly regarded keyboard player, was primarily known for his keyboard studies and variations.

Paulson, Gustaf   Swedish   1898-1966
Liten Serenade, Op. 22; 1939; SMI; 8 mins; 1111
Paulson, a prolific composer of music for orchestra, voice and chamber groups, shows the influence of Sibelius and Nielsen in his music.

Quartet, Op. 73; 1953; SMI; 1111

Paulus, Stephen Harrison   American   1949-
Wind Suite; c1977; SHA; 1111; D
Paulus, a student of Paul Fetler, received B.A., M.A. and Ph.D. degrees from the University of Minnesota and in 1983 became a composer-in-residence of the Minnesota Orchestra. He later served as composer-in-residence of the Atlanta Symphony and Dale Warland Singers and has had numerous commissions from major symphonies.

Pethel, Stan   American   20th C.
Harvest Blessing; SHA; 2020; C
The flute parts could be performed on oboe.

Petyrek, Felix   Czech   1892-1951
Gute Nacht, O Welt; c1962; DBM; 0111/1
Petyrek, a student of Schreker, used advanced contemporary techniques in his music.

Pillin, Boris   American   1940-
Scherzo for Woodwind Quartet; 1969; WIM; 1111; D
Pillin received degrees from the University of California in Los Angeles and the University of Southern California and is perhaps best known for his book about Schoenberg's music. He has written music for orchestra, piano, and chamber ensembles. Regarding his music, Pillin states: "I feel that my music in imbued with an urban quality, reflecting the complexity and multi-faceted moods of the big city, often in a jazz-like manner."

Pisk, Paul Amadeus   Austrian/American   1893-1990
Elegy and Scherzo, Op. 70 #2; 1951; AMC; 0121
Pisk describes his style as "linear, not atonal but free in tonal centers
and using the traditional structures and motivic development."

Little Woodwind Music; 1945; AMP; 0121

Placheta, Hugo
Quartet, Op. 10; c1963; DBM; 0111/1

Platz, Robert H.   German   1951-
Zusammenfinden; ESM; flexible instrumentation; E
Any three or four woodwind instruments could be used.

Pleyel, Ignaz   Austrian   1757-1831
Quartet in E-Flat Major; MRI; 1021; B/C
Pleyel studied with Haydn but is perhaps best known for his
manufacturing of pianos. A prolific composer, he wrote symphonies,
symphonie concertantes, concertos and chamber music.

Poot, Marcel   Belgian   1901-1988
Music for Wind Quartet; c1971; PRC; 1111; D/E
Poot studied piano with Arthur De Greef, a close friend of Grieg, and
composition with Mortelmans, Gilson and Dukas. Poot's music is
strongly rhythmic and basically tonal, brilliant and vigorous. His
works include several important orchestral works and many compositions for piano.

Praag, Henri C. Van   Netherlands   1894-1968
Quartet; DNA; 1111; C

Prokofiev, Serge   Russian   1891-1953
Fleeting Moments, Op. 22; CFI; 1111
Prokofiev studied with Rimsky-Korsakov, Lyadov and Tcherepnin at
the St. Petersburg Conservatory. His music also shows the influence of
Scriabin, Debussy and Strauss. He wrote a great quantity of music for
opera, ballet, film, orchestra, chamber ensembles and piano.

Visions Fugitives; 1915-1917; MMM; 1111
Originally written for piano, this work is like a quick drawing by a
master artist in their vivid expression. It uses a combination of Prokofiev's favorite compositional devices.

Provinciali, Emilio
Danse Villageoise; PRC; 2 mins; 1111; C

Prowse
Folk Song Suite; ESM; 1111; C

Purcell, Henry   English   1659-1695
Fantasia #1; Schmidt; WIM; 0021/1; C
Purcell was one of the greatest composers of the Baroque period.

Ralston, Alfred   American   1875-1952
Nocturne Sentimentale; ESM; 1021; C
The bassoon part could be performed on bass clarinet.

Sailors Hornpipe Fugues; ESM; 1021; C
Bassoon part could be played on bass clarinet.

Rameau, Jean-Philippe   French   1683-1764
Rigadon; Dawn; c1955; BHI; 1111
Rameau, best known for his operatic works, is known for his expressive melodies and rich harmonies.

Raphael, Gunther   German   1903-1960
Quartet, Op. 61; 1945; BAR; 15 mins; 1111
Raphael studied composition in Berlin with Robert Kahn, then later taught at the Hochschule für Musik in Cologne. He wrote five symphonies, several concertos and numerous chamber music pieces.

Raphling, Sam   American   1910-1988
Square Dance; c1952; ESM; 2 mins; 1111; C
Raphling has composed numerous works for opera, orchestra, concertos, piano and chamber ensembles.

Reger, Max   German   1873-1916
Abschied; Schmidt; c1966; WIM; 2 mins; 0111/1; B/C
Reger was a student of Hugo Riemann at the Sondershausen Conservatory and later at the Wiesbaden Conservatory. His prolific output includes music for orchestra, voice, chamber, organ and piano.

Fugue Op. 56, #2; Brown; WIM; 1111; C

Regner, Hermann   1928-
Serenade; c1959; PTE; 0111/1

Reicha
Variations for Wind Quartet; ESM; 1111 or 1021; C/D

Rekola, Jukka   Swedish   1948-
Blaskvartet; 1978; SMI; 0111/1

Renzi, Armondo   Italian   1915-
Cinque Bagatelle; de Santis; 1111

Riegger, Wallingford   American   1885-1961
Three Canons for Woodwinds, Op. 9; 1932; NME; 1111
Riegger has won numerous awards and grants including the
Koussevitzky and New York Music Critics' Circle. He studied at the
Institute of Musical Arts (now the Juilliard School) and then pursued
post graduate work at Berlin's Hochschule für Musik. His composi-
tional style includes twelve-tone techniques and atonality within more
traditional Neo-Classic structures.

Riisager, Knudage   Danish   1897-1974
Quartet, Op. 40A; 1941; PTE; 1111

Rivier, Jean   French   1896-1987
Trois Espaces Sonores; 1979; ESM; 1111

Roeckel, Joseph Leopold   1838-1923
Air du Dauphin; Leonard; c1974; CPP; 1111; B

Rossini, Gioachino   Italian   1792-1868
Andante and Variations; 1804; HEU, PRC; 1011/1; C
Recognized as one of the greatest Italian composers of his time, he is
best known for his operas.

Six Quartets; Berr/Zachert; 1804; EAM; 1011/1; C/D
The first five quartets were originally for two violins, cello and bass.
They were subsequently renumbered and transcribed for wind quartet by
Berr. The last of these quartets is the composer's work for wind quartet
sometimes listed as *Andante and Theme with Variations in F Major.*

Roy, Klaus George   Austrian/American   1924-
Sterlingman Suite; c1969; PRC; 1111; D
Roy studied at Boston University and Harvard. He is best known as a
writer and teacher. His works include music for chamber opera, orchestra and chamber ensembles.

Rubbra, Edmund   English   1901-1986
Notturno; c1962; ESM; 2110; C
This work requires piccolo, and bassoon may be substituted for clarinet.

Runnstrom, William   Swedish   1951-
Forspel til Scen 5, Op. 6; 1980; SMI; 10 mins; 1111

Ryker, Robert
Four Elizabethan Pieces, Op. 7; 1965; BML; 2020; C

Sabatini, Guglielmo   1877-1949
Puppet Waltz; COR; 0111/1

Sadler, Helmut   German   1921-
Quartettino; c1967; PTE; 1111

Sagvik, Stellan   Swedish   1952-
Liten Danssvit, Op. 40; 1974; SMI; 5.5 mins; 2110
Piccolo is required.

Salzedo, Carlos   French/American   1885-1961
Bailbles; ESM; 0301
English horn is required. There are alternate parts for bass oboe and oboe d'amore.

Sarkozy, Istvan   Hungarian   1920-
Salmo e Gioco: Quartetto per Fiati di Legno; 1970; EMB; 1111
Sarkozy studied composition with Kodaly, Farkas and Viski at the Budapest Academy of Music and was later appointed to that faculty.

Saunders, Rosamund
The Imp (A Whimsical Piece); CFI; flexible instrumentation
Various instrumentation options using flute, oboe, clarinet, bassoon and bass clarinet may be used.

Savina, Carlo   Italian   20th C.
Una Musica per Suonare Insieme; ESM; 1111; C

Scarlatti, Domenico   Italian   1685-1757
Scarlattiana; Rosenthal; WIM; 1111; D
A prolific composer, Scarlatti composed over 500 works for solo keyboard. The oboe and bassoon parts have optional flute and bass clarinet parts respectively.

Sonata VIII Pastorale in F Major; Rocereto; c1931; Volkwein; 1111

Scarmolin, Anthony Louis   Italian/American   1890-1969
Danse Grotesque; c1953; BHM; 1111; B/C
After studies at the New York College of Music and serving in the U.S. Army in WW 1, Scarmolin wrote more than 200 works for opera, orchestra and chamber groups.

Will-O'-the-Wisp; c1956; BHM; 1111; B

Schenk, Johann Baptist   Austrian   1753-1836
Quartet in F Major; c1968; DBM; 1201; C/D
Schenk, primarily known for his stage works, studied with Wagenseil in Vienna. This work requires two English horns instead of oboes.

Schickele, Peter   American   1935-
Seven Bagatelles; 1959; EVI, PRC; 6 mins; 1111; B/C
There are few areas of music in which Peter Schickele has not been involved. In a long and active career he has written and arranged for classical, jazz, rock, and folk ensembles. He studied composition with Persichetti, Bergsma, Roy Harris and Milhaud. The movements of this work are titled *Three-Legged March, Serenade, Waltzing Piece, Country Song, Game, City Song* and *River*.

Schmidt, William   American   1926-
Three Liturgical Preludes; c1975; WIM; 1111; C/D
Schmidt, best known as a saxophonist and music publisher, writes in a compositional style influenced by Halsey Stevens and Ingolf Dahl. The three preludes are titled *Tribulations, Wondrous Love* and *Aberystuyth*.

Schneider, Willy   1907-1983
Kleines Quartett; MOS; 1110/1

Schubert, Franz   Austrian   1797-1828
Ballet Music 1 from Rosamond; Schmidt; WIM; 0111/1; C
Schubert produced great masterpieces in virtually every field of composition. His music is rich in melody and expressive harmony.

Hirtenmelodien aus Rosamunde, Op. 26; BKH; 0021/1

Impromptu Theme and Theme from Trout Quintet (D667); Sutton; 1819; 1120; B
Bass clarinet is required.

Six Antiphonal Choruses; Schmidt; WIM; 0111/1; C

Six Schubert Waltzes; Feldsher; TMP; 1111; B/C

Three Schubert Dances; ESM; flexible instrumentation; B/C
This arrangement includes interchangeable parts for flute, oboe, clarinet, horn and bassoon in various combinations.

Schumann, Robert   German   1810-1856
Album for the Young; Winn; PRC; 1111
Schumann was a central figure of the Romantic period.

Landliches Lied and Jagerliedchen; Loffler; ESM; 1111

Suite from "Kinderszenen" (Scenes from Childhood), Op. 15; North; 1838; INT; 0111/1; C
These five selections from Schumann's famous piano pieces include *Curious Story, Blindman's Bluff, Perfectly Contented,* the famous *Reverie (Traumerei)* and *At the Fireside.*

Schurink, Bart   Netherlands   1947-1979
Quartet; DNA; 8 mins; 1111
Alto flute, English horn and bass clarinet are required.

Schwegler, Johann   1759-1817
Quartet in E-Flat Major; WIM; 2000/2; D

Schweinitz, Wolfgang von   German   1953-
Adagio, Op. 22; 1983; BHI; 6 mins; 0111/1
This work requires English horn and basset horn.

Schweizer, Klaus   1939-
Konversationsszene; BHI; 10 mins; 1111
This work requires E-flat clarinet.

Sehlbach, Oswald Erich   German   1898-1985
Quartet, Op. 91; c1962; MOS; 1111
Sehlback, winner of the 1952 Arts Prize of the City of Wuppertal, studied with Krehl and Karg-Elert at the Leipzig Conservatory. He served on the staff at Essen Folkwangschule teaching composition and counterpoint. His style is similar to Schoeck and Hindemith, but still very much his own.

Seiber, Mátyás   English   1905-1960
Dance Suite; de Haan; ESM; 1111; C
There is an alternate saxophone part in place of bassoon.

Seyfrit, Michael Eugene   American   1947-
Portal; AMC; 0211
English horn is required.

Siegmeister, Elie   American   1909-1991
Ten Minutes for Four Players; 1989; CFI; 10 mins; 1111
Siegmeister's music shows a strong American folk identity and his
devotion to Nationalism written in a modern romantic style. *Ten
Minutes* began as a single movement work called *Four Minutes* and
was later expanded to the current three-movement work that
incorporates fugato style, a blues-like melody and a virtuosic finale.

Singer, Lawrence   American   1940-
New Dimensions; SUV; 1111

Sitsky, Larry   Australian   1934-
Woodwind Quartet; !963; BHI; 1111
Perhaps best-known as a concert pianist, Sitsky wrote music for opera,
orchestra and chamber groups.

Sontag, Herbert O.
Quartet on Old Tunes for Woodwinds; c1950; KAL, PRC; 1111

Sousa, John Philip   American   1854-1932
Washington Post March; Holcombe; 1889; MPI; 3 mins; 1111; C
An effective arrangement for wind quartet, this well known work is
great for pops concerts.

Sperry
Chorale and Fugue for Four; TMP; 1111; B

Spinner, Leopold   Polish   1906-1980
Sonatina for Four Wind Instruments, Op. 23; 1971; BHI; 11 mins;
0111/1

Stahl, Sonya Leonore   American   1981-
March of the Penguins; M21; 3 mins; 0220
Stahl, a versatile young violinist and composer, is currently a student
at the University of Florida. Regarding this work, she states on the
score: "The penguins march to the cliff, dive into the sea for a little

ragtime swimming, then head out of the water again and march away
down the icy shores of Antarctica. Lots of echoing because penguins
aren't very creative."

Stamitz, Carl   Bohemian   1745-1801
Quartet in E-Flat, Op. 8 #2; Schuller, Weigelt; 1785; MMM, ESM;
10 mins; 0111/1; C
Stamitz was considered an exceptional violist and wrote a large number
of compositions for orchestra, sinfonie concertante, concertos and chamber ensembles. His style is outstanding for its melodic wealth, formal
elegance and harmonious tonal beauty.

Starer, Robert   Austrian/Israeli   1924-
Woodwind Quartet; C1972; MCA; 1111
Starer studied with Partos and Copland.

Stark
Serenade, Op. 55 ; SCH; 0022; C/D
There is an alternate bass clarinet part for the second bassoon.

Steiner, Heinrich   1903-
Ich Hatt; Einen Kameraden; BBM; 0022

Stevens, Halsey   American   1908-
Eight Pieces; 1966; AMC; 13 mins; 1111
Stevens studied with Berwald and Bloch and later taught at the University of Southern California in Los Angeles. A prolific composer, Stevens has written for a wide variety of choral and instrumental combinations. His music features vigorous rhythms, clear tonal centers and
brilliant writing.

Stolzel, Gottfried Heinrich   German   1690-1749
Adagio; CON; 1111
Primarily known for his operas and vocal works, Stolzel also wrote a
large quantity of instrumental music in traditional Classic style.

Storgards, John   Finnish   20th C.
Hommage to Shostakovich; 1979; FMC; 1111

Strang, Gerald   American   1908-1983
Divertimento; AMC; flexible instrumentation
Strang was among the early California modernists, headed by Henry
Cowell. After teaching at several California universities, Strang founded

the music department at California State University at Northridge. His music, while using new resources available in acoustics, electronics and computers, is still clearly formal in structure.

Strauss, Johann   Austrian   1825-1899
A Suite from the Bat; Schmidt; PRC; 0111/1; C/D
Johann Strauss, the most famous of the Strauss musical family, is known for his inspired melodic invention and wide, sweeping melodies in dance music.

Stravinsky, Igor   Russian/American   1882-1971
Pastorale; Maganini, Schmidt; 1933; EDM, WIM; 1 min; 1111, 0111/1 or 0211; C
Stravinsky's music went through several changes, often startling and sometimes disturbing to the public. His early years show the Russian influence, then Neo-Classical which eventually evolved into serial techniques in his later years. The *Pastorale* was originally a vocal work and was arranged by the composer for voice with winds and violin with winds. There is an alternate version using English horn instead of flute.

Stroud, Richard   1929-
Sketch for Woodwind; c1969; SEE; 1111

Sutermeister, Heinrich   Swiss   1910-
Serenade #15; EAM; 1111
Sutermeister studied with Orff and Courvoisier and later achieved international renown as a composer of operas that are dramatically effective and melodically pleasing.

Swack, Irwin   American   20th C.
Divertimento; ISM; 21 mins; 0111/1
Swack's music shows the influence of popular culture expressed through the idioms of jazz, dance and folk music. He attended the Cleveland Institute, Juilliard School, Northwestern University and Columbia University.

Swift, Frederic Fay   American   1907-
Folk Song Suite; KED; 1020/1; B
This work requires bass clarinet.

Tang, Jordan Cho-Tung   American   1948-
Little Suite; SEE; 15 mins; 1111

Tardos, Bela   Hungarian   1910-1966
Divertimento; 1963; EMB; 6 mins; 1111; C/D
Tardos studied with Kodaly at the Academy of Music in Budapest. He
wrote a great amount of choral music using Hungarian folk themes.

Tausch, Franz J.   German   1762-1817
Five Pieces, Op. 22; Beyer; c1994; KZE; 0021/1
Tausch was a violinist and clarinetist in the Mannheim Court Orchestra
at the early age of eighteen years. He later entered the Royal Prussian
service and founded a conservatory for wind instruments in 1805.
Among Tausch's compositions are concerti for clarinet and orchestra
and a variety of chamber works.

Tavener, John   English   1944-
Little Missenden; Calm; 1984; CHE; 0111/1
Tavener studied with Berkeley and Lumsdaine at RAM. Most of his
music is religious, influenced by late Stravinsky. He wrote many works
for chorus, chamber ensemble and opera.

Tchaikovsky, Peter   Russian   1840-1893
Chanson Triste; ESM; 1021; B
Tchaikovsky had a gift for beautiful melodies unmatched by his
contemporaries and wrote in every musical genre including stage, orchestra, chamber, piano and songs. He is widely regarded as the leading
nineteenth-century Russian composer. Bass clarinet may replace bassoon.

First Suite for the Young; ESM; 2020; B
This may also be performed with four flutes.

Folk Songs from Tchaikovsky; Erickson; BEL; 1111; B

Sarabande; von Kreisler; SMC; 0021/1; C

Second Suite for the Young; ESM; 2020; B
This may also be performed with four flutes.

Telemann, George Philip   German   1681-1767
Six Minuets; Polnauer; c1970; PRC; 1111, or 0211; B
Telemann was the most prolific composer of this time and is widely
regarded as Germany's leading composer in the early to mid-eighteenth
century.

Six Sonatas, Op. 2; Kynaston; ESM; 1120; C/D

Thybo, Leif   Danish   1922-
Non si Levava Ancor: Quartet; HAN; 1101/1
Thybo studied at the Conservatory in Copenhagen and the University
of Copenhagen, later teaching at both schools. This work requires
recorder in A instead of flute and English horn instead of oboe.

Trafford, Edmund   American   20th C.
Isolate/Set/Pattern; 1973; 4.25 mins; 1111

Tschemberdschi
Concertino; ESM; 1111; C/D

Turechek, Edward   1886-
Divertissement in F Minor; c1933; WBP; 1111

Tustin, Whitney   American   1907-
Improvisation #1; c1954; BHM; 1111; B/C

Uber, David   American   1921-
Novelette; c1995; ALE; 1111; C
Uber's career ranges from award-winning composer to trombonist,
college professor to band director. He was professor of music at Trenton
State College for more than three decades. He received both masters and
doctoral degrees from Columbia University. This delightful work for
wind quartet is written in a light, Neo-Romantic style. Each of the four
woodwinds has been given short solo motifs and there is a marked
degree of interchange in all parts.

Three Sketches; PIC; 1030
This work could also be performed with four flutes.

Vellere, Lucie   Belgium   1896-1966
Quartetto; ESM; 1111; D/E

Verdi, Giuseppe   Italian   1813-1901
Bella Figlia d'Amore; Benyas; INT; 0111/1
This is an arrangement of the famous *Rigoletto* quartet with bassoon
and horn sharing the Count's glorious tenor line.

Vidosic, Tihomil   Croatian   1902-1973
Istrian Scherzo; CMI; 0202
Vidosic was a student of Odak and Bersa at the Zagreb Academy of
Music. He was a teacher and conductor of military bands and choruses.

His music has a pleasing, communicative musical style that incorporates elements of Istrian folk music.

Villa-Lobos, Heitor   Brazilian   1887-1959
Quartet; 1928; PRC; 15 mins; 1111; D
Villa-Lobos, one of the most original composers of the twentieth century, had a remarkable ability to recreate native melodies and rhythms in large instrumental and choral forms. This work shows Villa-Lobos as the abstract musician and Classicist. Folk songs and dance are not apparent.

Three Fairy Tales; Schmidt; WIM; 0111/1; C

Vivaldi, Antonio   Italian   1678-1741
Allegro, Op. 8 #4a; CON; 1111
Vivaldi is considered the most original and influential Italian composer of his time.

Giga; Maganini; ESM; 1111; B

Sinfonia al Santo Sepulcro; ESM; 1111; B
The clarinet part could be played on horn.

Winter from *The Four Seasons*; Beal; ESM; 1111; B

Vogel, Vladimir   Russian/German   1896-1984
Horformen; 1974; GER; 12 mins; 1111
Vogel, a student of Heinz Tiessen and Busoni, taught at the Klindworth-Scharwenka Conservatory in Berlin and later moved to Switzerland. Much of his music is written in Neo-Classical format, but with some elements of serialism.

Voirin, J.
Deux Petites Pieces; ESM; 1111

Noctilugue, Batifolage; CHO; 1111

Vries Robbe, Willem de   Netherlands   1902-
Quartet; DNA; 15 mins; 1111

Walckiers, Eugene   French   1793-1866
Cinquieme Quatuor, Op. 7; ESM; 1011/1; D

Quartet Op. 7 #1; ESM; 1011/1; D

Quartet Op. 7 #3 ; ESM; 1101/1; D
There is an alternate clarinet part in place of oboe.

Walentynowicz, Wladyslaw   Polish   1902-
Small Quartet in Classical Style; c1958; PWM; 1111

Walshe, Michael   1932-
Holiday Pieces; c1989; ESM; 1111; C/D

Walthew, Richard   English   1872-1951
A Miniature Quartet; ESM; 1111; D

Warren, Elinor Remick   American   1900-1991
Three Pieces for Four; SCI; 1111; B
Warren was a student of Frank LaForge, Clarence Dickinson and Nadia Boulanger. Her music was inspired by the beauty of nature, particularly the West, where Warren lived and worked most of her life. She was a prolific composer with more than 200 works for orchestra, ensembles, voice and chorus.

Waters, Charles   English   1895-
Two Miniatures; PTE; 1111

Watson, Walter Robert   American   1933-
Scherzo for Winds; LMP; 1111

Weait, Christopher   Canadian   20th C.
Four Marches from the American Revolution; c1973; MMM; 2101; B/C
There are additional parts for flute/piccolo, oboe, English horn, clarinet and bass clarinet.

Weisgall, Hugo   Czech/American   1912-1997
Lines; PRC; 1111; C
Weisgall is one of America's most important opera composers. His early style used non-tonal classicism and later works used serialism and atonality.

Pastorale; 1966; PRC; 1 min; 1111; B/C
This work was originally written for a CBS documentary called *Of Heaven and Earth*.

Wenth, Johann N.   1745-1801
Quartetto Concertante; c1972; EKB; 11 mins; 0211; C/D
English horn is required. The clarinet part was originally for bass oboe.

Werner, Jean-Jacques   French   1935-
Quatre Chants Canadians; c1980; PRC; 6 mins; 1111; C
The four movements are titled *Je le mene bien, mon Devidoy; Marie-Calumet veut se marier; A la claire fontaine;* and *Vive la Canadian.*

Wetzel, Muller H.   1858-1928
A Gay Serenade; VLO; 0111/1; C
This work includes three dance movements titled *Polka, Waltz* and *March.*

White, Terrence E.   American   1953-
Quartet for Woodwinds; SEE; 1111

Wieslander, Ingvar   Swedish   1917-1963
Missologi: Liten Svit; SMI; 4 mins; 0022
Wieslander studied at the Royal Academy of Music in Stockholm and later served as the director of the Sundbyberg Orchestra Society and the Malmo Municipal Theatre. His music followed the Scandinavian Romantic style while maintaining Baroque structure.

Wilkinson, Philip G.
Suite for Woodwind Quartet; NOV; flexible instrumentation
This may be performed by varying combinations of flute, oboe, clarinet and bassoon.

Wilson, Keith
Nocturne; c1940; CPP; 1111

Winters, Geoffrey
Dance and Double-Hop; PRC; 1111
This work is included in a set of music by Jacob, Wright and Parfrey.

Wright, Geoffrey   English   20th C.
Various Original Pieces; PRC; 1111

Suite for Woodwinds; PRC; 1111
This piece is part of a set of music by Jacob, Parfrey and Winters.

Wuorinen, Charles   American   1938-
Sonatina; 1111
Wuorinen began playing piano and composing at age five and received
the Young Composers Award from the New York Philharmonic at age
sixteen. He taught at Columbia University and the Manhattan School
of Music. He won the Pulitzer Prize in 1970 for a work using
synthesized sound. His music is serialistic and shows the influence of
Schoenberg, Stravinsky and Varese.

Zaninelli, Luigi American   American   1932-
Burla and Variations; c1977; SHA; 10 mins; 1111; D
Zaninelli is a graduate of the Curtis Institute where he studied with
Menotti and   Martinu. He has over 200 published works. The
following description of this work is printed on the score: "This is a
work based on a short, puckish theme. The variations, which are
uninterrupted, begin with a graceful duet for clarinet and bassoon that
develops to include flute and oboe. A bassoon monologue follows,
preparing a pointilistic section, where the theme is viewed vertically
through staggered stacking. After a dialogue for flute and bassoon, an
agitated perpetual motion moves to an abrupt interruption. A myster-
ious waltz appears, evolving to a section of lyric polyphony. The perpetual motion returns with a calm but insistent oboe dominating the
texture. Following an abrupt cadence, the piece comes to a quiet close."

Zonn, Paul   American   1938-
Composition for Quartet; 1967; ACA; 17 mins; 1111

Divertimento #3; 1965; ACA; 5 mins; 0121
One bass clarinet required.

Zur, Menachem   Israeli   1942-
Concertino for Woodwind Quartet; SEE; 1111
Zur received a BM from Mannes College, an MFA from Sarah
Lawrence College and DMA from Columbia University. He has written
music for opera and chamber ensembles.

FIVE WINDS

Aspelmayr, Franz   Austrian   1728-1786
Partita in D Major; Pulkert; c1962; LKM; 0201/2; C
Aspelmayr (also spelled Aspelmeier) wrote music for ballet, melodrama, singspiel, orchestra and numerous chamber ensembes which contributed significantly to the early Viennese instrumental style.

Partita in F Major; Pulkert; c1962; LKM; 0201/2; C

Bach, Johann Christian   German   1735-1782
Wind Symphonies: Vol. 1 and 2; BBL; 0021/2
This traditional melody with a counter-melody and harmony, arranged for woodwind quartet, is suitable for contests or light programs.

Bach, Johann Sebastian   German   1685-1750
Quintet; Maros; ESM; 0021/2; C
The most famous member of the Bach family, Johann wrote primarily sacred music and works for keyboard. He also was a master organist and in-structor.

Four Quintets; Sadie; BHI, ESM; 0021/2; C

Beck, Jochen   1941-
Blaserquintett; MOS; 2011/1
Piccolo is required.

Beethoven, Ludwig van   German   1770-1827
Quintet in E-Flat Major; 1793; EAM; 0101/3; D

Menuetto, Op. 18 #5; Greist; MCA; 0101/3; B/C
Beethoven's early achievements show him to be extending the Viennese Classical tradition. Later he began to compose in an increasingly individual musical style, and at the end of his life he wrote his most sublime and profound works. This work requires bass clarinet.

Elf Modlinger Tanze; ESM; 1040; C

Bissell, Keith W.   Canadian   1912-1992
Folksong Suite; c1963; BHI; 4 mins; 1121 or 2030; B/C
Bissell studied composition with Leo Smith at the University of Toronto. He wrote music specifically intended for amateur performance.

Boellmann, Leon   French   1862-1897
Menuet Gothique; DUR; 0211/1
Boellmann studied organ with Gigout. He wrote music for orchestra, solo instruments, piano and chamber ensembles. Originally written for

organ, this is a movement from *Suite Gothique*. English horn is required.

Cowles
Suite Quintessential; ESM; 2030; C

Daquin, Louis-Claude   French   1694-1772
The Cuckoo; Gordon; c1933; WBP; 1121
Daquin, a student of Bernier, was regarded as the best organist of his generation.

Degastyne, Serge   1930-
Partita for Winds; FER; 2021

Dittersdorf, Karl Ditters von   Austrian   1739-1799
Three Partitas, # 2, #4 and #20; BKH, ESM; 0201/2; C/D
Dittersdorf wrote extensively in many genres including orchestral, chamber, keyboard, church, oratorio and opera. His music frequently has unexpected phrases, deceptive cadences and rhythmic surprises which display a wit very similar to Haydn. His music is largely diatonic and often include folk elements in the melodies.

Divertimento in B dur; Wojciechowski; c1954; SIK; 0221

Doppler, Franz   Polish/Hungarian   1821-1883
Bird of the Forest, Op. 21; c1984; MMM, ESM; 1000/4; D/E
Doppler's music combines the influences of Italian, Russian and Hungarian music. He wrote music for opera and ballet.

D'Rivera, Paquito   Cuban   20th C.
Alborada and Son; INT; 0302
These two movements from the *Aires Tropicales* provide a unique addition to the repertoire for double reed ensembles. English horn is required.

Druschetsky, Georg   Bohemian   1745-1819
Partita; EKB; 0022/1; C
Druschetsky's style is high Classicism and he composed primarily for wind instruments, for which he wrote particularly well.

Partita in F Major, #9; Weinmann; BKH; 0201/2; C

Partita in F Major, #10; Weinmann; BKH; 0201/2; C

Partita in B-Flat Major, #13; Weinmann; BKH; 0201/2; C

Partita in G Major, #21; Weinmann; BKH; 0201/2; C

Eaton, John   American   1935-
Concert Piece; 1956; SCI; 18 mins; 1220
Eaton is an eclectic composer who uses varied techniques including jazz, serialism, microtonal and electronic music. He studied with Babbitt and Sessions, received two Guggenheim Fellowships and won three successive American Prix de Rome.

Elgar, Edward   English   1857-1934
Music for Wind Quintet: Adagio; McNichol; c1977; CPP ; 2111; D
Elgar was considered one of the top European Romantic composers. He drew inspiration for this music from the culture and landscape of his country. He wrote in all the major forms except opera.

Fiala, Joseph   Czech   1748-1816
Three Quintets; Janetzky; c1970; BBL, HOF; 0201/2
Fiala was a friend of Mozart and an oboist in orchestras in Munich, Salzburg and Vienna. He composed a number of string quartets, symphonies and concertos, as well as numerous wind serenades which Mozart described in glowing terms. This piece requires two English horns.

Flothuis, Marius   Dutch   1914-
Quintet, Op. 13; 1941-42; DNA; 22 mins; 1121
Flothuis's music is usually lyrical and intimate, tonal and very contrapuntal. This work requires bass clarinet.

Frid, Geza   Hungarian/Dutch   1904-1989
Serenade, Op. 4; 1928; DNA; 14 mins; 1021/1
A student of Bartok and Kodaly, Frid was a prolific composer with works for opera, orchestra, chorus, keyboard and chamber ensembles.

Golabek, Jakub   Polish   1739-1789
Partita; Ochlewski; PWM; 0021/2

Grieg, Edvard Hagerup   Norwegian   1843-1907
Gnomes' Parade; Skinder; PWM; 1121
One of Norway's most important musical figures, Grieg is perhaps best known for *Peer Gynt* on which he collaborated with Ibsen.

Gyrowetz, Adalbert   Bohemian   1763-1850
Serenata, Op. 3, #1; Pratt; 1790; NOV, ESM; 0021/2; C
Gyrowetz (also spelled Jirovec), a student of Haydn, composed in a
style very similar to his teacher though he was also closely associated
with the Czech nationalistic style. In his younger years he was a very
popular composer and a good many of his works were printed during
his lifetime. However, by 1820 he was already practically forgotten
because of his inability to adapt to the change in musical taste.

Hallnas, Eyvind   Swedish   1937-
Blaskvintett; 1985; SMI; 11 mins; 1220
English horn and bass clarinet are required.

Handel, George F.   German/English   1685-1759
Two Arias; MRI, ESM; 0201/2; C
Handel's music featured grand design, lush harmonies and a certain
eloquence. He wrote for opera, oratorios, chamber ensembles and orchestra.

Hanmer, Ronald   1917-1995
Five for Five; ESM; 1121 or 2030; B/C

Woodwind Quintets; ESM; 1130 or 2030; B/C

Hansen, Theodore Carl   1935-
Toccata for Winds; SEE; 2111

Haydn, Franz Joseph   Austrian   1732-1809
Divertimento in D Major, Hob. II/5 or #32; Hellyer; 1765; ESM;
0021/2; C
Haydn is considered the creator of the classical form of the symphony
and string quartet. He played a historic role in the evolution of
harmony by adopting four-part writing as the compositional foundation.
A prolific composer, Haydn wrote music for orchestra, chamber ensem--
bles, concertos, dramatic works, masses and oratories. This work was
originally for two clarinets and two horns.

Hugues, Luigi   1836-1913
Allegro Scherzoso in D Major, Op. 92; Cavally; c1883; ESM, SMC;
2111; C/D

Jones, Parry   Welsh/English   1891-1963
Winnie the Pooh Suite; ESM; 1121; C/D
Alternate parts are available for French horn and bass clarinet.

Kalinsky, Jan
Andante; c1992; ESM; 0401; C/D
Parts three and four are for English horn rather than oboe.

Karg-Elert, Sigfrid   German   1877-1933
Quintett in C Moll, Op. 30; 1904; HOF; 0121/1
Karg-Elert studied at the Leipzig Conservatory with Reinecke and
Jadassohn. Later Grieg championed his work and many of Karg-Elert's
early works show this influence. He developed a compositional style
inspired by the Baroque but with impressionistic devices. He is best
known for his harmonium and organ compositions.

Kim, Yong-Jin   1930-
Three Movements; c1974; SEE; 1201/1
English horn is required in this work.

Krommer, Franz   Czech   1759-1831
Parthia; COM; 7 mins; 0021/2; C
Krommer was one of the most successful Czech composers in Vienna in
the early twentieth century. Of Krommer's (sometimes spelled Kramar)
more than 300 compositions, at least forty of these are partitas for wind
ensemble. He was a very popular composer and even Beethoven regarded him to be a serious competitor. This work features a solo clarinet
with the other instruments in an accompanying role.

Lee, Eugene   1942-
Compositions for Five Woodwind Instruments; 1971; 14 mins; 1211
English horn is required.

LeFleming, Christopher   English   1908-1985
Homage to Beatrix Potter; c1971; CHE, HAN; 1121; B/C
Le Fleming studied at the Brighton School of Music and the Royal
School of Church Music, later holding several teaching positions. He
wrote music for orchestra, chorus, piano and songs.

Luening, Otto   1900-1996
Fuguing Tune; SCI; flexible instrumentation
Luening has been an influential musical force for most of the twentieth
century. His diverse musical activities have included composition,
conducting, writing and teaching. This work may be performed with
any five woodwind instruments.

Lunden, Lennart   Swedish   1914-1966
Rondino; c1960; HAN; 1121

Three Swedish Tunes; HAN; 1121

The Wheatear; HAN; 1121

Masek, Vaclav Vincenc   Bohemian   1755-1831
Notturno; SNK; 0201/2; D/E
Vaclav, the most celebrated member of his musical family, was a prolific composer, writing some forty partitas for wind ensemble. These
compositions were so successful that they were performed by the best
wind ensembles in Austria and Germany. Especially appealing in Masek's works is the style, which balances Classical and Romantic periods. His name is sometimes spelled Mascek or Machek. This octet is
a brilliant, but highly demanding work with a very high first horn part
and many virtuoso passages for the woodwinds.

Miscellaneous
Ten Little Pieces by Classical Composers; Bonisch; ESM; 2021; C

Monteverdi, Claudio   Italian   1567-1653
Madrigal: Oh, Let Me Die; Nelhybel; PRC; flexible instrumentation
Monteverdi established the foundations of modern opera and was the
first to use string tremolos and pizzicato as well as dominant seventh
chords. Various instruments may be used including oboes, clarinets,
and bassoons.

Mozart, Wolfgang A.   Austrian   1756-1791
Adagio in B-Flat Major, K.411/K.484a; 1783; MRI; 0032; C/D
This solemn, elegant work, originally written for two clarinets and
three basset horns, was probably written for some Masonic Ceremony.
This may also be played using four clarinets and bassoon.

Il Mio Tesoro; Sutton; MidSx; 2030; B

Parfrey, Raymond   English   1928-
Suite for Five; ESM; 1130; C
Parfrey was a choirboy for five years before being drafted into the army
where he learned to play the standard popular tunes of the day from his
fellow servicemen. After leaving the military, he studied with Alan
Bush and began writing music for wind ensembles, choir, piano, organ
and string orchestra.

Ralston, Alfred   American   1875-1952
Seven Norwegian Miniatures; BHI; 1121

Rameau, Jean-Philippe   French   1683-1764
La Poule; Wiggins; FML, ESM; 1121; C/D
Rameau, best known for his operatic works, is known for his expressive melodies and rich harmonies.

Regner, Hermann   1928-
Ein Kleine Waldmusik; c1960; MOS; 0111/2

Reid, John   Scottish   1721-1807
A Set of Minuets and Marches; ESM; 0201/2; B/C

Rosetti, Antonio   Czech   1750-1792
Quintet in E-Flat Major; 1785; EKB; 1211
English horn is required.

Rossini, Gioachino   Italian   1792-1868
Harmonie; COM, ESM; 0021/2; C/D
Recognized as one of the greatest Italian composers of his time, Rossini is best known for his operas.

Roussakis, Nicolas   Greek/American   1934-1994
March, Song and Dance; c1966; MCA; 1121
Roussakis studied at Columbia University with Luening, Beeson, Cowell, Ben Weber, Shapey and Jarnach. He was on the faculty at Rutgers University and co-founded the American Composers Orchestra. While his music is generally accessible to audiences, he uses advanced contemporary techniques.

Rummel, Christian   German   1787-1849
Quintuor in B-Flat Major, Op. 41, Tire des oeuvres de Mozart; c1820; EAM; 0121/1
Basset horn is required in this work.

Salieri, Antonio   Italian   1750-1825
Picciola Serenata Angermuller; c1977; DBM, ESM; 0201/2; C
Only in our time has the life of the Imperial Court Kapellmeister Salieri begun to be seen in a new light and his work to be reassessed. Not a great deal of Salieri's work was published during his lifetime. Many of his successes were short-lived, and much of his music reflects the taste of his public, the aristocracy, and the members of the imperial court.

Salieri's importance as a teacher is, however, incontestable. Composers such as Beethoven, Mozart and Schubert quite rightly spoke proudly of having studied with him.

Serenade in E-Flat Major; SUV; 0201/2

Schubert, Franz   Austrian   1797-1828
Minuet und Finale Eines Oktetts, F Major; BKH; 0211/1 or 2011/1; C
Schubert produced great masterpieces in virtually every field of composition. His music is rich in melody and expressive harmony. This is an arrangement of Schubert's wind octet.

Schubert Favorites; Milnes; PIP; flexible instrumentation; C
There are parts for flute, oboe, clarinet, horn, saxophone, bassoon and bass clarinet in varying combinations.

Skinder , Kazimierz
Miniatury Romantyczne; c1958; PWM; 1121

Stamitz, Carl   Bohemian   1745-1801
Twelve Serenades, Op. 28; Lebermann; SIK; 2001/2
Stamitz was considered an exceptional violist and wrote a large number of compositions for orchestra, sinfonie concertante, concertos and chamber ensembles. His style is outstanding for melodic wealth, formal elegance and harmonious tonal beauty.

Steffan, Joseph   Czech   1726-1797
Harmonie in E-Flat Major; ESM; 0021/2; C
A pupil of Wagenseil, Steffan (sometimes spelled Stepan) settled in Vienna where he was a renowned teacher. Steffan composed in a tuneful Classical style and was especially renowned for his keyboard works, although his music became neglected after his death.

Stock, David Frederick   American   1939-
Keep the Change; 1981; MMB; flexible instrumentation
Stock studied with Berger and Shapero and played trumpet in various orchestras. His works include music for orchestra and chamber group. This work may be performed by any five treble instruments.

Stone, David   1922-
Prelude and Scherzetto; c1956; NOV; 1121

Sulpizi, Fernando   1936-
Quintetto; EDB; 1021/1

Telemann, George   German   1681-1767
Overture-Suite in D Major; Hinnenthal; LKM; 0201/2; C/D
Telemann was the most prolific composer of this time and is widely regarded as Germany's leading composer in the early to middle eighteenth century.

Villa-Lobos, Heitor   Brazilian   1887-1959
Quinteto para Instrumentos de Sopro; 1928; PRC; 1211
Villa-Lobos, one of the most original composers of the twentieth century, had a remarkable ability to recreate native melodies and rhythms in large instrumental and choral forms. English horn is required.

Wanhal, Johann Baptist   Bohemian   1739-1813
Divertimento in C Major; Steinbeck; c1970; PTE; 0201/2
A student of Dittersdorf, Wanhal was a prolific composer with works for piano, orchestra, chorus and chamber groups.

SIX WINDS

Acker, Dieter Rumanian/German 1940-
Attituden; 1968/71; GER; 0022/2
Acker studied composition at the Cluj Conservatory and later taught at the Hochschule für Musik in Munich. He wrote music for orchestra, piano and chamber ensembles.

Adler, Samuel German/American 1928-
Seven Epigrams; c1970; OUP; 2121
Adler was one of tne most prolific American composers with hundreds of compositions for chorus, chamber, orchestra and stage. He studied with Fromm, Piston, Hindemith, Fine and Copland. This work requires bass clarinet.

Ahlberg, Gunnar Swedish 1942-
Fluente; 1984; SMI; 3.5 mins; 2031
Bass clarinet is required.

Allers, Hans Gunther 1935-
Suite; c1964; MOS; 1111/2

Altmann, Eddo German
Kleine Tanzsuite; HOF; 1111/2

Bach, P.D.Q. American 1935-
Fugue of the Volgo Boatmen; PRC; 2.5 mins; 2202; C/D
Piccolo and English horn are required.

Baur, Jurg German 1918-
Pour rien fur Blasersextett; 1980; BKH; 0022/2
Baur studied wtih Jarnach in Cologne and taught at the Dusseldorf Conservatory and in Cologne. His music, though conservative, shows the influence of the younger composers in the 1950s.

Becker, Gunther German 1924-
Quasi una Fantasmagoria; 1980-81; BKH; 0022/2
This work is based on Robert Schumann's *Sphinxes*.

Beethoven, Ludwig van German 1770-1827
Sextet in E-Flat Major, Op. 71; 1796; BKH, IMC; 11 mins; 0022/2; D
Beethoven's early achievements show him to be extending the Viennese Classical tradition. Later he began to compose in an increasingly individual musical style, and at the end of his life he wrote his most

sublime and profound works. The opening movement *Adagio* is followed by an *Allegro* which features a delightful conversation among several instruments. The lovely *Adagio* in which the winds simulate strings is followed by a minuet with recognizable *Eroica* aspects. And the final *Allegro* uses a miniature march for its thematic substance.

Cadow, Paul   1908-
Pastorale im Alten Stil; TBM; 0302/1
This work requires English horn.

Castil-Blaze, Francois Henri J.   French   1784-1857
Sextet; MRI; 0022/2; C/D
Perhaps best known for his writings about music, Castil-Blaze contributed greatly to French opera in the early nineteenth century through his book *De l'opera en France* published in 1820.

Danzi, Franz   German   1763-1826
Sextet in E-Flat Major; SIK; 0022/2
Perhaps best known for his many singspiels, Danzi also wrote wind chamber music, symphonies, concertos, oratorio, sacred music, piano pieces and songs.

Davies, Sir Peter Maxwell   English   1934-
Alma Redemptoris Mater; c1965; EAM; 1121/1
Davies studied at the Royal Manchester College of Music and Manchester University, with later studies under Petrassi in Rome. Much of his music reveals his interest in pre-Baroque styles. He has written music for stage, chamber ensembles, piano and organ.

Devasini, G.   1822-1878
Sextett; 1843; RIC; 1121/1

Druschetsky, Georg   Bohemian   1745-1819
Partita in E-Flat; EKB, EAM; 0022/2
Druschetsky's style is high Classicism and he composed primarily for wind instruments, for which he wrote particularly well.

Dubois, Pierre Max   French   1930-1995
Sinfonia da Camera; c1965; LDA; 1121/1; D
Dubois studied at the Paris Conservatoire and won the Prix de Rome in 1955. His music shows the influence of Milhaud, Francaix and Prokofiev. His works for orchestra, dance and chamber ensembles are written in a light, humorous style, with chromatic scales, unusual harmonies and lively rhythms. One clarinet must double on saxophone.

Elgar, Edward   English   1857-1934
Serenade, Op. 20 ; Newhill; 1892; ESM; 1121/1; D
Elgar was considered one of the foremost European Romantic composers with music in all the major forms except opera. He drew inspiration for his music from the culture and landscape of his country. This work was originally for string orchestra.

Faure, Gabriel   French   1845-1924
Nocturne; LDA; 1111/2
Faure's style evolved with clear influences from late Romanticism to early twentieth century, but there are certain traits that can be found in nearly all his music such as his handling of harmony and tonality.

Fiala, Joseph   Czech   1748-1816
Parthia in F Major; ESM; 2202; C/D
Fiala was a friend of Mozart and an orchestral oboist in Munich, Salzburg and Vienna. He composed a number of string quartets, symphonies and concertos, as well as numerous wind serenades which Mozart described in glowing terms. This piece has an optional contrabassoon part.

Francaix, Jean   French   1912-1997
Sixtuor; 1992; EAM, ESM; 17 mins; 1121/1; D/E
A brilliant piano virtuoso, Francaix's music shows an innate gift for invention and an ability to express the freshness and wonder of childhood. This five movement work requires bass clarinet.

Froschauer, Helmuth   1933-
Sextet; c1962; DBM; 1121/1

Genzmer, Harald   German   1909-
Sextet; c1970; PTE; 10 mins; 0022/2; C/D
This work has four movements titled *Largo allegro, Andante molto tranquillo, Intermezzo* and *Finale*.

Giefer, Willi   1930-
Diskontinuum; GER; 12 mins; 0022/2

Gow, Niel   Scottish   1727-1807
Dances from Casterbridge; PIP, ESM; 2121; C

Gursching, Albrecht   German   1934-
Stops; c1976; PIC; 0022/2
A student of Karl Marx and Gunter Bialas, Gursching was an oboist and wrote music for orchestra and chamber groups.

Hagstrom, Robert   Swedish   1950-
Suono per fiati; 1979; SMI; 11 mins; 1211/1
English horn or alto sax is required; piccolo doubling required.

Haydn, Johann Michael   Austrian   1737-1806
Divertimento in D Major, P.95; DBM; 7 mins; 0202/2; C
Johann Michael Haydn, younger brother of Joseph, was best known in
his lifetime as a master of church music. He was, however, a respected
and prolific composer of instrumental works as well. This work, comprised of four movements, is written in standard classical sonata form.

Haydn, Joseph   Austrian   1732-1809
Divertimento #1 in F Major; DBM ; 0202/2; C/D
Haydn is considered the creator of the classical form of the symphony
and string quartet. He played a historic role in the evolution of
harmony by adopting four-part writing as the compositional foundation.
A prolific composer, Haydn wrote music for orchestra, chamber ensembles, concertos, dramatic works, masses and oratories.

Divertimento #3 in C Major, H.II, 7; 1765; DBM; 4 mins; 0202/2; C

Divertimento #5 in D Major; Rainer; c1969; DBM; 0202/2; C/D

Divertimento #6 in G Major; 1763; DBM; 0202/2; C/D

Divertimento #7 in G Major; 1765; DBM; 0202/2; C/D

Divertimento #8 in D Major; 1765; DBM; 0202/2; C/D

Feldpartie in C Major; 1761; BHI; 6 mins; 0202/2; B/C
This work is remarkable for the transparent instrumental color and
charm of its construction, inviting comparison with Mozart's *Serenade
in C Minor*. The melody content is well divided among all the instruments, the first horn in particular having important melodic passages in
the serene *Adagio*.

Feldpartie in F Major; BHI; 0202/2; B/C

Parthia #4 in B-Flat Major; BHI; 0202/2; B/C

Hidas, Frigyes   Hungarian/American   1928-
Five Miniatures; c1991; DMP; 6 mins; 0022/2; C/D

Hoffmeister, Franz Anton   Austrian   1754-1812
Partita in E-Flat Major; c1996; KZE; 0022/2; C/D
Hoffmeister, a well-known music publisher in his time, was also a
prolific composer. He wrote works for orchestra, concertos, stage and
chamber ensembles.

Janacek, Leos   Czech   1854-1928
Die Jugend: Mladi-Youth; 1924; IMC; 17 mins; 1121/1; E
In the jaunty first movement, which is in the form of a free rondo, the principal theme is derived from the speech melody of the sigh, "Youth, golden youth." The somber, almost dirge-like second movement is a reflection on his unhappy moments in the Brno monastery with its isolation and strict regulations. All suggestions of gloom are dispelled in the third movement, a scherzo, with a perky piccolo tune taken from Janacek's *March of the Blue-Boys*. The "blue-boys" were the boys of the Brno monastery, who sang and whistled as they marched along. In the buoyant, affirmative finale, the principal theme of the opening movement is recalled once more in combination with new material. Bass clarinet is required.

Janssen, Guus   Dutch   1951-
Muziek voor Six Houtblazers; c1976; DNA; 6 mins; 1131

Josephs, Wilfred   English   1927-1997
Papageno Variations, Op. 153; 1989; NOV; 12 mins; 1121/1; D/E
Inspired by Mozart's *Der Vogelfanger bin ich ja* from *The Magic Flute*, this work requires one bass clarinet and piccolo.

Kabelac, Miloslav   Czech   1908-1979
Blasersextett, Op. 8; 1940; SUP; 15 mins; 1121/1
Kabelac studied composition with Jirak. His music uses modern idioms but remains fairly tonal. This work requires piccolo, English horn and bass clarinet.

Kleinsinger, George   American   1914-1982
Design for Woodwinds; c1946; SCI; 1121/1
A student of Philip James, Jocobi and Wagenaar, Kleinsinger is perhaps best known for his children's musicals such as *Tubby the Tuba* and *Archy and Mehitabel*.

Krommer, Franz   Czech   1759-1831
Parthia in B-Flat; COM; 15 mins; 0022/2; C/D
In this work, an arrangement of the quintet for two clarinets, bassoon and two horns, the first clarinet is the soloist with the others used as accompaniment.

Partita in C Minor; HOF; 12 mins; 0022/2; D

Lefebvre, Charles Edouard   French   1843-1917
Second Suite, Op. 122; 1908; LDA; 1121/1
Lefebvre studied at the Paris Conservatory, won the Prix de Rome in 1870 and twice won the Prix Chartier. While highly regarded by the

French critics during the late nineteenth century, he was not an innovator. The style and texture of his instrumental music can be compared to Mendelssohn.

Lessel, Franciszek   Polish   1780-1838
Sextet in E-Flat Major; Fendt; c1996; MRI; 0022/2

Lunden, Lennart   Swedish   1914-1966
Quadrille; HAN; 2031
Bass clarinet is required.

Queen Christina's Song; HAN; 2031
Bass clarinet is required.

Lunden-Welden, Gunnar   Swedish   1914-1988
Four Smabitar; 1976; SMI; 12 mins; 2121

Lyons, Graham
Pastorale; ESM; 2040

Manicke, Dietrich   German   1923-
Sextett; 1962; PRC, ESM; 11 mins; 0022/2; D
Manicke followed the examples of Reger and Hindemith. His works are characterized by color and variety.

Masek, Vaclav Vincenc   Bohemian   1755-1831
Partita in F Major; SNK; 1122; D/E
Vaclav, the most celebrated member of his musical family, was a prolific composer, writing some forty partitas for wind ensemble. These compositions were so successful that they were also performed by the best wind ensembles in Austria and Germany. Especially appealing in Masek's works is the style, which balances Classical and Romantic periods. His name is sometimes spelled Mascek or Machek. Basset horn is required.

Mayr, Johann Simone   German   1763-1845
Divertimento in E-Flat Major; PRC; 8 mins; 0122/1; C/D

Michael, David Moritz   German   1751-1827
Parthia IV; BHI; 14 mins; 0022/2; C

Molterc, Johann Melchior   German   1696-1765
Concerto in D Major; Sherman; MED; 7 mins; 0211/2; C

Moniuszko, Stanislaw   Polish   1819-1872
Canzone aus "Halka"; 1846-47; VLO; 0122/1
Moniuszko is considered the most outstanding Polish opera composer
of his generation. This is an arrangement of a piece from his opera
Halka.

Mozart, Wolfgang A.   Austrian   1756-1791
Adagio from Serenade #11, K.375 ; 1781; BHI; 5.5 mins; 0022/2; C
This is from the well-known wind octet, here arranged for sextet.

Adagio in G Minor, K.516; PTE; 1121/1
This was originally written for string quartet.

Divertimento #8 in F Major, K.213; 1775; KAL; 11 mins; 0202/2;
C/D
The opening *Allegro* of this work is in miniature sonata form with a
subtly varied recapitulation. The *Andante* is a graceful ballet, the
Menuetto has a very Haydn-like quality and the finale, *Contredanse en
Rondeau,* is one of Mozart's most exuberant movements.

Divertimento #9 in B-Flat Major, K.240; 1776; KAL; 12 mins;
0202/2; C/D
This work is the second in the "table music" series. The *Allegro* is
more extended than in the first of the series; the *Andante grazioso* has a
dancing lilt of a gavotte; the *Menuetto* is remarkable for the high horn
writing; and the final *Allegro* is robust.

Divertimento #12 in E-Flat Major, K.252/240a; 1776; KAL; 13 mins;
0202/2; C/D
This work is the third in the "table music" series. In this work Mozart
provides variety by opening with an *Andante,* a graceful *Sicilian,* but
with an unusual amount of dynamic marks. The *Menuetto* is one of the
gayest movements, the *Trio* is written in the more solemn character of
A-flat major, the *Polonaise* is a delightful swagger and the *Finale* is a
brilliant conclusion.

Divertimento #13 in F Major, K.253; 1776; BKH; 15 mins; 0202/2;
C/D
This work is the fourth in the "table music" series. Only two other
works of Mozart's open with a variation movement (K.298 and K.331),
but its position in this work is the only unconventional feature of this
movement. The *Menuetto* is noble and expressive, the *Trio* is more
playful and dancing and the *Finale* combines bravura with delicacy.

Divertimento #16 in E-Flat Major, K.289 (271g); 1777; BKH; 13
mins; 0202/2; C/D
This is the sixth, and last, of the "table music" series. The first movement opens with a solemn adagio introduction to the allegro section.
The *Menuetto* is a rollicking Haydnesque dance and trio. The *Adagio*

has strong melodic links with other movements and the *Finale* is a brilliant and exhilarating movement.

Minuet and Trio in G Minor, K.516; PTE; 1121/1
This work was originally written for string quartet.

Non Piu Andrai; Sutton; 2031 or 2040; B

Serenade #2; MRI; 0022/2

Serenade in B-Flat Major, K.196f; Spiegl; EAM; 0022/2; D
There is a later version of this work for octet, adding two oboes and making significant changes in the other parts.

Serenade in E-Flat Major, K.375; Spiegl; 1781; EAM, OUP; 0202/2; D
This is the original work on which the octet version of K.375 is based.

Serenade, K.525; de Smet; PTE; 0222; D
This is an arrangement of one movement from *Eine Kleine Nachtmusik.*

Sextet, K.407; ESM; 0022/2; D
This work was originally for horn and strings.

Unser Dummer Pobel Meint, K.455, Variations on a Theme by Gluck; Druschetzky; EKB; 15 mins; 0022/2
This work was originally for piano.

Nelhybel, Vaclav   Czech/American   1919-1996
Impromptu; 1963 GMP; 2121
Nelhybel, best known for his symphonic band music, used harmonic dissonance with tonal centers. Piccolo is required.

Parchman, Gen. Louis   1929-
Sextet; SEE; 1112/1
This is a bassoon solo with quintet accompaniment.

Pleyel, Ignaz   Austrian   1757-1831
Sextet in E-Flat Major; MRI; 0022/2
Pleyel studied with Haydn but is perhaps best known for his manufacturing of pianos. A prolific composer, he composed symphonies, symphonie concertantes, concertos and chamber music.

Reinecke, Carl H.   German   1824-1910
Sextet in B-Flat Major,Op. 271; 1904; COM, MMP; 20 mins; 1111/2; D
Reinecke was a highly regarded pianist, composer and teacher in Leipzig. His many works in every genre are written in Classic form and

show refined craftsmanship. This work is among the very few substantial, handsomely crafted works for winds written between Beethoven's *Sextet Op. 71* of 1796 and Hindemith's *Klein Kammermusick* of 1922.

Ringbom, Nils-Eric   Finnish   1907-1998
Sextet; 1951; FMC; 0221/1
After studies at the Turku Academy, Ringbom played violin and later became director of the Sibelius Festival and managing director of the Helsinki Philharmonic. The first work by a Finnish composer to be performed at the International Festival for Contemporary Music, this work requires English horn and bass clarinet.

Rosetti, Antonio   Czech   1750-1792
Parthia in D Major; BBM; 0121/2
Rosetti was one of the leading members of the German branch of Czech composers. His contemporaries ranked him with Haydn and Mozart.

Partita in B-Flat Major; PTE; 0121/2

Partita in C Major; Peruzzi; PTE; 9 mins; 0022/2

Schroeder, Hermann   German   1904-1984
Sextett, Werk 49; 1975; GER; 16 mins; 0022/2

Schubert, Franz   Austrian   1797-1828
Shepherd Dance; Schoenbach; PRC; 1221
This arrangement from *Rosamunde, Incidental Music* requires English horn and bass clarinet.

Schweinitz, Wolfgang von   German   1953-
English Serenade, Op. 24; 1985; BHI; 16 mins; 0022/2

Seiber, Matyas   Hungarian/English   1905-1960
Serenade; 1925; HAN, CHE; 15 mins; 0022/2; C/D
Folk music is a frequent theme in Seiber's music and Kodaly was a strong influence on his style. He wrote music for opera, chorus, orchestra, chamber and instrumental solo music.

Shimazu, Takehito   Japanese   1949-
Neoplasma; 1979; BKH; 1111/2

Steffan, Joseph   Czech   1726-1797
Harmonie in E-Flat; Rhodes; PIP; 9 mins; 0022/2; C
A pupil of Wagenseil, Steffan (sometimes spelled Stepan) settled in Vienna where he was a renowned teacher. Steffan composed in a tuneful Classical style and was especially renowned for his keyboard works,

although his music became neglected after his death. He composed two
Harmonies for wind instruments.

Stumpf, Johan Christian   German   1740-1801
Harmonie in E-Flat Major; PIP; 0022/2; C/D

Svensson, Sven E.   Swedish   1899-1960
Sextett for Blasinstrument; 1960; SMI; 1121/1
Bass clarinet is required.

Swack, Irwin   American   20th C.
Themes and Variations; ISM; 23 mins; 2121
Swack's music shows the influence of popular culture expressed
through the idioms of jazz, dance and folk music. He attended the
Cleveland Institute, Juilliard School, Northwestern University and
Columbia University. Piccolo and bass clarinet are required.

Tchaikovsky, Peter I.   Russian   1840-1893
Adagio; COM; 0222
Tchaikovsky had a gift for beautiful melodies unmatched by his
contemporaries. He wrote in every musical genre including stage, orchestra, chamber, piano and songs. He is widely regarded as the leading
nineteenth-century Russian composer. Bass clarinet and English horn
are required.

Autumn Song, Op. 37; PWM; 0132

Templeton, Alex   Welsh   1909-1963
Passepied; Rhoads; PRC; 1221
Templeton studied at the Royal College of Music and the Royal Academy of Music, settling in the United States in 1935. He is perhaps
best known for his work as a radio pianist with humorous musical
sketches. This work requires English horn and bass clarinet.

Thomson, Virgil   American   1896-1989
Barcarolle (A Portrait of Georges Hugnet); 1944; SCI; 1221
Winner of the Pulitzer Prize in 1949, Thomson was a sophisticated and
eclectic composer who used many different styles from the past and
present. English horn and bass clarinet are required. This work was
originally for piano.

Voorn, Joop   Dutch   1932-
Sucevita Chorals; 1974; DNA; 7 mins; 0231
Voorn studied at the Brabant Conservatory and later taught there. Bass
clarinet is required.

Waters, Charles   English   1895-
Solemn Minuet; PTE; 1122

Weber, Carl Maria   German   1786-1826
Adagio and Rondo in B-Flat Major; Sander; c1973; EAM, MRI;
0022/2; D
Weber is an important founder of the Romantic movement in Germany
and one of its leading composers.

Woolfenden, Guy   English   1937-
Prelude, in Memoriam and Finale; ESM; 1121/1; D/E
Woolfenden, as head of the Royal Shakespeare Company, composed
more than 150 scores for the group. He conducted orchestras in Canada,
Germany, Japan, the United States and France. He also wrote music for
ballet, musicals, ensembles, band and concerti. Bass clarinet is
required.

Zehm, Friedrich   German   1923-
Musica Pastorale; c1966; Simrock; 2102/1

Bach, Carl Philipp Emanuel   German   1714-1788
Six Little Sonatas; MRI; 18 mins; 2021/2; C/D
Son of Johann Sebastian Bach, Carl departed from the polyphonic
writing of his father and adopted the "intimate expressiveness" of the
North German School. He wrote music for solo piano, concertos,
chamber ensembles, voice and chorus.

Bach, Johann Sebastian   German   1685-1750
Sarabande; Kennaway; ESM; 2131; B/C
The most famous member of the Bach family, Johann wrote primarily
sacred music and works for keyboard. He also was a master organist
and in-structor.

Three Sarabandes; Emerson; ESM, PRC; 2131; B/C

Baton, Rene Emmanuel   French   1879-1940
Aubade, Op. 53; c1940; DUR; 1122/1

Cruft, Adrian   English   1921-1987
Stilestone Suite, Op. 62A; c1976; Joad; 2122
Cruft, a student of Jacob and Rubbra, wrote sacred works as well as
music for chorus, orchestra and band.

Donizetti, Gaetano   Italian   1797-1848
Larghetto in F Major; BSE; 2021/2; C
Donizetti, best known for his Italian operas, also wrote songs, sacred
music, chamber music and pieces for piano. This work requires two
basset horns.

Doppelbauer, Josef Friedrich   1918-1989
Divertimento; c1974; DBM; 1221/1
This work requires English horn and bass clarinet.

Driessler, Johannes   German   1921-
Aphorismen, Op. 7A; 1948; BAR; 1221/1
English horn and bass clarinet are required.

Dubois, Theodore   French   1837-1924
Au Jardin, Petite Suite; c1908; COM, HEU; 6 mins; 2121/1; B/C
Dubois is representative of the Classical School of French musicians at
the end of the nineteenth century. He was a popular composer during
his life-time, even though he made no significant contribution to the
musical innovation of his day. Today many of his motets and masses
are still performed in French churches. Equally important are his

educational publications, in which field he is still regarded as an authority. He wrote three works for wind ensembles of which *Au Jardin* offers a typical example of his uncomplicated Neo-Classical style. While it may lack musical depth, it certainly is effective in pleasing both players and audience. This work is written in three movements titled *Les Oiseaux, Les Petites Visites* and *Gouttes de Pluie*.

Flament, Edouard   French   1880-1958
Fantasia con Fuga, Op. 28; MMM; 1212/1
Flament studied at the Paris Conservatory with Caussade and Lenepveu. The second oboe part is actually for English horn.

Frommel, Gerhard   German   1906-1984
Blaser Suite in C Major, Op. 18; ESM; 1121/2; C/D

Habert, Johannes Evangelista   Bohemian   1833-1896
Scherzo, Op. 107; BKH; 1112/2
Habert is best known as a composer of church music, but he also wrote some orchestral and chamber music, piano pieces and songs.

Hanmer, Ronald   1917-1995
Serenade for Seven; c1979; ESM; 2131; B/C

Suite for Seven; c1973; ESM; 2131; B/C

Indy, Vincent d'   French   1851-1931
Chansons et Danses in B-Flat Major, Op. 50; 1898; DUR; 15 mins; 1122/1; D
D'Indy was a composer, teacher, theorist and writer. Chiefly remembered as founder of the Schola Cantorum though his contributions to the French musical renaissance is significant. He studied with Franck at the Paris Conservatory and was greatly influenced by Wagner's works. This septet is d'Indy's most lyrical chamber music. The blending of horn tone with that of the woodwinds is masterly, which is understandable since d'Indy was a horn player.

Mayr, Sebastian   1845-1899
Am Morgen, Idyll; Andraud; VLO; 1122/1
Trumpet could replace horn.

Miscellaneous
Baroque Music; Keszler/Kovacs; ESM; 2121/1; B

Mouquet, Jules   French   1867-1946
Suite; c1910; LEM,COM; ; 1122/1
Mouquet studied at the Paris Conservatory with Leroux and Dubois.
He won the Prix de Rome in 1896 and later became professor of har-
mony at the Conservatory.

Paisiello, Giovanni   Italian   1740-1816
Divertissement; SCI; 2021/2
Paisiello, a prolific composer of comic operas, is known for music that
has lyrical grace and inventive melodies.

Petrassi, Goffredo   Italian   1904-
Tre Per Sette; 1966; SUV; 10 mins; 3220
Petrassi studied with Donato and Bustini, then later taught at the Aca-
demia of Santa Cecilia. His later works use twelve-tone technique.
Requires piccolo, alto flute, English horn and E-flat clarinet.

Pierne, Gabriel   French   1863-1937
Preludio et Fughetta in C Minor, Op. 40 #1; LDA, IMC; 4 mins;
2112/1; C/D
Pierne studied at the Paris Conservatory with Massenet and was
awarded the Grand Prix de Rome in 1882. His expert craftsmanship is
apparent in his music for opera, oratorio, orchestra, piano and chamber
ensembles.

Praag, Henri C. Van   Netherlands   1894-1968
Schetsen #3 for Seven Winds; DNA; 1222

Reicha, Joseph   Czech   1752-1795
Parthia in D Major, WV3.504; c1993; Edition Engel; 10 mins;
0221/2; C
This interesting work is written in standard Classic, four movement
form.

Roentgen, Julius   Dutch   1855-1932
Serenade in A Major, Op. 14; c1878; BKH; 1112/2; C/D
Roentgen was a prolific composer of the late Romantic school. This
early work shows the influence of Schumann.

Rosetti, Antonio   Czech   1750-1792
Parthia #3 in D Major; Kneusslin; c1964; EKB; 0221/2; C/D
Rosetti was one of the leading members of the German branch of Czech
composers. His contemporaries ranked him with Haydn and Mozart.

Written in three movements, there are two alternate English horn parts for the clarinets.

Parthia in B-Flat Major; Janetsky; c1976; PTE; 5 mins; 0302/2; C/D

Parthia in F Major; Janetsky; BBM; 0401/2
This work is for solo oboe with accompanying winds.

Salieri, Antonio   Italian   1750-1825
Serenade in B-Flat Major; c1981; SUV; 0023/2; C
Only in our time has the life of the Imperial Court Kapellmeister Salieri begun to be seen in a new light and his work to be reassessed. Not a great deal of Salieri's work was published during his lifetime. Many of his successes were short-lived, and much of his music reflects the taste of his public, the aristocracy, and the members of the imperial court. Salieri's importance as a teacher is, however, incontestable. Composers such as Beethoven, Mozart and Schubert quite rightly spoke proudly of having studied with him. Five original wind ensemble pieces by Salieri exist. Double bass could be used instead of contrabassoon.

Schoenberg, Arnold   Austrian/American   1874-1951
Verklarte Nacht; Schweitzer; 1899; MSM; 1221/1; D/E
Schoenberg's music may be divided into four periods. The first is tonal, the second atonal, the third is serialism, and the fourth is marked by greater diversity including occasional returns to tonal music. *Verklarte Nacht* was originally for string sextet. English horn and bass clarinet are required.

Schubert, Franz   Austrian   1797-1828
Scherzo and Trio in F; Emerson; c1975; ESM; 2131; B/C
Schubert produced great masterpieces in virtually every field of composition. His music is rich in melody and expressive harmony. Horn may be used in place of one clarinet.

Scherzo and Trio in G Minor; Emerson; ESM; 3 mins; 2131; B/C

Strang, Gerald   American   1908-1983
Lost and Wandering; AMC; 2211/1
Strang was among the early California modernists, headed by Henry Cowell. After teaching at several California universities, Strang founded the music department at California State University at Northridge. His music, while using new resources available in acoustics, electronics and computers, is still clearly formal in structure. This work requires two English horns.

Strang, Kenneth   Swedish   1955-
Associations for Winds, Op. 3; 1984; SMI; 0141/1
Bass clarinet is required.

Telemann, George Philip   German   1681-1767
Overture-Suite; COM; 0201/4; C
Telemann was the most prolific composer of his time and is widely
regarded as Germany's leading composer in the early to mid-eighteenth
century.

Vern, A.
Nocturne en Harmonie; ESM; 1022/2; C/D
There are optional parts for two oboes, contrabassoon, trumpet and
trombone.

Verrall, John   American   1908-
Septet; 1965; Highgate press; 1122/1
Verrall studied with Donald Ferguon and Kodaly, later teaching at
Hamline University, Mt. Holyoke College and the University of Wash-
ington. This work, originally written in 1941, was completely revised
in 1971 to include new second and fourth movements.

EIGHT WINDS

Alpaerts, Flor　　　　　　Belgian　　　　　　1876-1954
Avondmuziek; CFI; 2222
Alpaerts studied at the Royal Flemish Conservatory with Block and Benoit. His music reflects a lush, late Romantic style similar to Debussy. This work requires clarinet in A.

Amos, Keith　　　　　　English　　　　　　20th C.
Concertino for Clarinet; c1983; ESM; 8.5 mins; 2221/1; C
This work is a clarinet solo with chamber ensemble accompaniment.

Prelude and Postlude; ESM; 1.5 mins; 2221/1; B

Andriessen, Louis　　　　　　Dutch　　　　　　1939-
Octuor: Divertissement; DNA; 12 mins; 2222
One of Europe's most eminent and influential composers, Andriessen's music shows the influence of jazz and his admiration of Stravinsky.

Sinfonia Dell'arte #6; c1976; DNA; 12 mins; 2222

Bach, Carl Philipp Emanuel　　German　　　　1714-1788
Six Sonatas; MRI; 2022/2; C/D
Son of Johann Sebastian Bach, Carl departed from the polyphonic writing of his father and adopted the "intimate expressiveness" of the North German school. He wrote music for solo piano, concertos, chamber ensemble, voice and chorus.

Bach, P.D.Q.　　　　　　American　　　　　　1935-
Octoot, S. 8; c1973; EVI,PRC; 8 mins; 2222; C/D
Using the pen name of P.D.Q. Bach, Peter Schickele writes this hilarious work in five movements titled *Fast, right away; Slow, at least; Minuet and, presently, trio; Song: All year long, hey, hey, hey;* and *All of a sudden the end.* In the fourth movement, the oboists play their reeds alone, one bassoonist plays on a reed with bocal alone and the other bassoonist uses the last two joints of the instrument as if they were a huge brass mouthpiece. The last movement features clicking of the instruments' keys, among other things.

Bach, Wilhelm Friedrich Ernst　German　　　1759-1845
Parthia in E-Flat Major; COM, ESM; 0222/2; C
W.F.E. Bach was a grandson of Johann Sebastian and few of his compositions have been published.

Baksa, Robert Frank   American   1938-
Octet in E-Flat Major, Op. 27; PRC; 18 mins; 2222
A graduate of the University of Arizona with a degree in composition, Baksa has written over 400 works and is best known for his chamber music and choral pieces. A student of Foss, Baksa began composing at the age of thirteen.

Beethoven, Ludwig van   German   1770-1827
Fidelio, Volumes 1 and 2; Sedlak; MRI; 0222/2; D
Beethoven's early achievements show him to be extending the Viennese Classical tradition. Later he began to compose in an increasingly individual musical style, and at the end of his life he wrote his most sublime and profound works. Written in two volumes, this arrangement of Beethoven's opera has an optional contrabassoon part.

Octet in E-Flat Major, Op. 103; 1792; KAL, BKH, MRI; 9 mins; 0222/2; D
The *Octet* is laid out in four movements. The initial *Allegro* proceeds rhythmically from a theme first stated by the oboe. The lyrical *Andante* is in the form of a three-part song. This is followed by a *Minuet* and then a *Finale* full of high spirits and mischief.

Rondino in E-Flat Major, WoO 25; 1792; IMC, EAM; 4 mins; 0222/2; C/D
This charming, single-movement work contains interesting instrumental effects, in particular the horn echo at the end.

Symphony #7; 1811-12; COM; 0222/2; C/D
There is an optional contrabassoon part.

Bialas, Gunther   German   1907-1995
Romanza and Danza; 1971; BAR; 15 mins; 0222/2
Bialas wrote in a omnitonal style with folklike modalities. His works include music for opera, stage, concertos, chorus and chamber ensembles. Contrabassoon is required.

Blake, David   English   1936-
Casssation for Wind Octet; 1979; NOV, SHA; 15 mins; 0222/2; D
This work, commissioned by the Whispering Wind Band in Sheffield, England, has six movements titled *Alla marcia, Scherzino, Ebb and Flow, Alla Tanza, Fughetta* and *Finale*. Doubling is required as follows: second oboe/English horn; B flat clarinet/soprano sax; A clarinet/bass clarinet/E flat clarinet; horns/maracas; conductor/claves optional.

Blake, Howard   English   1938-
Serenade for Wind Octet; FMI; 0222/2; D/E

Bonsel, Adriaan   Dutch   1918-
Octet; 1975; DNA; 16 mins; 1222/1
Bonsel studied at the Amsterdam Conservatory and has written music
for orchestra and chamber ensembles. This work requires doubling on
piccolo.

Bonvin, Ludwig   Swiss/American   1850-1939
Romanze, Op. 19A; BHI; 1122/2
Bonvin, primarily known as a choral conductor and scholar, wrote
sacred music, as well as works for orchestra, piano, voice and violin.

Bozza, Eugene   French   1905-1991
Octanphonie; c1972; LDA; 0222/2; D/E
Bozza studied with Busser, Rabaud. Capet and Nadaud at the Paris
Conservatory where he won the Premiers Prix for the violin (1924),
conducting (1930) and composition (1934), and also the Prix de Rome
(1934). Though his larger works have been successfully performed in
France, his international reputation rests on his large output of chamber
music for winds. His works display at a consistently high level the characteristic qualities found in mid-twentieth century French chamber
music: elegant structure, melodic fluency and an awareness of the capabilities of the instruments for which he writes.

Brahms, Johannes   German   1833-1897
Variations on a Theme of Haydn; Bowman; ESM; 0222/2; D/E

Callhoff, Herbert   1933-
Movimenti; 1973; GER; 7 mins; 1222/1

Carpenter, Gary   1951-
Ein Musikalisches Snookersspiel; 1991; PRC, ESM; 10 mins; 0222/2;
D/E

Chagrin, Francis   English   1905-1972
Seven Petite Pieces; c1969; NOV; 2122/1

Chandler
Cassation; ESM; 0222/2; D

Cimarosa, Domenico   Italian   1749-1801
Marcia "Da Suonarsi sotto l'Abero Delia Liberta"; PRC; 2 mins;
0222/2; B/C

Druschetsky, Georg   Bohemian   1745-1819
Six Partitas; Weinmann; c1969; DBM; 0222/2; C
Druschetsky's style is high Classicism and he composed primarily for
wind instruments, for which he wrote particularly well.

Dubois, Theodore   French   1837-1924
First Suite; c1898; KAL, HEU; 2122/1; C
Dubois is representative of the Classical school of French musicians at
the end of the nineteenth century. He was a popular composer during
his life-time, even though he made no significant contribution to the
musical innovation of his day. Today many of his motets and masses
are still performed in French churches. Equally important are his
educational publications, in which field he is still regarded an
authority.

Second Suite; 1898; LDA; 2122/1; C
There are five movements titled *Ronde des archers, Chanson les-
bienne, Petite valse, Stella matutina* and *Menuet.*

Dvorák, Anton   Czech   1841-1904
Slavonic Dance, Op. 46 #8; 1878; BHI; 0222/2; D
This work was originally for orchestra. There is an optional contrabas-
soon part.

Slavonic Dance, Op. 72 #1; 1886-87; BHI; 0222/2; D
This work was originally for orchestra. There is an optional contrabassoon part.

Slavonic Dance, Op.72 #7; 1886-87; BHI; 0222/2; D
There is an optional contrabassoon part.

Eichner, Ernst   German   1740-1779
Divertissement in C Major; 1776; COM, ESM; 0222/2; C
During his short lifetime, Eichner, a virtuoso bassoonist, wrote a significant number of pieces for orchestra, solos, chamber ensembles and
voice. His music shows a solid craftsmanship and an eclectic style. He
sought to combine the forms and idioms of his time, incorporating
ideas from many divergent musical schools. Consequently, he does not
fit the style of a particular school, but was instead a rather solitary
figure who sought to give structure and substance to the new genre of
"concert symphony."

Ek, Gunnar   Swedish   1900-1981
Oktett; 1970; SMI; 8.5 mins; 2222
After studies at the Stockholm Conservatory, Ek played cello and organ professionally. He wrote music for orchestra and chamber ensembles.

Elliott, Willard   American   1926-
Five Impressions; c1989; NOV; 0222/2; E
Elliott, a renowned bassoonist, studied at North Texas State University and Eastman School. The five movements in this work are titled *Autumn Haze, Dust Devils, Enchanted Forest, Foxfire* and *Helios.*

Farkas, Ferenc   Hungarian   1905-2000
Contrafacta Hungarica; 1977; ESM; 10 mins; 0222/2; C/D
Farkas studied with Leo Weiner and Albert Siklos at the Academy of Music in Budapest and later with Respighi in Rome. He has served on the faculties of several schools including the State Conservatory at Szekesfehervar and the Academy of Music. The title *Contrafacta* refers in this instance to a designation used not so much in the music but rather in the literature of the Middle Ages and the Renaissance. Creative imitation was one of the basic principles of the aesthetics of late Humanism. The first movement adds two further bars to the original two bars of a melody notated by Pominoczky in 1520 and builds upon theme variants in the manner of the "basse danses" of the time. The second movement is a setting of a piece by Bakfark. In the third movement, two pieces along with their variations are combined. The fourth movement forms a rondeau around a melody by Tinodi. The fifth movement, *Intermezo,* is a modified folk song and the last movement, *Haiduks' Dance,* is another rondeau.

Fauré, Gabriel   French   1845-1924
Nocturne; Grovlez/McAlister; MMP; 1122/2
Faure's style evolved with clear influences from late Romanticism to mid-twentieth century, but there are certain traits that may be found in nearly all his music such as his handling of harmony and tonality.

Febonio, T.G.
Octet for Winds; ALE; 0222/2; C
This three-movement work is suitable for contests or recitals.

Gabrieli, Giovanni   Italian   1557-1612
Sonata Pian' e Forte; Ephross; c1968; PRC; 4220
A nephew of Andrea Gabrieli, Giovanni's music is primarily sacred or instrumental works. This work requires two piccolos.

Gershwin, George   American   1898-1937
Porgy and Bess; Skirrow; 1935; PRC; 4 mins; 0222/2; C/D
Perhaps one of America's best-known composers of music for stage, Gershwin's musical style ranges from diatonic to chromatic with the clear influence of jazz. This is an arrangement of many of the memorable tunes from this well-known opera.

Gipps, Ruth   English   1921-1999
Wind Octet, Op. 65; ESM; 0222/2; D/E
A pupil of Vaughan Williams, Gipps wrote symphonies, concertos, chamber and choral music.

Gouvy, Louis Theodore   French   1819-1898
Octet, Op. 71; McAlister; 1882; COM, MMP; 1122/2; C/D
Gouvy wrote works in various genres. His music, frequently compared to Mendelssohn's, is usually elegant and substantial. While traditional in form, it is well constructed and typically has lively melodies.

Granados, Enrique   Spanish   1867-1916
Lament of the Maia and the Nightingale from "Govescas"; Elliot; BMP; 0222/2
Granados, a composer, teacher and pianist, studied in Paris and with Pedrellin in Barcelona. This work was originally for piano.

Grieg, Edvard Hagerup   Norwegian   1843-1907
Four Lyric Pieces; Elliot; BMP; 0222/2
Grieg, best known for *Peer Gynt* on which he collaborated with Ibsen, was one of Norway's most important musical figures.

Gursching, Albrecht   German   1934-
Octet; 1974; PIC; 0222/2
A student of Karl Marx and Gunter Bialas, Gursching was an oboist and wrote music for orchestra and chamber groups.

Haan, Stefan de   1921-
Woodwind Octet; ESM; 2222; D

Haeffner, J.C.F.   Swedish   1759-1833
Allegro non Molto in F Major; UUB; 0222/2

Allegro non Tanto—Tempo Allemande in E-Flat Major; UUB; 0222/2

Maestoso; UUB; 0222/2

March in C Major; UUB; 0222/2

Partie in E-Flat Major; UUB; 0222/2

Sinfonia in C Major; UUB; 0222/2

Handel, George   German/English   1685-1759
Music for the Royal Fireworks; Campbell; 1749; ESM; 0222/2; C
Handel's music featured grand design, lush harmonies and a certain eloquence. He wrote music for opera, voice, chamber ensembles and orchestra.

Sinfonia from Solomon, "The Arrival of the Queen of Sheba"; ESM;
0222/2; C/D

Hawes, Jack   1916-
Pieces of Eight; c1979; ESM; 12 mins; 2222; C/D
The five movements are titled *Preludio, Arietta, Scherzetto and Trio,
Chorale* and *Alla Burlesca.*

Haydn, Franz Joseph   Austrian   1732-1809
Divertimento #1; ESM; 0222/2; C
Haydn is considered the creator of the classical form of the symphony
and string quartet. He played a historic role in the evolution of harmony by adopting four-part writing as the compositional foundation. A
prolific composer, Haydn wrote music for orchestra, chamber ensembles, concertos, dramatic works, masses and oratorios. This work,
based on the *St. Anthony Chorale*, requires contrabassoon.

Feldpartie in B-Flat Major, Hob. II:43 or #11; May; 1780s; EAM;
0222/2; C
This work was presumably written for Prince Eszterhazy's Feldhar-
monie (open-air wind band). The horn parts include the original scoring in high B-flat as well as an easier version for horns in F.

Octet in F Major, Hob11:7 or #19 Lyman;   IMC,   PTE;   7   mins;
0222/2; D
This work may have actually been written by Wranitzky, but it is attri-
buted to Haydn.

Symphony #75; COM, ESM; 2022/2; C/D
There is an optional contrabassoon part.

Henneberg, Richard   Swedish   1853-1925
Serenade; SMI; 1122/2
Henneberg studied piano with Liszt and later became a well-known
conductor. He wrote music for ballet, chorus, chamber ensembles and
an opera.

Henze, Hans Werner   German   1926-
Sonata per Otto Ottoni; EAM, SCL; 0222/2

Hoffmeister, Franz Anton   Austrian   1754-1812
Serenade in E-Flat Major; c1962; PTE; 10 mins; 0223/2; C/D
Hoffmeister, a well-known music publisher in his time, was also a pro-
lific composer. He wrote for orchestra, stage and chamber ensembles.
Flutes may substitute for oboes in this work. Contrabassoon is re-
quired.

Jacob, Gordon   English   1895-1984
Divertimento in E-Flat Major; 1969; MRI; 7 mins; 0222/2; C/D
Jacob studied with Stanford and Howells at the Royal Academy of
Music and Dulwich College and later joined the faculty of the RAM.
His works are deeply rooted in tradition and display fine craftsmanship.
Written with three movements titled *March, Sarabande on a Ground*
and *Rondo*, this is a nice addition to the octet repertoire.

Serenade for Woodwinds #2; 1950; BHI; 24 mins; 2222; C/D
Piccolo and English horn are required.

Three Elizabethan Fancies; c1978; ESM; 7 mins; 0222/2; C/D
These three charming movements are titled *The Carman's Whistle, A
Toye* and *Quodling's Delight.*

Joplin, Scott   African American   1868-1917
The Chrysanthemum; ESM; Flexible instrumentation; C/D
Named the "King of Ragtime," Joplin was largely self-taught though
he briefly attended the Smith College for Negroes in 1895 to gain technical skills in composition.

Koetsier, Jan   Dutch   1911-
Octet; 1968; DNA; 20 mins; 0222/2; C/D
A pianist and conductor now living in Munich, Koetsier writes in the
Neo-Classic tradition of northern Europe. His music is influenced by
Hindemith and is characterized by solid craftsmanship and invention.

Krol, Bernhard   German   1920-
Linzer Harmoniemusik, Op. 67; 1978; BBM; 17 mins; 0222/2; D
Krol, composer and horn player, studied at the Mohr Conservatory and
the Internationales Institute.

Krommer, Franz Czech   1759-1831
Octet in Bb Major, Op. 67; Hellyer; c1970; MRI, ESM; 0222/2; C/D
All of these octets by Krommer may be found variously listed as *Octet,
Partita* or *Harmonie*.

Octet in F Major, Op. 57; MRI; 0222/2; C
In this work, an arrangement of the quintet for two clarinets, bassoon
and two horns, the first clarinet is the soloist with the others used as
accompaniment. There is an optional contrabassoon part.

Octet, Op. 69; Hellyer; c1970; MRI; 0222/2; C/D
There is an optional contrabassoon part.

Octet, Op. 79; Hellyer; c1971; MRI; 22 mins; 0222/2; C/D
There is an optional contrabassoon part.

Partita in B-Flat Major, Op. 13 #1; ESM; 0222/2; D
There is an optional contrabassoon part.

Partita in E-Flat Major, "La Chasse"; DBM; 0222/2; D

Partita in E-Flat Major, Op. 13 #2; ESM; 0222/2; D
There is an optional contrabassoon part.

Partita in E-Flat Major, Op. 13 #4; ESM, COM; 0222/2; D
There is an optional contrabassoon part.

Lachner, Franz   German   1803-1890
Octet in B-Flat Major, Op. 156; 1850; MRI; 12 mins; 1122/2; C/D
Brother of Theodore, Franz was the most celebrated of this German
family of musicians.

Laderman, Ezra   American   1924-
Octet for Winds; 1957; PRC, OUP; 0222/2; C
Laderman studied with Wolpe, Miriam Gideon, Luening and Moore,
received three Guggenheim fellowships and taught at several colleges

before becoming dean at Yale University School of Music. His music incorporates a lyrical style into a contemporary context, using tonal material in combination with atonal and aleatory elements and seeking out unusual formal structures.

Lalo, Aleksander   French   1948-
Albanian Folk Dances; ESM; 2222; D

Lawrance
Boogie for Wind Octet; ESM; 0222/2; D/E

Riffs for Wind Octet; ESM; 0222/2; D/E

Lazzari, Sylvio   Austrian/French   1857-1944
Octuor in F Major, Op. 20; 1890; SMC; 1212/2
Lazzari studied with Franck and Guiraud at the Paris Conservatory and wrote music for opera, orchestra, voice, piano and chamber groups. English horn is required.

Loudova, Ivana   Czech   1941-
Don Giovanni's Dream; 1989; COM; 3 mins; 0222/2; C/D
Loudova studied composition at the Prague Conservatory and the Prague Academy of Music, and later studied with Messiaen and Jolivet in Paris. Her music has evolved from tonal themes to serialism and aleatory forms. About *Giovanni's Dream* Ivana Loudova writes: "I wanted to create a 'dream fantasy' of the story of Don Giovanni. With the oboe as solo instrument and the English horn replacing the second oboe, space is given to other solo instruments. The tutti passages sound differently, with a timbre like in normal classical works. In that manner I composed the fantasy for wind octet, which is not easy to play, but it does give the players the possibility to show their quality and master." English horn is required.

Lowe, Thomas   English   1911-
Suite of Dances; c1976; ESM, PRC; 7 mins; 2131/1; C
This work features four movements titled *Minuet, Polonais, Sarabande* and *Tarantella*.

Lutyens, Elisabeth   English   1906-1983
The Rape of the Moone, Op. 90; 1973; ESM, KAL; 0222/2; E
Lutyens attended the Royal College of Music where she studied with Darke. Her music incorporates twelve tone technique and other twentieth-century devices.

Masek, Vaclav Vincenc Bohemian 1755-1831
Serenata in E-Flat Major; c1990; ESM; 10 mins; 0222/2; C/D
Vaclav, the most celebrated member of his musical family, was a prolific composer, writing some forty partitas for wind ensemble. These compositions were so successful that they were performed by the best wind ensembles in Austria and Germany. Especially appealing in Masek's works is the style, which balances Classical and Romantic periods. His name is sometimes spelled Mascek or Machek. Contrabassoon or string bass is required.

Mills, Charles Borromeo American 1914-1982
Concerto Sereno, Op. 77; 1948; AMC; 0222/2
A student of Garfield, Copland, Sessions and Harris, Mills wrote music primarily in a contrapuntal style with formal clarity, though his later works adopt serialism.

Miscellaneous
Christmas Pieces; Emerson; ESM; 2131/1; B/C
This set of arrangements for winds includes music by Mendelssohn, Humperdinck, Scarlatti, Tchaikovsky and Cornelius.

Three Renaissance Pieces; Schweikert; BMP; 0222/2

Mozart, Wolfgang Amadeus Austrian 1756-1791
Alla Turca, K.331; Mayer; DBM; 0222/2; C
Originally for piano, this is a movement from *Sonata in A Major*.

Divertimento, K.226/196e; Einstein; PTE, MRI; 20 mins; 0222/2; D
This divertimento first appeared as the second of a set of *Three Pieces d'Harmonie*. It was one of a number of works for wind band found in Prague by Mozart's first biographer Niemetschek. Opinions as to its authenticity have been divided. Kochel assigned it to the appendix of doubtful works as Anh. 226, perhaps as no autograph score had survived. In the third edition of Kochel's catalogue (1937), Alfred Einstein identified it as one of the works Mozart wrote for the Munich Carnival in 1775, renumbering it K.196e. However, the latest edition of Kochel has relegated it once more to the appendix.

Divertimento in B-Flat Major, K.227; 1775; PTE; 9 mins; 0222/2; C/D
The authenticity of this work, like *K.226*, has not been established. The quality of the writing in the various movements is extremely uneven. The melodic lines frequently require long phrases and the part writing is faulty in places. There are portions that may be by Mozart,

but it seems very doubtful that the works in their entirety were composed in this form by Mozart.

Divertimento in B-Flat Major #14, K.270; 1777; KAL; 12 mins; 0202/2; C/D
This divertimento shows a refined chamber music style, particularly in the *Andante* and the *Minuet*. It ends with a *Rondo* in the rhythm of a German dance.

Harmonie: Cosi Fan Tutti; Wendt; MRI; 0222/2
Arrangements of music from the opera are included in this set.

Harmonie: Don Giovanni; Triebensee; 1791; MRI; 0222/2; D
This is a two-volume arrangement of music from the opera.

Harmonie: Figaro; Wendt; MRI; 0222/2
Arrangements from the opera are included in this set for octet.

Harmonie: Magic Flute; Heidenreich; 1791; MRI; 12 mins; 0222/2
This is a two volume set of musical arrangements from the opera.

Harmonie: Seraglio; MRI; 0222/2

Harmonie: Titus; MRI; 0222/2

Idomeneo Overture; Sheen; 1781; KAL; 0222/2; D

Impresario Overture; Sheen; KAL; 0222/2; D

La Clemenza di Tito; Triebensee; 1791; MRI; 0222/2; D
This is a two-volume set of musical arrangements from the opera. There is an optional contrabassoon part.

La Clemenza di Tito Overture; Sheen; 1791; KAL; 0222/2; D

Selections from *Cosi fan Tutti*; Topilow; 1790; CON; 0222/2

Serenade #11 in E-Flat Major, K.375; Spiegl; 1781; PRC; 24 mins; 0222/2; D
The *Serenade* exists in two different versions for wind ensembles. The first version is scored for wind sextet and was completed in 1781. In the following year Mozart wrote a new version of the work, this time adding two oboes to the group to make it a standard wind octet. The two outer movements and the central slow movement are completely reworked and the octet version even has an extra bar at the end of the slow movement. The two minuet movements, however, simply have oboe parts superimposed on the sextet score.

Serenade #12 in C Minor, K.388/384a; 1782; PRC; 24 mins; 0222/2; D

Mozart's last wind serenade, this piece absolutely belongs among the most subtle chamber music of the mature composer. The *Nacht Musique,* as he called it in a letter, is unrelentingly somber until the *Minuet* when the coda gives way to a bright C major finale.

Serenade in B-Flat Major, K.196f; EAM; 0222/2

Originally for wind sextet, this octet version adds two oboes and makes significant changes in the other parts.

Serenade in B-Flat Major. K.182/370a; Einstein; 1781; PTE; 11 mins; 0222/2

This work was originally for thirteen winds and is believed to have been reduced to an octet by the composer.

Serenade, K.448; ESM; 0222/2; D

This work was originally for two pianos.

Sinfonia Concertante; EAM, SCL; 0222/2; D

This is an octet arrangement of the well-known work for wind quartet and orchestra.

Sonata in F Major, K.497; Rudolph; COM; 27 mins; 0222/2; D

This was originally for piano four hands.

Mysliveczek, Josef   Czech   1737-1781

Three Octets; ESM; 0222/2

Perhaps best known for his operas, Mysliveczek studied with Giovanni Pescetti in Venice. He was one of the most significant Bohemian composers of his time and even Mozart expressed admiration of his talent.

Noble

Hertfordshire Suite; ESM; 2222; C/D

Novacek, Rudolf   Czech   1860-1929

Sinfonietta, Op. 48; Dishinger; 1888; MMM, ESM; 1122/2; D

Novacek was a violin teacher and conductor in Rumania, Bulgaria and Russia. The *Sinfonietta* is perhaps his best known work.

Piccinini, Alessandro   Italian   1566-1638

Marcia; PRC; 0222/2

Piccinini came from a family of musicians and served at the Ferrarese court.

Pleyel, Ignaz   Austrian   1757-1831
Octet; MRI; 0222/2
Pleyel studied with Haydn but is perhaps best known for his manufacturing of pianos. A prolific composer, he wrote symphonies, symphonie concertantes, concertos and chamber music.

Poot, Marcel   Belgian   1901-1988
Octuor—Mosaique; 1948; EAM, UNE; 17 mins; 2222; C
Poot studied at Brussels Conservatory with Sevenants, Lunssens and
de Greef, where he later was on the staff and was director from 1949
until his retirement. His music is primarily tonal and is striking in its
rhythmic vivacity.

Radziwill, Prince Maciej   Polish   1751-1800
Divertissement; ESM; 2222; D/E

Reicha, Joseph   Czech   1746-1803
Partita in D Major; c1989; COM; 1221/2; D
Reicha (also spelled Rejcha) wrote music that is pleasing to both the
performers and their audiences. His uncle, Anton Reicha, is famous for
his twenty-five wind quintets. This work features the flute.

Reinecke, Carl Heinrich   German   1824-1910
Octet in B-Flat Major, Op. 216; 1892; IMC; 22 mins; 1122/2; D
As a composer Reinecke is mainly known for his numerous compositions for piano. His compositional style is closer to Schumann's than
to Mendelssohn's writing. His operas met with little success, but his
chamber music found wide recognition. His later works contain a
warmth similar to music by Brahms.

Righini, Pietro   Italian   1907-
Octet: Parthia; MRI; 0222/2
Righini is the author of several books on a variety of musical topics.

Rossini, Gioachino   Italian   1792-1868
Tancredi Overture; 1813; COM; 1122/2; D
Optional contrabassoon.

Ruppert, Anton   German   1936-
Reprisen; 9 mins; 0222/2

Saint-Saens, Camille Charles   French   1835-1921
Feuillet d'Album, Op, 81; Taffanel; 1887; DUR; 1122/2
Saint-Saens was a gifted and prolific composer whose music exemplifies the essential French qualities of clarity and order. This work is originally written for piano four hands.

Salieri, Antonio   Italian   1750-1825
Harmonia per un Tempio della Notte; Ranier; c1981; DBM, SUV; 3
  mins; 0222/2; C
Only in our time has the life of the Imperial Court Kapellmeister Salieri begun to be seen in a new light and his work to be reassessed. Not a great deal of Salieri's work was published during his lifetime. Many of his successes were short-lived, and much of his music reflects the taste of his public, the aristocracy, and the members of the imperial court. Salieri's importance as a teacher is, however, uncontestable. Composers such as Beethoven, Mozart and Schubert quite rightly spoke proudly of having studied with him. Five original wind ensemble pieces by Salieri exist. This one-movement piece is reminiscent, in its three-part structure, of the da capo aria, and it reminds us that the composer gave precedence to the operatic stage in his works.

Schickele, Peter   American   1935-
Octoot; 1983; EVI; 8 mins; 0222/2; C/D
Schickele wrote this piece under his fictional name of P.D.Q. Bach.

Schneider
Harmonie #1; ESM; 2022/2; D/E

Harmonie #8; ESM; 2022/2; D/E

Schubert, Franz   Austrian   1797-1828
Minuet and Finale in F Major, D.72; 1813; NPR; 0222/2; C/D
Schubert produced great masterpieces in virtually every field of composition. It is rich in melody and expressive harmony. These two movements are from the *Wind Octet in F Major*.

Minuets #1-#6; BAR; 1122/2

Octet in F Major, D.72; Weait/Hoorickx; 1813; MMM; 12 mins; 0222/2; C
The first two movements of this work were completed after Schubert's death by Hoorickx. Combined with the original *Minuet* and *Finale* by Schubert it becomes a complete concert work.

Schwertsik, Kurt   Austrian   1935-
Am Ende steht ein Marsch, Op. 59; 1991; BHI; 21 mins; 0222/2

Shewan, Douglas
Wind Octet; c1975; HAN; 2221/1

Short, Michael   English   1937-
Three Pieces; 1981; ESM; 10 mins; 0222/2
This multimeter work is in three movements titled *Badinage, Cortege* and *Burlesque.*

Small, A.
Delicate Blues; CFI; 2033
Contrabassoon is required.

Stadlmair, Hans   Austrian   1929-
Octet; c1971; PTE; 0222/2
Stadlmair received his musical training in Linz and Vienna and later settled in Munich where he founded the Munich Chamber Orchestra. He wrote mostly instrumental works in a Neo-Baroque style.

Stamitz, Carl   Bohemian   1745-1801
Parthia in E-Flat; 1777; ESM; 0222/2
Stamitz was considered an exceptional violist and wrote a large number of compositions for orchestra, sinfonie concertante, concertos and chamber ensembles. His style is outstanding for melodic wealth, formal elegance and harmonious tonal beauty.

Stearns, Peter Pindar   American   1931-
Octet; AMC; 2222
This work requires piccolo, English horn, bass clarinet and contrabassoon.

Steffan, Joseph   Czech   1726-1797
Serenata Parthia in E-Flat Major; Rhodes; ESM; 0222/2; C
A pupil of Wagenseil, Steffan (sometimes spelled Stepan) settled in Vienna where he was a renowned teacher. Steffan composed in a tuneful Classical style and was especially renowned for his keyboard works, although his music became neglected after his death. He composed two *Harmonies* for wind instruments.

Harmonie in D Major; ESM; 0222/2; C

Tansman, Alexandre   Polish/French/Amer.   1897-1986
Four Impressions; c1950; MCA; 2222
Tansman's early music shows the influence of Chopin, Stravinsky and Ravel. Later works may be compared to Milhaud in the use of folk themes and of different instrumental combinations.

Tchaikovsky, Peter   Russian   1840-1893
Humoreske; Skirrow; PRC, ESM; 0222/2; B/C
Tchaikovsky had a gift for beautiful melodies unmatched by his contemporaries and wrote in every musical genre including stage, orchestra, chamber, piano and songs. He is widely regarded as the leading nineteenth-century Russian composer.

Nutcracker Overture; Emerson; ESM; 5120; C

Three Pieces from "Album for the Young," Op. 39; Cuninghame; 1878; ESM; 3131; C
Originally written for piano, this arrangement requires alto flute.

Triebensee, Joseph   Austrian   1772-1848
Menuetto con Variazioni in F Major; Brown; c1979; NPR; 0222/2; C/D
Oboist Joseph Triebensee was the son of George, who was solo oboist for the Schwarzenberg Court both in Wittengan and in Vienna. Joseph is best known for the prolific number of arrangements for wind octet that he wrote after becoming the Director of Prince Alois Lichtenstein's octet in 1796. Although the majority of these were of music by other composers, these original variations display not only his skill as a writer, but also the technical skill of the Lichtenstein musicians.

Tull, Fisher Aubrey   American   1934-1994
Scherzino; c1973; BHI; 4004; C/D
Piccolo and bass clarinet are required.

Verdi, Giuseppe   Italian   1813-1901
La Traviata Highlights; North; TRI; 1122/2
This arrangement features music from the first act.

Weber, Carl Maria   German   1786-1826
Five Weber Movements; Campbell; ESM; 0222/2; C/D
Weber is an important founder of the Romantic movement in Germany and one of its leading composers.

Freischutz Overture; 1817-21; COM; 0222/2; C/D
This work has optional contra-bassoon and trumpet parts.

Freischutz, Part 1 and 2; 1817-21; ESM; 0222/2; C/D
This arrangement has optional contrabassoon and trumpet parts.

March from "Turandot"; Elliot; BMP; 0222/2; C/D

Peter Schmoll Overture; Elliot; BMP; 0222/2; C/D

Weilland
Harmonie; ESM*;* 0222/2; C/D

Wenth, Johann N. 1745-1801
Parthia in E-Flat Major; c1989; ESM; 0222/2; C/D

Whitlock, Percy English 1903-1946
Folk Tune; Emerson; c1974; ESM; 2 mins; 2131/1; B/C
Taken from a larger work entitled *Five Short Pieces*, this pleasant
movement is good for young ensembles.

Woolfenden, Guy English 1937-
Suite Francaise; ESM; 2222; C/D
Woolfenden, as head of the Royal Shakespeare Company, composed
more than 150 scores for the group. He conducted orchestras in Canada,
Germany, Japan, the United States and France. He also wrote music for
ballet, musicals, ensembles, band and concerti.

Wranitzky, Paul Czech 1756-1808
Harmonie in F Major; ESM; 2022/2 ; C/D
Wranitzky, best known for his symphonies and chamber music, composed in a somewhat simplified form of the Classical period. The two
flute parts may be played on oboe.

Ahmas, Harri 20th C.
Tango Flautando; 1990; FMC; 3 mins; 0405
English horn and contrabassoon are required.

Albeniz, Isaac Spanish 1860-1909
Tango from Espana; Campbell; 1890; EAM; 1222/2; D
Albeniz, one of the most important figures in Spain's musical history, helped create a national idiom and an indigenous school of piano music. Virtually all his music written for piano is inspired by Spanish folklore. He is credited with establishing the modern school of Spanish piano literature which is derived from original rhythms and melodic patterns, rather than imitating the Spanish music by French and Russian composers. He studied with Reinecke, Dukas and d'Indy. This is a movement from *Espana, Op. 165* solo piano collection, here arranged for wind nonet.

Bach, P.D.Q. American 1935-
No-No Nonette; PRC; 14 mins; 1222/2; C/D
Various toys are required for performance.

Bartos, Jan Zdenek Czech 1908-1981
Divertimento I, Op. 79; c1960; PAN; 1222/2
Bartos studied with Jirak and Kricka in Prague. He has written opera, ballet, choral works and chamber music.

Beethoven, Ludwig van German 1770-1827
Adagio in F Major; Hess; c1957; BKH; 1222/2; C/D
Beethoven's early achievements show him to be extending the Viennese Classical tradition. Later he began to compose in an increasingly individual musical style, and at the end of his life he wrote his most sublime and profound works.

Andante Cantabile from Quintet, Op. 16; Triebensee; COM; 0223/2; C/D
Contrabassoon is requied.

Sonata Pathetique; Druchetsky; 1798-99; COM; 0223/2; D
Contrabassoon is requied.

Bonvin, Ludwig Swiss/American 1850-1939
Melodie; BKH; 1222/2
Bonvin, primarily known as a choral conductor and scholar, wrote sacred music as well as works for orchestra, piano, voice and violin.

Boyce, William   English   1711-1779
Symphony #4 in F Major; Taylerson; 1760; ZER; 0223/2; C/D
Boyce's style has a fresh energy that is apparent in this work. He used middle movements that are quick, light and soft rather than slow. In the 19th century Boyce's reputation depended mainly on his Cathedral Music, a three-volume collection of sacred music by English masters of the sixteenth through eighteenth centuries. However, in the early twentieth century interest in his music was revived when a number of Boyce's overtures were published by Constant Lambert. Contrabassoon or string bass is required.

Brahms, Johannes   German   1833-1897
Hungarian Dances #3 and #7; 1872; BHI; 0223/2; C/D
One of the greatest masters of music, Brahms composed music for orchestra, voice, piano, chorus and chamber ensembles. Contrabassoon is required.

Intermezzo, Op. 117 #1; Skirrow; 1892; PRC; 1222/2; C/D
In spite of powerfully Romantic characteristics in his music, he used a traditional sense of order in his music and was true to the central German musical tradition.

Variations, Op. 23; Connolly; 1861; NOV, SHA; 1222/2; D

Brautigam, Helmut   German   1914-1942
Kleine Jagdmusik, Op. 11; c1939; BKH; 1222/2

Bresgen, Cesar   German   1913-1988
Jagdkonzert; EAM; 2123/1
Bresgen studied with Haas at the Munich Academy. His works include music for opera, concerto grosso and piano. Contrabassoon is requied.

Brun, Herbert   German/American   1918-
Passacaille, Op. 25; LEM; 2122/2
Brun studied with Wolpe and later taught electronic music at the University of Illinois. Contrabassoon is requied.

Chaun, Frantisek   Czech   1921-1981
Divertimento; CHF; 1222/2
Chaun, a professional pharmacist and avocational painter, studied composition with Feld and Slavicky in Prague. His works show the influence of Stravinsky with their Neo-Classical style. Two bass clarinets are required.

Cherubini, Luigi   Italian   1760-1842
March in F Major; Ballola; EAM; 0223/2
Cherubini studied with Sarti and is best known for his operas and sacred music.

Cianchi, Emilio   1833-1890
Nonetto; 1868; COM; 0223/2; D/E
This work has the traditional Classic form; however, the music itself recalls the atmosphere of the Romantic Italian opera through appealing bel canto melodies and truly virtuoso passages. Contrabassoon is required.

Cole, Hugo   English   1917-1995
Serenade for Nine Wind Instruments; NOV; 1123/2
Contrabassoon or string bass is required.

Debussy, Claude A.   French   1862-1918
Three Pieces from Children's Corner; Sheen; 1906-08; KAL; 1222/2; D
Debussy studied with Chopin and later at the Paris Conservatory with Durand. He wrote music for opera, ballet, orchestra, piano and chamber ensembles. This work, originally written for piano, requires English horn, bass clarinet and contrabassoon.

Donizetti, Gaetano   Italian   1797-1848
Sinfonia; Townsend; 1817; PTE; 4.5 mins; 1222/2; C/D
Donizetti, best known for his Italian operas, also wrote songs, sacred music, chamber music and works for piano. As used by Donizetti, the term "sinfonia" does not refer to a four-movement composition for orchestra, but to a short instrumental work similar to the opera overture of his day.

Dubois, Pierre Max   French   1930-1995
Huit Plus Un; c1977; BIL; 8 mins; 1222/2; D
Dubois studied at the Paris Conservatoire and won the Prix de Rome in 1955. His music shows the influences of Milhaud, Francaix and Prokofiev. He has written music for orchestra, dance and chamber ensembles. The five movements are titled *Amorce, Bucolique, Serenade Cassee, Gavotte and Gaillard* and *Toccata*.

Dvořák, Antonín   Czech   1841-1904
Slavonic Dance, Op. 46 #2; Clements; 1878; ESM, PRC; 6 mins;
1222/2; C/D
Dvořák's musical style is diverse, with his early works reflecting the
influence of Beethoven and Schuber, then Wagner and later Brahms.
This work was originally for violin and piano.

Gounod, Charles   French   1818-1893
Petite Symphonie in B-Flat Major, Op. 90; 1888; IMC, BIL; 19 mins;
1222/2; D
Gounod, a leading figure in the revival of chamber music in France
during the 1870s, wrote this piece specifically for the famous flute virtuoso, Paul Taffanel. It has been compared with the divertissements of
Mozart and the septet and octet of the youthful Beethoven. The
freshness and clarity of both melody and part-writing are inspired by
those works.

Gouvy, Louis Theodore   French   1819-1898
Petite Suite Gaulouise, Op. 90; 1898; UNE; 1222/2; D
Gouvy's music, frequently compared to Mendelssohn's, is usually
elegant and substantial. While traditional in form, it is well constructed
and typically has lively melodies.

Grovlez, Gabriel   French   1879-1944
Nocturne; Sansone; 1222/2
A student of Gedalge and Faure, Grovlez was active in Paris as a
performer and teacher. He wrote opera, ballets, choral and solo vocal
music, chamber and piano music.

Gyrowetz, Adalbert   Bohemian   1763-1850
Parthia in E-Flat Major; 1801; COM; 11 mins; 0223/2; C
Gyrowetz (also spelled Jirovec), a student of Haydn, composed in a
style very similar to his teacher though he was also closely associated
with the Czech Nationalistic style. In his younger years Gyrowetz was
a very popular composer. A good many of his works were printed
during his lifetime. However, by 1820 he was already practically forgotten because of his inability to adapt to the change in musical taste.
A particularly remarkable feature of this *Parthia* is the demanding horn
part. The first horn is often called upon to perform the melodic line,
which gives the instrumentalist technical and musical demands that go
far beyond the usual function of the horn in the Classic period.
Contrabassoon is required.

Haydn, Franz Joseph   Austrian   1732-1809
Twelve Short Pieces; Skinder; c1965; PWM; 2232

Hekster, Walter   Dutch   1937-
Relief #3 for Nine Winds in Three Groups; DNA; 8 mins; 1222/2
After graduation from the Amsterdam Conservatory, Hekster was a clarinetist with the Connecticut Symphony Orchestra and later taught clarinet and composition at Brandon University (Canada), Utrecht Conservatory and Arnhem Conservatory.

Holbrooke, Josef   English   1878-1958
Nocturne; SMC; 2322
Holbrooke studied composition with Corder at the Royal Academy of
Music. He wrote operas, symphonies, concertos, chamber and piano
music. English horn is required.

Holloway, Robin   English   1943-
Divertimento #2, Op. 18; 1972; BHI; 1222/2
Holloway studied at Oxford and Cambridge. He wrote music for opera,
orchestra, concertos, chamber music and voice. Flute doubles on piccolo and English horn is required.

Horovitz, Joseph   Austrian/English   1926-
Fantasia on a Theme of Couperin; 1962; NOV; 1222/2; D
Horovitz studied at New College in Oxford and wrote music for opera,
ballet, orchestra and chamber ensembles. This work was originally for
strings. English horn is required.

Hummel, Johann Nepomuk   Austrian   1778-1837
Octet: Parthia in E-Flat Major; MRI; 0223/2; D/E
A student of Mozart, Hummel was considered one of the great
composers and piano virtuosos of his time and was often declared to be
the equal of Beethoven. His compositions demonstrated fine craftsmanship, melodic inventiveness and harmonic and contrapuntal skill of
the highest caliber. Contrabassoon is required.

Keler, Bela   Hungarian   1820-1882
Overture: "Lustspiel," Op. 108; ZER; 1222/2; D
Keler served in numerous posts as conductor, violinist and composer.
This is an arrangement of his most successful work, originally for or-
chestra. There is an optional contrabassoon part.

Kozeluch, Leopold   Bohemian   1747-1818
Parthia a la Camera; c1989; COM; 8 mins; 0322/2; C/D
Kozeluch was one of the leading representatives of Czech music in
eighteenth-century Vienna. His musical output is almost entirely
secular. His in-strumental music uses Viennese Classical style with
later works show-ing some Romantic lyricism. This piece features
bassoon and oboe with other instruments primarily used as
accompaniment. His name is sometimes spelled Kotzeluch or Kozeluh.

Two Suites for Wind Nonet; 1802; PRC; 8 mins; 0223/2; C/D
Contrabassoon or string bass is required.

Kraus, Joseph Martin   Swedish   1756-1792
Intermedes pour Amphitryon; 1784; SMI; 0232/2

Krommer, Franz   Czech   1759-1831
Harmonie in B-Flat Major, Op. 78; ESM; 0223/2; D
Krommer was one of the most successful Czech composers in Vienna in
the early twentieth century. Of Krommer's (sometimes spelled Kramar)
more than 300 compositions, at least forty of these are partitas for wind
ensemble. He was a very popular composer and even Beethoven regarded him to be a serious competitor. Contrabassoon is required.

Harmonie in C Major, Op. 76; 1820; ESM; 8 mins; 0223/2; C/D

Harmonie in E-Flat Major, Op. 71; 1807-1810; ESM; 0223/2; D
Contrabassoon is required.

Harmonie in F Major, Op. 73; ESM; 0223/2; D
Contrabassoon is required.

Harmonie in F Major, Op. 77; ESM; 0223/2; D
Contrabassoon is required.

Harmonie in F Major, Op. 83; ESM; 0223/2; D
Contrabassoon is required.

Nonet, Op. 79; Janetzky; BBL; 23 mins; 0223/2; D
Contrabassoon is required.

Lange, Friedrich   Norwegian   1861-1939
Nonetto in F Major; 1879; SEE, COM; 12 mins; 1222/2; D
Lange's influence in Norway is still noticeable, since many of today's
teachers had a personal relationship with him. This work uses the Classical masters as its example.

Lefebure-Wely, Louis   French   1817-1869
Sortie in B-Flat Major; ZER; 1222/2; C/D
After studies with Berton and Halevy at the Paris Conservatory, Lefebure-Wely was an organist at the Madeleine and St. Sulpice.

Lortzing, Albert   German   1801-1851
Overture to Zar and Zimmermann; WBP; 0223/2; C/D
There are two optional trumpet parts.

Marteau, Henri   Swedish   1874-1934
Serenade in D Major, Op. 20 ; c1922; STE; 2232
Regarded as one of the great violinists of his time, Marteau composed works for orchestra, chorus, chamber, concertos and opera. Bass clarinet is required.

Mendelssohn, Felix   German   1809-1847
Koncertstuck in D Minor, Op. 114; Sheen; ESM; 1222/2; D
Mendelssohn's music emphasizes clarity and adherence to the Classical tradition. This arrangement is for clarinet and bassett horn soloists with wind septet.

Methfessel, Albert Gottlied   1785-1869
Variationen; Funck; ZIM; 0223/2
Contrabassoon is required.

Miscellaneous
Four Encores; COM; 0223/2; D
Contrabassoon or string bass is required.

Mozart, Wolfgang Amadeus   Austrian   1756-1791
Canzonetta from Don Giovanni; Taylerson; ESM; 0223/2; C/D
Mozart was a musical genius whose works in virtually every genre are unmatched in lyrical beauty and rhythmic variety. Contrabassoon is required.

Fantasia in F Minor, K.608; Pillney; c1967; BKH; 1222/2; C/D
Originally for mechanical organ, there is an optional contrabassoon part in this version.

Symphony #39; 1788; COM; 0223/2; D
This is an arrangement of the first movement. Contrabassoon is required.

Oliver, Stephen   English   1950-1992
Ricercare 2; NOV, ESM; 11 mins; 0223/2; D
Contrabassoon is required.

Otten, Ludwig   Netherlands   1924-
Divertimento #3; DNA; 16 mins; 1222/2

Parry, Charles Hubert   English   1848-1918
Nonet, Op. 70; 1877; COM; 12 mins; 1222/2; D
This splendid *Nonet* is a welcome addition to the scarce Romantic repertoire for wind ensemble. The greater part of Parry's compositions
consists of vocal works. His instrumental works include four symphonies, a piano concerto, symphonic suites and poems, music for piano
and organ and some chamber music. Of great importance are his
treatises on music. English horn is required.

Reiner, Karel   Czech   1910-1979
Kleine Suite; 1960; CHF; 1222/2
During WW II, Reiner was sent to the camps of Dachau and Ausch-
witz, but survived and continued his work as a composer and pianist.
His early music was atonal, but after 1945 he wrote mostly traditional
music and then later returned to avant garde techniques. He wrote
operas, concertos, symphonies and chamber music.

Rossini, Gioachino   Italian   1792-1868
L'Italiana in Algeri Overture; 1813; RIC, ESM; 8 mins; 0223/2; D
Recognized as one of the greatest Italian composers of his time, he is
best known for his operas. Contrabassoon or string bass is required.

William Tell Overture; 1829; COM; 11 mins; 0223/2; D
The third bassoon part is for contrabassoon or string bass.

Rummel, Christian   German   1787-1849
*Two Grandes Pieces d'Apres des Motifs de Kalkbrenner, Dussek et
Weber, Op. 52*; EAM; 0223/2
Contrabassoon is required.

Variations, Op. 40 (Romance de Joseph); EAM; 0223/2
Contrabassoon is required.

Saint-Saens, Camille Charles   French   1835-1921
Deuxieme Suite; Baxter-Northrup; 2122/2
Saint-Saens was a gifted and prolific composer whose music exemplifies the essential French qualities of clarity and order. This work was
originally written for piano four hands.

Salieri, Antonio   Italian   1750-1825
Two Wind Serenades; Bailey; 2203/2; C
Contrabassoon or string bass is required.

Schildknecht, Bjorn   Swedish   1905-1946
Fugerat Forspel; SMI; 2221/2

Schreck, Gustav   German   1849-1918
Nonett, Op. 40; c1905; COM, BKH; 2122/2; D
Schreck was not a progressive or innovative composer, but in a very natural way he applied sound technical skill as a composer. In this respect the light-hearted *Nonett* is a valuable addition to the Romantic repertoire for wind ensemble.

Schubert, Franz   Austrian   1797-1828
Sixteen German Dances; KAL; 1222/2; C/D
Schubert produced great masterpieces in virtually every field of composition. His music is rich in melody and expressive harmony. Contrabassoon is required.

Siebert, Friedrich   1906-
Scherzetto; c1966; EUL; 2222/1
This is a solo horn piece with accompanying winds.

Strauss, Johann   Austrian   1825-1899
Die Fledermaus Overture; Newhill; 1874; ESM; 1222/2; C/D
Strauss achieved international recognition early in life and was hailed as the successor to Brahms and Wagner. Although he wrote extensively for theatre, Strauss's biggest achievements were in the dance genre such as this work which is an arrangement of the overture from his best operetta.

Triebensee, Joseph   Austrian   1772-1848
Partita in B-Flat Major; COM; 0223/2; C/D
Oboist Joseph Triebensee was the son of George, who was the solo oboist for the Schwarzenberg Court both in Wittengan and in Vienna. Joseph is best known for the prolific number of arrangements for wind octet that he made after becoming the Director of Prince Alois Lichtenstein's octet in 1796. This partita is written in a purely classical style. Contrabassoon or string bass is required.

Tscherepnin, Ivan   French/American   1943-
Wheelwinds; 1966; EAM; 3231; E
Starting with a simple scheme of nine notes brought through a circle of fifths, the resulting twelve sections are arranged to allow the instruments to be heard in all possible registers. The conductor is considered a performer with a section composed as a "conductor's solo." This work requires alto flute, English horn, E-flat clarinet and bass clarinet.

Vomacka, Boleslav   Czech   1887-1965
Nonett; 1957; CHF; 1222/2
Vomacka, a student of Vitezslav Novak, wrote music in a strong nationalistic style.

Weait, Christopher   Canadian   20th C.
Two Canadian Folksongs; c1974; COM; 0223/2; C/D
Contrabassoon is required.

TEN WINDS

Amos, Keith   English   20th C.
Theme and Variations; c1986; ESM; 11.5 mins; 2222/2; D

Andriessen, Jurriaan   Dutch   1925-
Concertino; DNA; 2222/2; C/D
Andriessen's music shows sound professional skill in a style that draws on diverse techniques without being bound to any specific system. This work features bassoon.

Respiration Suite; 1962; DNA; 10 mins; 2222/2; C/D
This suite contains four movements titled *Blood Air-Dialogue, Deep Sea Sarabande, Menuet at High Altitude* and *Flowing Air.*

Baker, Michael Conway   American/Canadian   1937-
Blow the Wind Southerly; ESM; 2222/2; D

Ballou, Esther Williamson   American   1915-1973
Suite for Winds; ACA; 2222/2
Ballou studied with Bernard Wagenaar at the Juilliard School and studied privately with Luening and Riegger.

Beethoven, Ludwig van   German   1770-1827
Two Minuets; Hill; ESM; 2222/2; B
Beethoven's early achievements show him to be extending the Viennese Classical tradition. Later he began to compose in an increasingly individual musical style, and at the end of his life he wrote his most sublime and profound works.

Bernard, Emile   French   1843-1902
Divertissement in F Major, Op. 36; 1895; MMM; 23 mins; 2222/2; D
Bernard studied at the Paris Conservatoire and was organist of the Notre Dame Cathedral from 1887 to 1895. The *Divertissement* was first performed at the Parisian Society of Wind Instruments in 1895. This difficult work from the late Romantic period is among the very best written for double quintet.

Bialas, Gunther   German   1907-1995
Partita; 1963; BAR; 20 mins; 1223/2
Bialas wrote in a omnitonal style with folklike modalities. He wrote for opera, stage, concertos, chorus and chamber ensembles. Contrabassoon is required.

Bird, Arthur   American/German   1856-1923
Suite in D Major; 1901; COM; 2222/2; C/D
Bird's music was well known in Germany, and most of it was
published there. Critics agreed that his music, late Romantic in style,
was pleasing and melodious, and that he was an excellent contrapuntist.

Blank, Allan   American   1925-
Paganini Caprice 24; c1978; SCI, ACA; 4 mins; 2222/2; C/D
Blank attended the Juilliard School then performed on violin with the
Pittsburgh Symphony before resigning to devote his time to composition. He has published more than sixty works and received numerous
grants and awards. This work is a theme and variation on the well-
known Paganini melody.

Boehm, Yohanan   Israeli   1914-
Divertimento; IMP; 2222/2

Byrd, William   English   1543-1623
Variations on Walsingham; Hodges; WWP; 2222/2; D/E
Byrd was a prolific composer of virtually all genres used in England
during his time.

Caplet, Andre Leon   French   1878-1925
Suite Persane; McAlister; 1900; COM; MMP; 8 mins; 2222/2; D/E
Caplet studied with Debussy and they remained close friends throughout their lives. This work is part of Caplet's small output of chamber
music.

Casadesus, François   French   1870-1954
London Sketches; 1924; SAL; 6 mins; 2222/2
Casadesus studied at the Paris Conservatory and later conducted the
Opera and the Opera-Comique. This work includes three movements
titled *The Policeman in the Zoo, Trafalgar Square Idyll* and *Children
Play.*

Chandler
Badinages; 1975; ESM; 2222/2; D/E

Clementi, Aldo   Italian   1925-
Intermezzo; SUV; 2222/2
Clementi studied composition with Sangiorgi and Petrassi at the Santa
Cecilia Conservatory in Rome. His music incorporates many twentieth
century devices.

Corghi, Azio   Italian   1937-
Actus I; SUV; 2222/2

Cossart, Leland A.   1877-
Suite; HEI; 2222/2

Debussy, Claude A.   French   1862-1918
Prelude; Holcombe; 1890-1905; MPI; 2222/2
Debussy studied with Chopin and later at the Paris Conservatory with
Durand. He wrote music for opera, ballet, orchestra, piano and chamber
ensembles. This is an arrangement from *Suite Bergamasque*.

Dvořák, Antonín   Czech   1841-1904
Slavonic Dance, Op. 46 #4; Taylerson; 1878; ZER; 1223/2; D
The third bassoon part is for contrabassoon. This work was originally
for orchestra.

Czech Suite, Op. 39; Sheen; 1879; KAL; 2222/2; D
Dvořák's musical style is diverse with his early works reflecting the
influence of Beethoven and Schubert, then Wagner and later Brahms.
The artistic stylization of natural folk dances in this five-movement
work is clear. The *Suite*, originally for orchestra, displays the light
mood of the Classical serenade though in thoroughly Czech musical
language.

Edlund, Mikael   Swedish   1950-
Music for Double Wind Quintet; 1984; SCI; 2222/2
Edlund studied composition with Lidholm and Mallnas and has writ-
ten music for ensembles and orchestra.

Enescu, George   Romanian   1881-1955
Dixtuor in D Major, Op. 14; 1906; MMM; 2222/2; D/E
Enescu, considered the foremost Romanian composer, studied at the
Paris Conservatory with Faure and Massenet. His style was basically
Neo-Romantic with occasional use of experimental techniques such as
quarter tones. Second oboe doubles on English horn.

Erod, Ivan   Hungarian/Austrian   1936-
Capriccio; c1980; DBM; 5.5 mins; 2222/2

Fiala, Joseph   Czech   1748-1816
Divertimento #3 in E-Flat Major; ZER; 12 mins; 0422/2; C/D
Fiala, a friend of Mozart, was an oboist in orchestras in Munich, Salzburg, and Vienna. He composed a number of string quartets, symphonies and concertos, as well as numerous wind serenades which Mozart
described in glowing terms. Two English horns are required.

Francaix, Jean   French   1912-1997
Elegy; 1990; EAM; 5 mins; 2222/2; D
A brilliant piano virtuoso, Francaix's music shows an innate gift for
invention and an ability to express the freshness and wonder of childhood. Alto flute, English horn, basset horn, bass clarinet and contrabassoon are required.

Nine Characteristic Pieces; 1973; EAM; 2222/2; D/E

Seven Dances from *Les Malheurs de Sophie;* 1970; EAM; 2222/2; D

Fucik, Julius   Czech   1872-1916
Der Alte Brummbar, Op. 210; Taylerson; ZER; 1223/2; D
Fucik studied composition with Dvorak and was a bassoonist and band
master. He wrote a large number of dances and marches, including the
well-known *Entry of the Gladiators*. This work, a comic polka, was
originally written for solo bassoon and orchestra. Contrabassoon is required.

Florentine March, Op. 214; Taylerson; ZER; 1223/2; C/D
Contrabassoon is required.

Gaalman, A.   1914-1986
Introduction and Burlesque; COM; 1223/2; D
This work requires English horn, bass clarinet and contrabassoon.

Gipps, Ruth   English   1921-1999
Seascape; c1961; ESM; 2222/2; E
A pupil of Vaughan Williams, Gipps wrote symphonies, concertos,
chamber and choral music.

Gounod, Charles   French   1818-1893
Funeral March of a Marionette; 1873; WIM; 5 mins; 2222/2; C
Due to his great popularity and stylistic influence on the next generation of composers, Gounod was perhaps the most important French
composer during the late nineteenth century. This work was originally
for orchestra.

Grieg, Edvard Hagerup   Norwegian   1843-1907
Two Elegiac Melodies; Dawson; c1974; SHA; 2222/2
One of Norway's most important musical figures, Grieg is perhaps best
known for *Peer Gynt* on which he collaborated with Ibsen.

Haydn, Franz Joseph   Austrian   1732-1809
Feldpartitur,Chorale St. Antoine, Hob. II:46; Pohl; 0224/2
Haydn is considered the creator of the Classical form of the symphony
and string quartet. He played a historic role in the evolution of harmony by adopting four-part writing as the compositional foundation.
A prolific composer, Haydn wrote music for orchestra, chamber ensembles, concertos, dramatic works, masses and oratories. Contrabassoon
or string bass is required.

Jacob, Gordon   English   1895-1984
Old Wine in New Bottles; c1960; OUP; 12 mins; 2222/2
Jacob studied with Stanford and Howells at the Royal Academy of Mu-
sic and Dulwich College and later joined the faculty of the RAM. His
works are deeply rooted in tradition and display fine craftsmanship.
Flute doubles on piccolo. There are optional parts for two trumpets and
contrabassoon. The work includes four old English tunes: *The Wraggle
Taggle Gypsies, The Three Ravens, Begone Dull Care* and *Early One
Morning.*

Jadassohn, Salomon   German   1831-1902
Serenade, Op. 104; c1990; COM; 2222/2; C/D
Jadassohn wrote more than 140 pieces including symphonies, concertos, chorus, vocal and chamber music. Although he was an excellent contrapuntist he also valued melodic beauty.

Jaeger, David   Canadian   1947-
Double Woodwind Quintet; CMC; 2222/2

Joplin, Scott   African American   1868-1917
Cascades; Taylerson; 1904; ZER; 1223/2; C/D
Named the "King of Ragtime," Joplin was largely self-taught though
he briefly attended the Smith College for Negroes in 1895 to gain technical skills in composition. Contrabassoon is required.

Easy Winners; Taylerson; ZER; 1223/2; C/D
Contrabassoon is required.

Lenot, Jacques   French   1945-
Comme au Loin; SUV; 2222/2

Liadov, Anatol Konstantinovich Russian   1855-1914
Eight Russian Folk Songs; 1906; WWP; 23 mins; 2222/2; C/D
Though he completed only a small number of works, primarily due to
laziness, Liadov was held in great affection by his fellow musicians.
This piece, originally for orchestra, requires doubling on English horn
and piccolo.

Lutyens, Elisabeth   English   1906-1983
Music for Wind; 1964; EAM; 2222/2
Lutyens attended the Royal College of Music where she studied with
Darke. Her music incorporates twelve tone technique and other
twentieth-century devices.

McCabe, John   English   1939-
Symphony for Ten Wind Instruments; 1964; NOV; 7 mins; 2222/2;
C/D
McCabe's music is eclectic, drawing on many contemporary styles and
techniques. Piccolo, alto flute and English horn are required.

Melin, Bengt   1928-
Menuet Badin; SMC; 2222/2

Milhaud, Darius   French   1892-1974
Dixtuor; UNE; 2222/2; D/E
Milhaud studied at the Paris Conservatory with Dukas, Widor and
Leroux. Perhaps more influential in his compositions were the friend-
ships of several writers and painters. His music persuasively captures
the Mediterranean spirit with many melodies having origins in the folk
songs of Provence, France. Piccolo, English horn and bass clarinet are
required.

Symphony #5; c1922; BHI; 2222/2; D
Piccolo, English horn and bass clarinet are required.

Mouquet, Jules   French   1867-1946
Symphonietta, Op. 12 in C Major; LEM; 2222/2
Mouquet studied at the Paris Conservatory with Leroux and Dubois.
He won the Prix de Rome in 1896 and later became professor of harmony at the Conservatory.

Moyse, Louis   French   1911-
Divertimento; MMM; 2222/2
Moyse, son of Marcel Moyse, is best known as a flutist.

Mozart, Wolfgang A.   Austrian   1756-1791
Adagio in C Major, K. 356; Taylerson; ZER; 1223/2; C/D
Contrabassoon is required. This work was originally written for glass
harmonica.

Andante, K.315; Taylerson; ESM; 1223/2; C/D
Mozart was a musical genius whose works in virtually every genre are
unmatched in lyrical beauty and rhythmic variety. Contrabassoon or
string bass is required.

Concert Rondo, K. 382; ZER; 1223/2; C/D
Originally for piano and orchestra, contrabassoon is required in this
version.

Divertimento #4, K.186; ESM; 0422/2; C/D
Two English horns are required.

Divertimento, K.166; 1773; BHI; 0422/2; C/D
Two English horns are required.

Duet from La Ci Darem; ZER; 1223/2; C
Contrabassoon is required.

Two Marches from The Magic Flute and Idomeneo; Taylerson; ZER;
1223/2; C/D
Contrabassoon is required.

Nocentini, Domenico   1848-1924
Sinfonia "Labor Omnia Vincit"; COM; 1223/2; D
Contrabassoon is required.

Symphonia in B-Flat Major; COM; 1223/2
Contrabassoon is required.

Pablo, Luis de   Spanish   1930-
Credo; 1976; SUV; 2222/2
After receiving a law degree, Pablo received musical advice from
Messiaen and Boulez and later taught at the Universities of Ottawa and
Montreal. While his early works shows the influence of de Falla, his
later music adopts advanced serial techniques.

Paganini, Niccolo   Italian   1782-1840
Caprice 24; Blank; 1805; AMP; 2222/2; D
Paganini, legendary violinist, wrote for orchestra, chamber ensembles
and violin concertos. One of his best works, the *Caprices* were originally written for solo violin.

Raff, Joachim   Swiss   1822-1882
Sinfonietta, Op. 188; 1873; KZE; 2222/2; D
Raff, a prolific composer influenced by Mendelssohn and Liszt, wrote
more than 400 works for opera, orchestra, and chamber ensembles.

Ravel, Maurice   French   1875-1937
Pavane pour une Infante Defunte; Baker; 1910; ESM; 5 mins; 2222/2;
D
Ravel studied at the Paris Conservatory with Pessard and Fauré. His
music shows the influence of Debussy and Schubert. This work was
originally for piano and later arranged for orchestra by the composer.
Two English horns are required.

Reicha, Joseph   Bohemian   1752-1795
Parthia in F Major; c1988; COM; 2222/2; D/E
Reicha (also spelled Rejcha) wrote twelve partitas for wind instruments.
He wrote music that is pleasing to both the performers and their
audience. A true highlight in this work is the lovely bassoon solo in
the second movement. This work is perfectly suited for a young wind
ensemble.

Reizenstein, Franz   German/English   1911-1968
Serenade in F Major, Op. 29; 1951; BHI; 25 mins; 1223/2; D
Reizenstein's output of Neo-Romantic music for wind instruments was
large. His clarity of style, melodic invention and underlying wit,
together with a natural understanding of the instruments, produced a
number of works which have become part of the standard repertoire.
When Reizenstein first submitted this work to Boosey & Hawkes, he
was asked by them to make an orchestral version, too, which he did a
year later, adding another flute, strings and timpani. This subsequent

version, Op. 29A, is only available as a rental. Written in five movements, the third movement features the flute and the second movement omits the flute and contrabassoon/double bass. The third bassoon part is for contrabassoon or string bass.

Rosetti, Antonio   Czech   1750-1792
Parthia in D Major; COM; 2222/2; C

Rossini, Gioachino   Italian   1792-1868
Overture to Mathilde di Shabran, ESM; 1223/2; D
Recognized as one of the greatest Italian composers of his time, he is best known for his operas. Contrabassoon is required.

Schibler, Armin   Swiss   1920-1986
Prologue; PRC; 2233
After studies with Willy Burkhard in Zurich, Schibler became the music director at the Kanton Gymnasium in Zurich. His music is typically Neo-Classical with occasional use of a modified twelve tone technique. Bass clarinet and contrabassoon are required.

Signal, Beschworung; PRC; 2332
English horn and bass clarinet are required.

Schmitt, Florent   French   1870-1958
Lied et Scherzo, Op. 54; c1912; DUR; 2222/2
Piccolo and English horn are required.

Schubert, Franz   Austrian   1797-1828
Ellens Zweiter Gesang; ESM; 0222/4; C
Schubert produced great masterpieces in virtually every field of composition. His music is rich in melody and expressive harmony.

Sims, Ezra   American   1928-
Serenade; ESM; 2222/2; D
English horn is required.

Siqueira, Jose   Brazilian   1907-
Divertimento for Double Wind Quintet; 1967; 6 mins; 2222/2; C/D
Siqueira's early music was Neo-Classical style, but later he turned to musical nationalism.

Sjoberg, Johan Magnus   Swedish   1953-
En Liten Hipp Serenade; 1993; SMI; 8 mins; 2222/2

Solere
Andantino from Concerto #3; Woolfenden; ESM; 2222/2; D/E

Sporck, Georges   1870-1943
Landscapes of Normandy; SMC; 2222/2
Sporck studied with Guiraud and Dubois at the Paris Conservatory and later with Vincent d'Indy. He wrote music for orchestra and chamber groups, and published educational editions of Classical works by famous composers.

Stamitz, Carl   Bohemian   1745-1801
Parthia in E-Flat Major; 1777; COM; 2222/2
Stamitz was considered an exceptional violist and wrote a large number of compositions for orchestra, sinfonie concertante, concertos and chamber ensembles. His style is outstanding for its melodic wealth, formal elegance and harmonious tonal beauty. This version has two optional flute parts to make it a double quintet.

Strauss, Johann   Austrian   1825-1899
Frauenherz Polka, Op. 166; Taylerson; 1855; ZER; 1223/2; D
Although he wrote extensively for theatre, Strauss's biggest achievements were in the dance genre such as this work. Contrabassoon is required.

Gypsy Baron Overture; Taylerson; 1885; ZER; 1223/2; D
Contrabassoon is required.

Sullivan, Sir Arthur   English   1842-1900
Were I Thy Bride; Sutton; ESM; 4051; C
Bass clarinet is required.

Suppe, Franz   Austrian   1819-1895
The Beautiful Galatea; 1865; ESM; 1223/2; D
Suppe, best known for his overtures for musical farces and operettas, wrote in a light, fluent style. This work is from the comic mythological operetta, *Galatea*. The third bassoon part is for contrabassoon or string bass.

Sutermeister, Heinrich   Swiss   1910-1995
Modeste Mignon: d'Apres une Valse d'Honore de Balzac; 1974; EAM
2222/2; D
Sutermeister studied with Orff and Courvoisier and later achieved international renown as a composer of operas that are dramatically effective
and melodically pleasing. This work is based on a waltz by Balzac.
Piccolo and E-flat clarinet are required.

Taneyev, Alexander   Russian   1850-1918
Andante for Double Woodwind Quintet; MMM; 2222/2; D
Taneyev studied with F. Reichel and Rimsky-Korsakov. His music,
written in a Romantic style, shows the influence of Tchaikovsky. His
last name is sometimes spelled Tanjew.

Vivaldi, Antonio   Italian   1678-1741
Concerto, Op. 3 #3; Taylerson; ZER; 1223/2; D
Vivaldi is considered the most original and influential Italian composer
of his time. This work features the flute as soloist. Contrabassoon or
string bass is required.

Wiernik, Adam   1916-
Variations; 1994; SMI; 11 mins; 2222/2

Wilby, Philip   English   1949-
And I Move Around the Cross; 1985; SCI; 8 mins; 2222/2
Wilby was a violinist who wrote music for voice, ensembles and or-
chestra.

Zamecnik, Evzen Czech   1939-
Eine Kleine Abendmusik; ESM; 0082; D/E
Zamecnik, a violinist, studied at the Janacek Academy and the Academy of Musical Arts in Prague. The two bassoon parts in this piece
could be played on bass clarinet.

ELEVEN OR MORE WINDS

Amelsvoort, Johannes van   1910-
Deux Elegies; ESM, COM; 2233/4 ; C/D
English horn and contrabassoon/string bass are required.

Anderson, Leroy   American   1908-1975
Suite of Carols; CPP; 3341
Anderson studied composition with Piston and Enescu at Harvard University. He specialized in light music for orchestra or band with charming melodies and popular dance rhythms. This arrangement requires piccolo, English horn, contrabassoon and alto clarinet.

Arnell, Richard   English   1917-
Serenade, Op. 57 ; 1973; ESM; 2223/2; D/E
Arnell studied with John Ireland at the Royal College of Music in London. His musical style is festive and decidedly English. The third bassoon part is for contrabassoon or string bass.

Arnold, Sir Malcolm   English   1921-
Trevelyan Suite, Op. 96; 1968; ESM; 3222/2; C/D
Arnold's music is basically diatonic and the main attraction lies in catchy tunes, interesting orchestration and the pleasure that the music gives to the performers. This work features three movements titled *Palindrome, Nocturne* and *Apotheosis.*

Brauer, Max   German   1855-1918
Pan; BHI; 2223/2
Contrabassoon or string bass is required.

Davis, Carl   American   1936-
Pickwick Papers; ESM; 2223/4; D
Contrabassoon is required.

Delden, Lex van   Dutch   1919-88
Sinfonia #7; 1964; DNA; 2232/2
Delden studied law then turned to music after WWII. Largely self-taught, he has written oratorios, symphonies, and chamber music. Bass clarinet is required.

Dvorák, Antonín   Czech   1841-1904
Romance; Taylerson; ESM; 2223/2; C/D
Dvorák's musical style is diverse with his early works reflecting the influence of Beethoven and Schubert, then Wagner and later Brahms. Contrabassoon or string bass and English horn are required.

Serenade in D Minor, Op. 44; 1878; KAL; 0225/3; C/D
This charming *Serenade*, first played in Prague when Dvorák made his conducting debut in a Prague concert of his works, actually requires two bassoons and contrabassoon with cello and double bass instead of the three bassoons and two contrabassoons listed here. However, this is considered such a standard for wind ensembles it is included here with this variation of instrumentation.

Ganz, Rudolf   Swedish/American   1877-1972
Woody Scherzo for 13 Instruments, Op. 33 #3; c1946; MCA; 2232
Ganz is perhaps best known as a conductor and champion of contemporary American composers. His small output of works, written in a conservative style, include music for piano, chamber ensembles and orchestra. This work requires two piccolos, two English horns, three bass clarinets and two contrabassoons.

Holst, Gustav   English   1874-1934
A Moorside Suite Emerson; ESM; 2223/4; C
Contrabassoon is required.

Janacek, Leos   Czech   1854-1928
Three Lachian Dances; Sheen; ESM; 2223/2; D
Janacek, like Smetana and Dvorak, was a composer who worked tirelessly for the advancement of the music of his native Czechoslovakia. He often made use of what he called "speech melody," melody whose contours were inspired by the characteristic rhythm and cadence of the Czech language. Contrabassoon is required.

Kalabis, Victor   Czech   1923-
Incantations, Op. 69; COM, ESM; 4 mins; 2223/4; C/D
Kalabis's early music frequently shows the influence of Brahms. He later develops a more individual style with brilliant feeling for color and sonority. English horn is required and there is an optional contrabassoon part.

Kohn, Karl   Austrian/American   1926-
Concert Music for Twelve Wind Instruments; 1956; CFI; 2332/2
Kohn studied at Harvard with Piston, Fine, Thompson and Ballantine.
His early music reflects his Harvard training and orientation toward
American Neo-Classicism with additional influence from Bartok. Dur-
ing the 1950s his music moved toward the twelve tone method while
later works blended Classicism and Romanticism with twentieth-cen-
tury techniques. English horn and bass clarinet are required.

Lewis, Peter   American   1932-
Sestina; ACA; 2232/2
The third clarinet part is for bass clarinet.

Lieberson, Peter   American   1946-
Wind Messengers; 1990; AMP; 3242/2
Lieberson's rather eclectic interests include English literature and Vaj-
rayana Buddhism. A student of Babbitt, Wuorinen and Martino, he is a
master of serial technique: shaping, coloring and modifying the basic
material in order to convey a wide range of emotions. His compositions
include music for orchestra, voice and chamber ensembles. This work
requires two bass clarinets.

Moser, Franz Josef   Austrian   1880-1939
Serenade, Op. 35 ; 1921; UNE; 2333/4

Mozart, Wolfgang Amadeus   Austrian   1756-1791
Cosi fan Tutte Overture; 1790; COM; 2223/2
Contrabassoon is required.

Idomeneo Overture, K.366; Emerson; 1781; KAL; 2223/2 ; C/D
Contrabassoon is required.

Serenade #10, Gran Partita, K.361/370a; Hellyer; 1781-82; ESM; 40
mins; 0243/4; C/D
Believed to be written by Mozart as a wedding present to his wife, this
extended work is a true masterpiece for winds. Even though the
clarinets often lead the melody, with the two pair of horns providing
the tonal foundation, all thirteen instruments nevertheless have fairly
equal parts. Two clarinets may replace the two basset horn parts and
there is an optional contrabassoon part.

Orff, Carl   German   1895-1936
Carmina Burana; 1937; EAM, ESM; 2223/2; D/E
All of Orff's major works, including *Carmina Burana*, were designed
as pageants for the stage. This arrangement includes five movements
from this well-known orchestral work. Contrabassoon is required.

Perilhou, Albert   French   1846-1936
Divertissement; 1904; HEU; 2222/4

Ponse, Luctor   Swiss/Dutch   1914-
Euterpe, Op. 37; 1964; DNA; 2232/2
Ponse won the Prix d'Excellence for theory at the Conservatory in Val-
enciennes, France.

Pragg, Henri C. Van   Netherlands   1894-1968
Music; DNA; 2232/2

Reger, Max   German   1873-1916
Serenade for Wind Ensemble; ESM; 3 mins; 2222/4; D
Reger was a student of Hugo Riemann at the Sondershausen Conservatory and later he studied at the Wiesbaden Conservatory. His prolific
output includes music for orchestra, voice, chamber, organ and piano.

Rorem, Ned   American   1923-
Sinfonia; c1957; PTE; 3343/2
Piccolo and English horn are required.

Rosetti, Antonio   Czech   1750-1792
Partita in F Major; OUP; 2222/3; C/D
Rosetti was one of the leading members of the German branch of Czech
composers. His contemporaries ranked him with Haydn and Mozart.
Written in three movements, there are alternate English horn parts for
clarinet.

Schubert, Franz   Austrian   1797-1828
March in D Major; Taylerson; ESM; 2223/2; C
Schubert produced great masterpieces in virtually every field of composition. His music is rich in melody and expressive harmony. Contrabassoon is required.

Stranz, Ulrich   German   1946-
Serenade; 1992; BAR; 18 mins; 2223/2
Contrabassoon is required.

Strauss, Johann   Austrian   1825-1899
Die Fledermaus Overture; Blomhert; 1874; ESM; 2223/2; D
This is an arrangement of the overture from his best operetta.

Strauss, Richard   German   1864-1949
Serenade in E-Flat Major, Op. 7; 1881; IMC; 9 mins; 2223/4; C/D
The *Serenade* is largely written in Classic style. Influenced by Mendelssohn and Brahms, it bears Strauss's individual melodic style
which is strongly evident in the very opening bar of the principal horn.
It was this remarkably fresh and well-scored piece which first attracted
general attention to the talent of Richard Strauss who was then only 18
years old. Contrabassoon or string bass is required.

Sonatina #1 in F Major for Winds, "From An Invalid's Workshop";
BHI; 23 mins; 2253/4; D/E
The opening *Allegro moderato* allows themes to flow effortlessly and
then develop, vary and sustain interest with tonal modulations. The
middle movement reveals again his love for singing melodic lines and
classical forms. The final movement uses a free fugue form. This work
requires bass clarinet, basset horn and either contrabassoon or double
bass.

*Symphony for Wind Instruments in E-Flat Major: From a Happy
Workshop;* 1944-45; BHI; 36 mins; 2253/4; D/E
Also titled *Sonatina #2*, Strauss dedicated this to "the spirit of the
immortal Mozart at the end of a life full of thankfulness." Reminiscent
of Mozart's serenades, harmonies and divertimenti, this work demonstrates Strauss's usual skill with charming melodies and Classical
forms. Written towards the end of his life, this work is clearly written
to please the audience and players. Bass clarinet, basset horn and either
contrabassoon or double bass are required.

Suite in B-Flat Major for 13 Winds, Op. 4; 1884; LKM; 23 mins;
2223/4; D
The opening *Allegretto* of this work is reminiscent of Strauss's *Serenade* using a sonata form without development. The last three movements, which use other Baroque forms, include *Romanze, Gavotte* and
Introduction and Fugue. Contrabassoon or string bass is required.

Suk, Josef   Czech   1874-1935
Serenade in E-Flat Major, Op. 6; Emerson; ESM; 2223/2; D/E
Contrabassoon is required.

Tikka, Kari   1946-
Logo; 1991; FMC; 3 mins; 0705
Tikka studied at the Sibelius Academy and is primarily known as a
conductor. The instrumentation in this work includes four oboes, one
oboe d'amore, two English horns, four bassoons and a contrabassoon.

KEY TO MUSIC SOURCES

ABM	Alberen Muziek	CPI	Conners Publications
ACA	American Composers Alliance	CPP	Columbia Pictures Publications
ALE	Alry Publications Etc.	CRA	Cramer Music
AMC	American Music Center	CRO	Croatian Music Information Center
AMP	Associated Music Publishers	DBM	Doblinger
		DCM	Da Capo Music Ltd.
ARP	Arsis Press	DNA	Donemus Amsterdam
BAR	Bärenreiter Verlag	DNP	Dorn Publications
BBL	Broude Brothers Ltd.	DUR	Editions Durand
BBM	Bote & Bock	DVM	Deutscher Verlag Musik
BEL	Belmont Music Pub.		
BHI	Boosey & Hawkes	DWP	Daniel Waitzman
BHM	Barnhouse Music	EAM	European American
BIG	Big Three Music	ECB	Edition Con Brio
BIL	Billaudot	ECS	ECS Publications
BKH	Breitkoph & Hartel	EDB	Edizioni Berben
BML	Berandol Music Ltd.	EDC	Edizioni Curci
BMP	Bruyere Music Publishers	EDH	Edition Helios
		EDM	Edition Musicus
BRU	Bruzzichelli, Aldo	EDN	Edition NGLANI
BVP	Broekmans & Van Poppel	EDP	Edition de Paris
		EDR	Editions Reimers
BSE	Bocaccini & Spada Editions	EDV	Editions Viento
		EDY	Ed. Doberman-Yppan
BXP	Brixton Publishers	EKB	Edition Kneusslin Basel
CAR	Carp Music		
CFI	Carl Fischer, Inc.	EKW	Edition KaWe
CHE	Chester Music Ltd.	EMB	Edition Musica Budapest
CHF	Cesky Hudebni Foundation		
		EME	Editions Max Eschig
CHO	Choudens	EMI	EMI Music
CMC	Canadian Music Center	EOL	Edition Oiseau-Lyre
		EPF	Ed. Philippe Fougeres
CMI	Czech Music Information Center	ESM	Emerson Editions
		EUL	Eulenberg Edition
CMU	Comus	EVI	Elkan-Vogel Inc.
COM	Compusic	FER	Fereol Publisher
CON	Consort Press	FLC	Forlivesi & Co.
COR	Cor Publishing Co.	FMC	Finnish Music Center
COS	Costallat	FMI	Faber Music, Inc.

FML	Fenton Music Ltd.	LMP	Ludwig Music Publishing Co.
FMP	Fema Music Publications	LKM	F.E.C. Leukart
GAL	Gallet	LYC	Harold Lyche
GER	Gerig, Musikverlag Hans	M21	Musica 21 Publishing
		MAR	Margun Music
GHP	G. Henle Publishers	MAU	J. Maurer
GLM	Galaxy Music	MBV	Merseberger Verlag
GMF	Gehrmans Musikforlag	MCA	MCA & Mills
		MED	Medici Music Press
GMP	General Music Publishing Co.	MER	Mercury Music
		MFS	Musikverlag F. Schulz
HAN	Wilhelm Hansen Musik	MJQ	MJQ Music
HAR	Hargail	MMB	MMB Music
HBM	Hans Busch Musikforlag	MMM	McGinnis & Marx
		MMP	Masters Music Pub.
HEI	Heinrichshofen	MNM	Merion Music
HEU	Heugel & Cie	MOB	Mobart Music
HNP	Henmar Press	MOS	Moseler Verlag
HOF	Hofmeister Musicverlag	MPI	Musicians Publications
HPC	Hildegard Publishing Co.	MRI	Musica Rara
		MSM	M. Schweitzer Music
HUS	Huset Musik	MSS	MSS Publishing
IMC	International Music Co.	MVH	Max Verlag Hieber
		NHP	Needham Publishing
IMP	Israeli Music Publisher	NOR	Nordiska Musikforlaget
INT	International Opus	NOV	Novello & Co. Ltd.
ISW	Irwin Swack Music	NPR	Nova Press
JMC	Jobete Music Co.	NVM	New Valley Music Publishers
KAL	Kalmus, Ltd.		
KED	Kendor Music Inc.	OPM	Opus Music
KER	Kerby Publishers	OUP	Oxford University Press
KIS	Kistner & Siegel		
KMC	Kjos Music Co.	PAN	Panton International
KZE	Kunzelmann Edition	PIC	Peermusic Classical
LDA	Alphonse Leduc	PIP	Piper Publications
LEM	Lemoine Editions	PMP	Providence Music Press
LMA	LEMA Musikforlag		

PRC	Theodore Presser Co.	TBM	Thomi-Berg
PTE	C.F. Peters Corp.		Musikverlag
PWM	Polskie Wydawn.	TGM	Trigram Music
	Muz.	TIE	Tierolff
REM	Ries & Erler		Muziekcentrale
RIC	Ricordi Americana	TMP	Tempo Music
RML	Rhodes Music Ltd.		Publishers
RON	Rongwen Music	TON	Tonos Editions
SAL	Salabert Editions	TRA	Transatlantiques
SAP	San Andreas Press		Edition
SCH	Mus. Hermann	TRI	Trillenium Music Co.
	Schmidt	TTP	Tritone & Tenuto
SCI	G. Schirmer Inc		Pub.
SCL	Schott & Co. Ltd.	UNE	Universal Edition
SEE	Seesaw Music Corp.	UUB	Uppsala
SEL	Selmer Editions		Universitetsbib.
SER	Serendipity Press	VLO	Verla Louis Oertel
SHA	Shawnee Press	VMP	Valley Music Press
SHF	Slovensky Hudbeny	WBP	Warner Brothers Pub.
	Fondation	WIL	Willis Music Co.
SIE	Sieber, G.	WIM	Western International
SIK	Hans Sikorski		Music
SKA	Skandinavisk	WMI	Wimbledon Music
	Musicforlag		Inc.
SMC	Southern Music Co.	ZAN	Zanibon, G.C.
SMI	Swedish Music	ZER	Zephr Music
	Information	ZIM	Zimmerman
SMP	Scotus Music Pub.		Musikverlag
	Ltd.		
SNK	Stati Nakadetelstvi		
	Krasne		
SPR	Spratt Woodwind		
SSP	Soundspells		
	Productions		
STE	Steingraber		
STU	Studio Music		
	Publishing Co.		
SUB	Subito Music		
	Publisher Inc.		
SUP	Supraphon		
SUV	Suvini Zerboni		

MUSIC PUBLISHERS

Acoma Nambe Editions
P.O. Box 62056
Victoria Terrance PO
Toronto ON   M4A 2W1
Canada
416-757-5966
Music@Acoma-Co.com
www.Acoma-Co.com

Alberen Muziek
Groot Hertoginnenlaan 182
2517 EV Den Haag
Netherlands
+31 70 3456000
+31 70 3614528

Alry Publications Etc., Inc.
P.O. Box 36542
Charlotte, NC   28236
USA
704-334-3413
FAX 704-334-1143
amyblu@aol.com
members.aol.com/alrypbl/

American Composers Alliance
73 Spring Street
Room 505
New York, NY 10012
USA
212-362-8900
212-925-0458
FAX 212-925-6798
info@composer.com
www.composers.com

American Music Center
30 W. 26 Street, #1001
New York, NY   10010 USA
212-366-5260
FAX 212-366-5265
www.amc.net

Arsis Press
170 NE 33rd St.
Ft. Lauderdale, FL   33334
USA
954-563-1844
FAX 954-563-9006
DocShaffer@aol.com
www.InstantWeb.com/~arsis

Associated Music Publishers
257 Park Ave. South
20th Floor
New York, NY 11010
USA
212-254-2100
FAX 212-254-2013
www.schirmer.com

Bärenreiter Verlag
P.O. Box 10 03 29
D-34003 Kassel
Germany
+49 (0)561 3105-179
FAX +49 (0)561 3105-176
info@baerenreiter.com
www.baerenreiter.com

Barnhouse Company
Box 680
205 Cowan Ave. West
Oskaloosa, IA   52577
USA
641-673-8397
FAX 641-673-4718
bbarnhouse@barnhouse.com
www.walkingfrog.com

Belmont Music Pub.
Box 231
Pacific Palisades, CA   90272
USA
310-454-1867

FAX 310-573-1925
belmus@primenet.com

Belwin Music
15800 NW 48th Avenue
Miami, FL 33014
USA
305-620-1500
FAX 305-625-3480

Berandol Music Ltd.
2600 John St., Unit 200
Markham ON L3R 3W3
Canada

Big Three Music
31 Gray
Montclair, NJ 07042
USA
201-744-0984

Billaudot Èditeur, Gérard
14 rue del Echiquier
75010 Paris Cedex 10
France
+33 1 47 701446
FAX +33 1 45 232254
info@billaudot.com

Bocaccini & Spado Ed.
(see Boosey & Hawkes)

Bongiovanni
Via Ugo Bassi 31/F
40121-Bologna BO
Italy
+39 051 550252
FAX +39 051 226128
andrea@bongiovanni70.com
www.Bongiovanni70.com

Boosey & Hawkes, Inc.
35 E. 21 Street
New York, NY 10010
USA

sales.us@boosey.com
212-358-5300
FAX 212-358-5303
www.boosey.com

Bosworth & Company Ltd.
14-18 Heddon Street
London W1R 8DP
UK

Bote & Bock
Hardenbergstrasse 9A
D-10623 Berlin
Germany
+49 30 3110030
FAX +49 30 3124281

Breitkopf & Hartel
Walkmühistraße 52
D-65195 Wiesbaden
Germany
+49 611 4500856
FAX +49 611 4500859

Brixton Publishers
404 W. Maxwell St.
Lakeland, FL 33803
USA

Broekmans & Van Poppel B.V.
Van Baerlestraat 92-94
1071 BB Amsterdam
Netherlands
+31 20 6796575
FAX +31 20 6646759
music@broekmans.com
www.broekmans.com

Broude Brothers, Ltd.
141 White Oaks Rd.
Williamtown, MA 01267
USA
413-458-8131
800-525-8559
FAX 413-458-5242

Bruyere Music Publishers
9538 Central Park
Evanston, IL 60203
USA

Bruzzichelli, Aldo
Borgo S. Frediano 8
50124-Firenze FI
Italy

Buried Treasures Ens. Press
342 Warren Avenue
Buffalo, NY 14217
USA
716-877-4236

Busch, Musikforlag H.
3 Stubbstigen
18146-Lidingo
Sweden

Canadian Music Center
Chalmers House
20 St. Joseph Street
Toronto ON M44 1J9
Canada
416-961-6601
FAX 416-961-7198
info@musiccenter.ca

Carp Music, Inc.
153 Seaman Avenue
New York, NY 10034
USA
212-567-2934

Carl Fischer, Inc.
65 Bleeker Street
New York, NY 10012 USA
212-777-0900
800-762-2328
FAX 212-477-6996
cf-info@carlfischer.com
www.carlfischer.com

Cesky Hudebni Foundation
(Czech Music Fund Found.)
Radlicka 99
CZ-150 00 Prague 5
Czech Republic
+420 2 573 200 08
FAX +420 2 534 234
www.musica.cz/asc/nchf

Chester Music Ltd.
8/9 Frith Street
London W1V 5TZ
UK
music@musicsales.co.uk

Charles Colin Music Public.
315 W. 53 Street
New York, NY 10019
USA
212-581-1480
FAX 212-489-5186
info@charlescolin.com
www.charlescolin.com

Choudens
(see C.F. Peters Corp.)
38 rue Jen Mermoz
75008 Paris
France

Columbia Pictures Public.
15800 NW 48th Ave.
Miami, FL 33014
USA
305-620-1500

Compusic, Edition
Amsterdam, Holland

Comus
Heirs House Lane
Colne, Lancashire BB8 9TA
UK

Conners Publications
503 Tahoe Street
Natchitoches, LA 71457-5718
USA
318-357-0924
FAX 318-357-3299
ALMEI@aol.com
hostnet.pair.com/conners

Consort Press
1755 Monita Dr.
Ventura, CA 93001
USA
800-995-7333
FAX 800-643-9051
office@consortpress.com
www.consortpress.com

COR Publishing Co.
67 Bell Place
Massapequa, NY 11758-4026
USA
516-798-7515

Costallat Editions
United Music Publishers
60 rue de la Chaussee d'Antin
Paris
France

Cramer Music Ltd.
23 Garrick Street
London C2E 9AX
UK

Croatian Music Info. Ctr.
Kneza Mislava 18
10 000 Zagreb
Croatia
+385 1 46 11 810
FAX +385 1 46 11 807
mic@zg.tel.hr
www.mic.hr

Czech Music Information Center
Besedni 3
118 00 Praha 1
Czech Republic
his@vol.cz
www.musica.cz/about.htm

Da Capo Music Ltd.
26 Stanway Rd.
Manchester M45 8EG
UK

Deutscher Verlag Musik
(see European American Music)
Lizenznummer 418-515
D 80878 Leipzig
Germany

Doblinger Musikverlag
Dorotheerg 10
A 1010 Vienna
Austria
+43 1 515 03-0
FAX +43 1 515 03-51
music@doblinger.at
www.doblinger-musikverlag.at

Donemus Amsterdam
Paulus Potterstraat 14
1071 CZ Amsterdam
Netherlands
+31 0 20 676 4436
FAX +31 0 20 673 3588
donemus@pi.net

Dorn Publications
P.O. Box 206
Medfield, MA 02052
USA
508-359-7004

ECS Publications
138 Ipswich St.

Boston, MA 02215-3534
USA
617-236-1935
FAX 617-236-0261
office@ecspublishing.com
www.ecspublishing.com

Edition Con Brio
Box 7457
S-103 22 Stockholm
Sweden
+46 571 407 45

Edition de Paris

Edition Helios
Erlinger Höhe 9
D-82346 Andechs
Germany
+49 (0)8 152 6671
FAX +49 (0)8 152 5120
webmaster@dingfelder-verlag.de
www.dingfelder-verlag.de/Katalog/
  Edition_Helios/edition_helios.
  html

Edition Kneusslin Basel
(see C.F. Peters)

Edition KaWe
see Musica Rara

Edition Moeck Verlag
Postfach 143
D 3100 Celle
Germany
+514-88530

Edition Musica Budapest
(see Boosey & Hawkes)
www.emb.hu

Edition Musicus
POB 1341
Stamford, CT 06904

USA
203-323-1401

Edition NGLANI
Box 5684
Takoma Park, MD 20913
USA

Edition Oiseau-Lyre
122 rue de Grenelle
Paris
France

Edition Philippe Fougeres

Editions Doberman-Yppan
C.P. 2021
St. Nicholas Estate QC G0S 3L0
Canada
418-837-1304
FAX 418-836-3645
doberman.yppan@videotron.ca
pages.infiniti.net/doyp

Editions Max Eschig
4-6 place de la Bourse
75008 Paris Cedex 02
France
+33 1 44 887373
FAX +33 1 44 887388
durand.eschig@bmgintl.com

Editions Musicales Durand
215 rue de Faubourg St. Honore
75008 Paris
France
+033 1 53 838450
FAX +033 1 53 838160

Editions Reimers
Box 15030
S-161 15 Bromma
Sweden
FAX + 46 8 662 50 45

Editions Viento
8711 SW 42 Ave.
Portland, OR 97219-3571
USA

Edizioni Berben
65 Via Redipuglia
60100 Ancona AN
Italy

Edizioni Curci
Galleria del Corso 4
20122-Milano MI
Italy
FAX +603-888-1762
lbt@true.mv.com

Elkan-Vogel, Inc.
(see Theodore Presser Co.)
800-304-0096
603-888-6444

Emerson Editions Ltd.
Windmill Farm, Ampleforth
North Yorkshire Y06 4HF
UK
JuneEmerson@compuserve.com

EMI Music
810 Seventh Ave., 3rd Floor
New York, NY 10019
USA
212-830-2000
FAX 212-830-5196

Eulenberg Edition
c/o Schott & Co.
48 Great Marlborough St.
London W1F 7BB
UK

European American Music
Distributors Corp.
15800 NW 48 Ave.
Miami, FL 33014

USA
305-521-1604
FAX 305-521-1638
eamdc@eamdc.com
www.eamdc.com

European Music Center
Ambachtsweg 42
1271 Am Huizen
Netherlands
+31 35 5242104
FAX +31 35 5242336
emcmusic@strengholt.nl
www.emc-scores.nl

Faber Music Inc.
3 Queen Square
London WC1 N3A
UK
information@fabermusic.co.uk

Falls House Press
P.O. Box 7121
Nashua, NH 03060-7121
USA
800-304-0096
603-888-6444
FAX 603-888-1762
lbt@true.mv.com
www.mv.com/ipusers/true/
    fallshousepress

Fema Music Publications
POB 395
Naperville, IL 60540
USA
312-35-0207

Fentone Music Ltd.
4 Fleming Rd., Corby,
Northants N17 4SN
UK
music@fentone.com
www.fentone.com

Fereol Publishers
POB 6007
Alexandria, VA 22306
USA

Finnish Music Info. Center
Lauttasaarentie 1
FIN-00200 Helsinki
Finland
+358 9 6810 1311
FAX +358 9 682 0770
info@mic.teosto.fi
www.fimic.fi

Foreign Music Distributors
13 Elkay Driver
Chester, NY 10918
USA
914-469-5790
FAX 914-469-5817
76573.1062@compuserve.com

Forlivesi & Co.
Via Roma
450123 Firenze FI
Italy

Galaxy Music
(see ECS Publications)

Gallet & Fils
6 Rue Vivienne
Paris
France

General Music Pub. Co. Inc.
145 Palisade St.
Dobbs Ferry, NY 10522
USA

Gerig, Musikverlag Hans
Frankenforster Str. 40
51427 Bergisch Gladbach
Germany
+49 02204 2003-0

FAX +49 02204 2003-33

Gehrmans Musikforlag
Box 6005
S-102 31 Stockholm
Sweden
FAX +46 8 31 42 44

Hal Leonard Publications
7777 West Bluemound Road
Milwaukee, WI 53213
USA
414-774-3630
FAX 414-774-3259
halinfo@halleonard.com
www.halleonard.com

Hansen Musik, Wilhelm
Bornholmsgade 1
DK-1266 Copenhagen
Denmark
+1-117888
FAX +1-148178

Hargail Music Press
POB 118
Saugerties, NY 12477
USA

Heinrichshofen Verlag
Postfach 1655
Liebigstraß 16
D 26356 Wilheimshaven
Germany
+49 0 44 21 92 67 0
FAX +49 0 44 21 20 20 07
info@heinrichshofen.de
www.heinrichshofen.de

Henle Verlag
Forstenrieder
Allee 122
D-81476 Munich
Germany
+49 89 7 59 82 0

FAX +49 89 7 59 82 40
info@henle.de
www.henle.de

Henmar Press
(see C.F. Peters)

Heugel & Cie
(see Alphonse Leduc)
175 rue Saint-Honore
F 75040 Paris Cedex 01
France

Hildegard Publishing Co.
POB 332
Bryn Mawr, PA 19010
USA
610-649-8649
FAX 610-649-8677
mail@hildegard.com
www.hildegard.com

Hofmeister Musicverlag
Karlstraß 10
04103 Leipzig
Germany
+49 0341 8600750
FAX +49 0341 9603055

Huset Musik
Karl Johansgt.45
Oslo
Norway
+02 33 48 97

International Music Co.
5 W. 37th Street, 6th Floor
New York, NY 10018
USA
212-391-4200
800-959-5972
FAX 212-391-4306

International Opus
P.O. Box 4852

Richmond, VA 23220
USA
800-720-0189
intlopus@aol.com
www.members.aol.com/intlopus/
   woodwind.html

Israeli Music Publications, Ltd
25 Keren Hayesod St.
P.O. Box 7681
Jerusalem 94188
Israel
+972 2 6241377
FAX +972 2 6241378

Jobete Music Co. Inc.
6255 Sunset Blvd.
Hollywood, CA 90028
USA
213-856-3507
FAX 213-461-2785

Kalmus, Alfred A., Ltd.
48 Great Marlborough Street
London W1V 2BN
UK
info@kalmus-music.com
www.kalmus-music.com

Kalmus, Edwin F. & Co.
P.O. Box 5011
Boca Raton, FL 33431-0811
USA
561-241-6340
800-434-6340
FAX 561-241-6347
efkalmus@aol.com
www.kalmus-music.com

Kendor Music, Inc.
21 Grove Street, POB 278
Delevan, NY 14042-0278
USA
716-492-1254
FAX 716-492-5124

customerservice@kendormusic.
      com
www.kendormusic.com

Kerby Publishers
198 Davenport Rd.
Toronto M5R 1J2
Canada
416-922-9934

Kistner & Siegel
505 Port Westhoven
Am Kielshof, Liepzig
Germany

Kjos Music Co., Neil A.
P.O.Box 178270
San Diego, CA 92117-8270
USA
858-270-9800
FAX 858-270-3507
email@kjos.com
www.kjos.com

Kunzelmann Edition
Haupstr. 35
D 79807 Lottstentten
Germany
+49 07745 8020
FAX +49 07745 7221
info@edition-kunzelmann.de
www.edition-kunzelmann.de

Leduc, Alphonse
175 rue Saint-Honore
75040 Paris Cedex 01
France
+33 (0)1 42 968911
FAX +33 (0)1 42 860283
alphonseleduc@wanadoo.fr
www.alphonse/educ.com

LEMA Musikforlag
Vetevagen 24
S-691 48 Karlskoga

Sweden
+46 586 35717
FAX +46 586 399 20

Lemoine Editions
41 rue Bayen
75017 Paris
France
+33 01 56 68 86 65
FAX +33 01 56 68 90 66
info@editions-lemoine.fr
www.editions-lemoine.fr/

Leukart, F.E.C.
Nibelungenstrasse 48
D-8000 Munich 19
Germany

Ludwig Music Pub. Co. Inc.
55767 E. 140th St.
Cleveland, OH 44110-1999
USA
216-851-1151
FAX 216-851-1985

Lyche, Harold
Postboks 2171 Stromso
N-3003 Drammen
Norway

Margun/Gunmar Music
167 Dudley Rd.
Newton Centre, MA 02159
USA
617-332-6398
FX 617-969-1079
margunmu@aol.com

Masters Music Publications
POB 810157
Boca Raton, FL 33481-0157
USA
561-241-6169
FAX 561-241-6347
mastersmus@aol.com

www.masters-music.com

Maurer, J.
Avenue du Verseau 7
B-1020 Brussels
Belgium

MCA & Mills/MCA Joint
Venture Editions
1755 Broadway, 8th Floor
New York, NY 10019
USA
212-841-8000
FAX 212-582-7340

**McGinnis & Marx Music
Publishers**
236 West 26th Street, #11S
New York, NY 10001-6736
USA
212-675-1630
FAX 212-254-2013

Medici Music Press
5017 Veach Rd.
Owensboro, KY 42303
USA
270-684-9233
ronalddishinger@yahoo.com
www.medicimusic.com

Mercury Music
(see Theodore Presser)

Merion Music
c/o Jerona music Center
POB 5010
Hackensack, NJ 07606
USA

Merseberger Verlag
(see C.F. Peters)

MJQ Music Inc.
200 W. 57th St.

New York, NY 10019
USA

MMB Music
3526 Washington Ave.
St. Louis, MO 63103
USA
800-543-3771
FAX 314-531-8384
mmbmusic@mmbmusic.com
www.mmbmusic.con

Mobart Music
(see Theodore Presser)

Moseler Verlag
Postfach 460
Hoffman von Fallerslebenstrasse 8
3340 Wolfenbuttel
Germany

MSS Publishing
806 N. 3rd St.
Jefferson, OR 97352
USA
517-327-3047

Music 21 Publishing
818 Woodhill Ct.
Palm Harbor, FL 34683
USA
727-786-4189
info@musica21.com
www.musica21.com

Music Publishers Association
PMB 246
1562 First Avenue
New York, NY 10028
USA
212-327-4044
mpa-admin@mpa.org
www.mpa.org

Music Sales Corp.
257 Park Avenue, So., 20th Fl.
New York, NY 10010
USA
212-254-2100
FAX 212-254-2013
yb@musicsales.com
www.schirmer.com/msg.html

Musica Rara
84170 Monteux
France
+33 90654751
FAX +33 90653390

Musicians Publications
1076 River Rd.
Trenton, NJ 08628
USA
609-882-8139
FAX 609-882-3182

Musikaliska Konstforeningen
(See Music Library of Sweden)

Musikverlag Max Hieber
Postfach 429
Kaufingerstrasse 23
Munich
Germany

Needham Publishing
c/o Dorn Publishing
POB 206
Medfield, MA 02052
USA

New Valley Music Press
of Smith College
Sage Hall 49
Northampton, MA 01063
USA
413-585-3105
FAX 413-585-3180

Nordiska Musikförlaget
Warner/Chappel Music Scand. AB
Box 533
S-182 15 Danderyd
Sweden
+46 862 20980
FAX +46 875 34888
leila-maj.palmer-
    hahne@warnerchappell.com

Nova Press
(see Schubert Press)

Novello & Co. Ltd.
8/9 Frith Street
London W1V 5TZ
UK
music@musicsales.co.uk

Opus Music Publishers
1318 Chicago Ave.
Evanston, IL 60201
USA
708-475-1541

Oxford University Press
Great Clarendon St.
Oxford OX2 HDP
UK
music@oup.org
www.oup.org

Panton International
Radlicka 99
115000 Praha 5
Czech Republic
+42 2 5155 3952
+42 2 5155 5994
panton@panton.cz

Peermusic Classical
(see Theodore Presser Co.)
810 Seventh Avenue
New York, NY 10019
USA

212-265-3910
FAX 212-489-2465
classicalny@peermusic.com
www.peermusic.com/classical

Peters Corporation, C.F.
170-30 80th Street
Glendale, NY 11385
USA
718-416-7800
FAX 718-416-7805
sales@cfpeters-ny.com
www.edition-peters.com

Piper Publications
Dochroyle Farm
Barrhill, Girvan
Ayrshire A26 0QG
Scotland
+44 01465 821 377

Polskie Wydawnictwo Musycne
Al Krasinakiego 11a
PL 31-111 Krakow
Poland

Presser Company, Theodore
588 N. Gulph Rd.
King of Prussia, PA 19406
USA
215-525-3636
FAX 215-527-7841
sales@presser.com
www.presser.com

Providence Music Press
251 Weyboset Street
Providence, RI 02903
USA

Roger Rhodes Music Ltd.
POB 855
Radio City Station
New York, NY 10019
USA

212-245-5045

Ricordi Edizioni
Via Salomon 77
20138-Milano MI
Italy
+02 8881 4314
+02 8881-4279
FAX +02 8881-4280
print@ricordi.it
ricordi@sminter.com.ar

Ries & Erler Musikverlag
Wandalenalle 8
14052 Berlin
Germany
+030 825 10 49
FAX +030 825 97 21
verlag@rieserler.de
www.rieserler.de

Rongwen Music
(see Broude Brothers)

Rubank
5544 W. Amstrong Ave.
Chicago, IL 60646-6514
USA

Salabert Editions
4-6 place de la Bourse
75080 Paris
France
+33 (0)1 44 887373
+33 (0)1 44 887388
info@salabert.fr

San Andreas Press
650-856-9394

Schirmer, Inc., G.
257 Park Avenue South
20th Floor
New York, NY 10010
USA

212-254-2100
FAX 212-254-2013
schirmer@schirmer.com
www.schirmer.com

Schmidt, Musikverlag Hermann
(See European American Music)

Schott & Co., Ltd.
48 Great Marlborough Street
London W1F 7BB
UK
info@schott-music.com
www.schott-music.com

Schubert Press
Goldsmid Mews
15a Farm Road
Hove, East Sussex BN3 1FB
UK

Schulz, Musikverlag F.
Freiburg im Bresgau
Germany

Schweitzer, Marsha
905 Spencer Street #404
Honolulu, HI 96822
USA
808-531-6617

Scotus Music Publications, Ltd.
Berlinerstrasse 26
D-6000 Frankfurt-am-main
Germany

Seesaw Music Corp.
2067 Broadway
New York, NY 10023
USA
212-874-1200

Selmer Editions
18 Rue de la Fontaine-au-Roi
75011 Paris

France

Shawnee Press
49 Waring Drive
Delaware Water Gap, PA 18327
USA
570-476-0550
800-962-8584
FAX 570-476-5247
shawnee-info@shawneepress.com
www.shawneepress.com

Sieber, G.
Paris, France

Sikorski, Hans
Johnsallee 23
D-20148 Hamburg 13
Germany
+49 40 41 41 00-0
FAX +49 40 41 41 00-41
contact@sikorski.de
www.sikorski.de

Skandinavisk Musicforlag
Gothersgade 9-11
DK-1123 Copenhagen
Denmark

Slovensky Hudbeny Found.
Bratislava, Yugoslavia

Soundspells Productions
86 Livingston St.
Rhinebeck, NY 12572
USA
914-876-6295

Southern Music Co.
P.O. Box 329
San Antonio, TX 78292
USA
800-284-5443
210-226-8167
FAX 210-223-4537

info@southernmusic.com
www.southernmusic.com

Spratt Woodwind Shop
Box 277
Old Greenwich, CT 06870-0277
USA
203-637-1176
FAX 203-673-7555
www.jacksprattwoodwindshop.com

Stati Nakadetelstvi Krasne

Steingraber
Auf der Riesweise 9
Offenbach

Studio Music Pub. Co.
4153 Brick Church Park
Whites Creek, TN 37189
USA

Subito Music Pub.
504 Bloomfield Ave.
Verona, NJ 07044
USA
973-857-3440
FAX 973-857-3442
mail@subitomusic.com
www.subitomusic.com

Supraphon
(see Bärenreiter)
Palackeho 1
112 99 Praha 1
Czech Republic
+004202-24 94 87 82
FAX +004202-24 94 87 28
supraphon@bonton.cz

Suvini Zerboni Edizioni
Via Quintiliano 40
I 20138, Milano MI
Italy
www.esz.it

Swack, Irwin
2924 Len Drive
Bellmore, NY 11710
USA
516-781-3305
swmusic@rcn.com

Swedish Music Inform. Ctr.
Box 27327
Sandhamnsgatan 79
SE-102 54 Stockholm
Sweden
+46 08 783 88 00
FAX +46 08 783 95 10
swedmic@stim.se
www.mic.stim.se

Tempo Music Publishers
3773 W. 95th St.
Leawood, KS 66206
USA
913-381-5088
FAX 913-381-5081
800-733-5066
tempo@tempomusic.com
www.tempomusic.com

Thomi-Berg Musikverlag
Postfach 1736
D 82145 Planegg Bei Munchen
Germany
+89 8599944
FAX +89 8593323
Thomi-Berg@t-online.de

Tierolff Muziekcentrale
Box 18
4700 AA Roosendaal
Netherlands
+31 165541255
FAX +31 165558339

Tonos Musikverlage
tonos@aol.com

Transatlantiques Edition
50 rue Joseph de Maistre
75018 Paris
France

Trigram Music
(see Wimbledon Music Inc.)
1888 Century Park East
Suite 1900
Los Angeles, CA 90067-1702
USA
310-284-6890
webmaster@wimbtri.com
www.wimbtri.com

Trillenium Music Company
Box 88
Turnbridge, VT 05077
USA
802-889-3354
800-889-5622
trillenium.music@trillmusic.
  com
www.trillmusic.com

Tritone Press & Tenuto Pub.
P.O. Box 5081, Southern Station
Hattiesburg, MS 39401
USA
(subsidiary of PRC)

Universal Edition AG
Bosendorferstrasse 12
A-1015 Vienna
Austria
+431 5058695
FAX +431 5052720

Universal Edition, Inc.
32 W. 39 Street
11th Floor
New York, NY 10018 USA
212-768-0003
212-937-6206
info@uenyc.com

www.uenyc.com

Uppsala Universitetsbibliotek
Box 510
S-751 20 Uppsala
Sweden
+47 1 39 00
FAX +47 1 39 13
www.uu.se

Verla Louis Oertel
Postfach 100
Eichenweg 11A
3006 Grossburgwedel Hannover
Germany

Valley Music Publishers
Northampton

Waitzman, Daniel
28-02 Parsons Blvd.
Flushing, NY 11354
USA
718-353-1936

Warner Brothers Publications
15800 NW 48th Ave.
Miami, FL 33014
USA
305-620-1500
FAX 305-621-4869

Western International Music
3707 65th Avenue
Greeley, CO 80634-9626
USA
970-330-6901
FAX 970-330-7733
wimbo@wiminc.com
www.wiminc.com

Willis Music Co.
P.O. Box 548
Florence, KY 41022-0548
USA

606-283-2050
800-354-9799
FAX 859-283-2050
orderdpt@willis-music.com
www.willismusic.com

Wimbledon Music Inc.
1888 Century Park East
Suite 1900
Century City, CA   90067-1702
USA
310-284-6890
webmaster@wimbtri.com
www.wimbtri.com

Zanibon, G.C.
(See C.F. Peters)
Piazza del Signori 24
Padua
Italy

Zephyr Music
5 Hume St.
Crows Nest NSW 2065
Australia
+61 029439 8900
+61 029437 4014
zephyr@ozemail.com.au

Zimmermann Musikverlag
Gaugrafenstrasse 19-23
Postfach 940183
D-6000 Frankfurt-am-main
Germany

BIBLIOGRAPHY

Baker, Theodore. *Biographical Dictionary of Musicians,* 8th ed. New York: Schirmer Books, 1991.

Cohen, Aaron I. *International Encyclopedia of Women Composers.* New York: Books & More, Inc., 1987.

Cummings, David, and Dennis McIntire. *International Who's Who in Music and Musicians Directory.* Cambridge: IWWM International Biographical Center, 1994.

Gifford, Virginia Snodgrass. *Music for Oboe, Oboe D'Amore and English Horn at the Library of Congress.* Westport: Greenwood Publishing Group, 1983.

Gilder, Eric. *The Dictionary of Composers and Their Music.* London: David & Charles Press, 1993.

Gillespie Jr., James E. *The Reed Trio: An Annotated Bibliography of Original Published Works.* Detroit: Detroit Studies in Music Bibliography, Information Coordinators, Inc., 1971

Hitchcock, H. Wiley and Stanley Sadie. *The New Grove Dictionary of American Music.* New York: Grove Dictionaries of Music Inc., 1986.

Jackson, Stephen. *Classic FM Lifelines: Franz Schubert, An Essential Guide to His Life and Works.* London: Pavilion Books Limited, 1996.

Kallmann, Helmut; Potvin and Winters. *Encyclopedia of Music in Canada.* Toronto: University of Toronto Press, 1981.

Randel, Don Michael. *The New Harvard Dictionary of Music.* Cambridge: Harvard University Press, 1990.

Sadie, Stanley. *The New Grove Dictionary of Music and Musicians.* London: Macmillan Publishers Ltd., 1980.

Sadie, Stanley. *The Norton/Grove Concise Encyclopedia of Music.* New York & London: W.W. Norton & Company, 1994.

Slonimsky, Nicholas. *The Concise Edition of Baker's Biographical Dictionary*. New York: Schirmer Books, 1993.

Slonimsky, Nicolas. *Bakers Biographical Dictionary of Twentieth Century Classical Musicians*. New York: Schirmer Books, 1997.

Southern, Eileen. *Biographical Dictionary of Afro-American and African Musicians*. Westport: Greenwood Press, 1982.

Zaslaw, Neal with Cowdery, William. *The Compleat Mozart: A Guide to the Musical Works of Wolfgang Amadeus Mozart*. New York: Mozart Bicentennial at Lincoln Center and W.W. Norton & Co., 1990.

COMPOSER INDEX

ABOUT THE AUTHOR

Barbera Secrist-Schmedes, founder of the Pandean Players chamber ensemble, lived in Washington, DC, and New York City for nearly a decade after undergraduate work at Georgia State University. While living there she performed with the Kennedy Center Opera Orchestra, Wolf Trap Orchestra, National Symphony, Amato Opera, and the American Chamber Orchestra. Since returning to Atlanta in 1985, Ms. Secrist-Schmedes has performed with the Knoxville (TN), Columbus (GA), Macon (GA), and Columbia (SC) symphonies. Ms. Secrist-Schmedes recently completed a master of arts at Florida State University's renowned School of Music and has served on the faculties of Morris Brown College and Agnes Scott College.

In addition to her role as artistic director and oboist with the Pandean Players, she currently plays English horn and oboe with the Augusta (GA) Symphony, manages the Atlanta Center for Arts and History Elderhostel Program, performs frequently with the Greenville (SC) Symphony and conducts statewide on-site evaluations of musical organizations for the Georgia Council for the Arts.

Ms. Secrist-Schmedes has worked as an arts consultant to a variety of organizations including the Cobb Chamber of Commerce, Atlanta Business Volunteers for the Arts, Cobb Arts Council, DeKalb Council for the Arts, Jubilee Arts Festival, Sunday Serenade Concert Series, Cobb County Grassroots Arts Project, Augusta Symphony, Rome Symphony and Cobb Symphony. She lives in Marietta, GA, with her husband, actor/director/playwright John Schmedes, son Eron, and their three cats.